"Practical. Encouraging. Motivating. God is the greatest giver of all, so it makes sense that He loves to honor stunning generosity. *Double Blessing* challenges us to reframe our perception of blessing, seeing God's gifts as opportunities for increased ministry. Mark Batterson calls all of us to not only receive God's blessings but also to excellently use what we've been given to bring glory to God and grace to those around us."

—Louie Giglio, pastor of Passion City Church, founder
of Passion Conferences, author of *Not Forsaken*

"I love Mark Batterson's transparency about his own journey toward incredible generosity. And his practical advice in *Double Blessing* will get you up and moving in the right direction before you know it. But I'll warn you to keep a pen handy. He's got some great one-liners that you'll want to remember—and probably claim as your own!"

—Dave Ramsey, bestselling author and nationally syndicated
radio show host

"The word *blessed* has been hijacked to mean something completely different from what God intended. In *Double Blessing,* Mark takes us to the root of the word and shows us how much better for us God's *true* blessing is than anything the world could ever give."

—Carlos Whittaker, author of *Kill the Spider*

"Through pure honesty and authenticity, Mark Batterson in *Double Blessing* reminds us of God's powerful call for us to bless others through the blessings that we've received and to remain generous through all occasions. When these principles of giving and receiving are put into practice, we glorify God and make a tremendous impact on the lives of others."

—Roma Downey, actress, producer, and *New York Times*
bestselling author

"We all aspire to glorify God in our daily lives, but we are sometimes unsure of what specific steps to take. Mark Batterson offers an honest and encouraging path to help us experience God's blessings in a refreshing way—by blessing others through the blessings that we've received. I highly encourage you to read *Double Blessing*."

—John C. Maxwell, bestselling author and speaker

"In this book, Mark Batterson has tapped into two things I am very passionate about: giving and prayer. If we all shift our focus from what we can get to what we can give, then God will, as Malachi 3:10 says, 'open the floodgates of heaven' in our lives."

—David Green, CEO of Hobby Lobby Stores, Inc.

"In *Double Blessing*, Mark Batterson skillfully describes the nature of a loving and compassionate Father who naturally desires to bless His children beyond their wildest dreams. Batterson simultaneously underscores the personal responsibility of believers to live obedient and benevolent lives. Your desire to discover and walk in your birthright as a believer will increase exponentially in reading this book, as will your desire to be a blessing unto others."

—John K. Jenkins Sr., pastor of First Baptist Church
of Glenarden, Maryland

"Whenever Mark teaches or writes, we are wise to listen or read. He seems to sense what we need to learn. This book is no exception. Thanks, Mark."

—Max Lucado, pastor and bestselling author of *How Happiness Happens*

"God has blessed Mark Batterson with the spiritual vision and godly insight to provide every reader with clear direction through *Double Blessing*. Receiving a blessing is wonderful, but receiving a double blessing is what God desires for us to enjoy and embrace."

—Kevin Warren, commissioner-elect of the
Big Ten Conference

DOUBLE
BLESSING

DOUBLE BLESSING

Don't Settle for Less Than You're Called to Bless

Mark Batterson

MULTNOMAH

DOUBLE BLESSING

To those who have generously invested their time, talent, and treasure in National Community Church. Once a shareholder, always a shareholder.

CONTENTS

ARIADNE'S THREAD

God blessed them and said, "Be fruitful and multiply."

GENESIS 1:28, NLT

In Greek mythology, there is a legend about a labyrinth that was unnavigable and inescapable. Those who entered never exited. For within the maze meandered the Minotaur, a fearsome creature that was half man, half bull. Every nine years, the evil king of Crete demanded that the Athenians send seven boys and seven girls to be sacrificed to the Minotaur. As you might imagine, the Athenians did not take well to this tradition.

On the occasion of the third Minotaur Games, the prince of Athens volunteered himself as tribute in the place of other young citizens. When Theseus landed on Crete, the daughter of the Cretan king, Princess Ariadne, fell head over ancient heels in love with him. She knew that no one who had ventured into the labyrinth had ever found a way out, so she devised a rather ingenious plan. Ariadne gave Theseus a sword to slay the Minotaur and, more importantly, a ball of thread. After tying one end to the entrance, Theseus unwound the ball of thread as he wove his way through the spiderweb of corridors. After successfully slaying the Minotaur, Theseus was able to moonwalk his way out of the labyrinth with the help of Ariadne's thread.[1]

Life is a labyrinth, is it not? It's full of relational twists and occupational turns we couldn't see coming. We zig through big decisions and zag through bad ones. There are situations we get ourselves into that we don't know how to get ourselves out of. And we all encounter some Minotaurs along the way!

Weaving your way through difficult seasons of life can feel as hopeless as trying to escape an ancient labyrinth, but there is a way out. There is a ball of thread waiting for you, but we must backtrack all the way to the beginning of human history to find its figure-eight knot.

Ancient Instinct

The Austrian psychologist Alfred Adler was famous for beginning counseling sessions with new clients by asking, "What is your earliest memory?" No matter how his patient replied, Adler responded, "And so life is."[2]

Adler believed that our earliest memories leave a profound imprint on our souls. For better or for worse, it can be very difficult to escape their gravitational pull. Our earliest memories have unusual staying power.

Imagine Alfred Adler sitting down with Adam, the first Adam, and asking his trademark question. Adam's early memories range from rib surgery to roaming the garden. Naming all the animals had to be an unforgettable experience, especially the pink fairy armadillo. Yes, it actually exists, and it lives up to its name! Then, of course, there was the awkwardness of nakedness after succumbing to the serpent's temptation. And, I'm sure, subsequent nightmares of being naked in public! But none of those moments represents Adam's earliest memory.

> God blessed them and said, "Be fruitful and multiply. Fill the earth and govern it. Reign over the fish in the sea, the birds in the sky, and all the animals that scurry along the ground."[3]

Before original sin, there was original blessing. And so life is! That first blessing sets the tone, sets the table. It establishes the emotional baseline and spiritual trend line of Adam's life. But it's not just Adam's earliest memory. It also reveals God's most ancient instinct.

Blessing is God's default setting—His first and foremost reflex. If you don't believe that, you'll doubt the goodness of God. And if you second-guess the goodness of God, you'll forfeit His blessing.

God wants to bless you beyond your ability to ask or imagine.

There. I said it. And I believe it. The question is, do you?

The blessing of God is Ariadne's thread, and we'll thread that needle from

Genesis to Revelation. What happened at the very beginning has more to do with your future than you might imagine. And my prayer is that this book will begin a new season of blessing in your life. Of course, you've got to position yourself for that blessing. And I'll show you how to do just that. But the blessing of God is more than a mystery to solve. It's a decision to make, a habit to form, and a mindset to establish.

Original Blessing

I'm not sure what your earliest memory is, good or bad. But for many, memories of their earthly father do not mirror Adam's experience. In fact, you may feel cursed rather than blessed by your family of origin. If that's true, if that's you, it can be difficult to conceive of a heavenly Father whose deepest desire is to bless you. There might even be a generational curse that needs to be broken. But believe it or not, *God has blessings for you in categories you cannot even conceive of.* If you're going to live the happy, healthy, and holy life God has called you to, you've got to get that in your gut. God is in the blessing business! And as His children, blessing is our birthright.

Now, I know what you may be thinking. Am I promising health, wealth, and prosperity? The answer to that is an unequivocal *no!* God promises us something so much better than physical health or material wealth. Plus, some of God's greatest blessings are blessings in disguise.

The blessing of God is not an immunity card against pain and suffering. Jesus said point blank, "In this world you will have trouble."[4] He Himself endured far more than His fair share of earthly troubles, including the Cross! What makes us think we can become like Jesus without going through some of the same struggles He did? But take note—this promise doesn't end with "trouble." Don't make the mistake of putting a period where God puts a comma! In the same breath, Jesus declared, "But take heart! I have overcome the world."[5] There are sacrifices to be made—no doubt. There is suffering to endure—no question. But there is a blessing on the other side, a double blessing!

I had better add this at the outset: God doesn't bless disobedience! God doesn't bless pride or greed or laziness either! We've got to position ourselves for God's blessing, and that's what this book is all about. But make no mistake about it—God has postured Himself to bless you from the very beginning. And this blessing is not just the opening act of Genesis.

A tag cloud is a visual representation of textual data, showing the importance of words by color and size of font. If you tag cloud the Old Testament, I'm not sure there is a word that is bigger or brighter than *blessing*. In fact, *blessing* is a flashing neon sign! If we're being honest, many of us have a hard time believing this because of the high volume of brutality and bloodshed before Christ. But the Hebrew word for "blessing," *barak,* is put on repeat 330 times! It means "to bless the one who blesses you."[6] And in the New Testament, we get two flavors—*makarios* and *eulogētos.*[7] The concept of blessing may be Greek to you, but by the end of this book, you'll know how to get it and how to give it. We'll explore the dimensions of blessing in much greater detail, but I want you to understand up front that blessing is the central storyline of Scripture from start to finish.

Blessed to Bless

The blessing of God isn't easy to quantify or qualify. It is tangible and intangible, timely and timeless. It is universally offered to everyone, but the blessing of God is as unique as your fingerprint. Some blessings are as simple and straightforward as the sunrise. Others are more difficult to discern, like the blessing of brokenness. But of this I'm certain: *the blessing of God is the solution to your biggest problem, the answer to your boldest prayer, and the fulfillment of your bravest dream.*

We'll explore *how to get the blessing* and *how to give the blessing.* There is an art and a science to both. But make no mistake—the endgame is not getting but giving! God doesn't bless us to raise our standard of living. God blesses us to raise our standard of giving. In the words of Winston Churchill, "We make a living by what we get, but we make a life by what we give."[8] That idea is as old as the Abrahamic covenant:

> I will make you into a great nation,
>   and I will bless you;
> I will make your name great,
>   and you will be a blessing.

I will bless those who bless you,
    and whoever curses you I will curse;
and all peoples on earth
    will be blessed through you.[9]

The covenant of blessing established with Abraham is as valid today as it ever was. Why? Because God keeps His covenants! Even better, the old covenant has been updated and upgraded by what Christ accomplished on the cross. But let's not get ahead of ourselves.

Simply put, *we are blessed to bless.* The way we turn a blessing into a double blessing is by flipping the blessing. The secret of the double blessing is simply this: *the way you get it is by giving it.* That is counterintuitive and counter-cultural, but that is the miracle at the other end of Ariadne's thread. And you will be a bigger blessing to more people because of it.

Whirlwind Tour

Before we embark on this pilgrimage of blessing, let me take you on a whirlwind tour from Genesis to Revelation. Remember, one end of Ariadne's thread must be tied to the original blessing: "Be fruitful and multiply."[10] The blessing of God then weaves its way from the Garden of Eden to Ur of Chaldeans where God establishes the covenant of blessing with Abraham. It is followed by a cryptic yet prophetic encounter with Melchizedek. The blood and wine offered to Abraham by the priest-king of Salem foreshadows the new covenant, and Abraham atones with a tithe of all his goods.[11] The blessing of God survives a soap opera known as Isaac and Jacob, proving itself bigger and better than any mistake we can make. The blessing turns Jacob into Israel, who then pronounces longer and stronger blessings on his twelve sons, the twelve tribes of Israel.[12]

During four hundred years of enslavement in Egypt, the blessing survives unspeakable suffering and indescribable setbacks. The blessing finds its voice at a burning bush on the back side of the desert, giving a man named Moses the holy confidence to confront Pharaoh.[13] On the eve of the Exodus, the blessing of God is the blood of the Passover lamb that provides a hedge of protection for God's people and delivers them out of bondage. During Israel's wanderings, the blessing becomes a cloud by day that gives shade and a fire by night that gives light.[14]

While in the wilderness, a priestly blessing is pronounced on the people of God.[15] That blessing sets them up and sets them apart. God doubles down with an elevated blessing on top of Mount Gerizim.[16] The blessing then parts the Jordan River, fells the walls of Jericho, and delivers the hill country called Hebron.[17]

Ariadne's thread then weaves its way through a shepherd's field, a fugitive's cave, and into the Valley of Elah where David defeats Goliath. The thousand year-old blessing that David inherited from the line and lineage of Judah, finds it's prophetic fulfillment in the Son of David, in the City of David a thousand years later.

The Lion of the tribe of Judah is birthed in Bethlehem—*God with us*. The blessing seems to take a wrong turn at the Garden of Gethsemane, down the Via Dolorosa, dead-ending at Calvary's cross. But that's where the curse is broken and the blessing is bestowed—*God for us*. The covenant of blessing becomes the cup of blessing, the bottomless cup of God's grace from which we drink every time we come to the Lord's Table and celebrate our communion with Christ.[18] The blessing is signed, sealed, and delivered on the third day with an empty tomb. With it, a fine-print footnote the Father had not forgotten: "I will give you the sacred blessings I promised to David."[19]

The last thing Jesus does, before His ascension, is raise His hands and bless His disciples just as the ancient priests of Israel did.[20] Adam's first memory becomes their last and lasting memory. Ten days later, a second blessing was bestowed on the disciples in an upper room. The Holy Spirit was poured out on the Day of Pentecost—*God in us*.

Eternal Blessing

What is the blessing of God? It's God—God *with* us, God *for* us, God *in* us. To reduce it to anything less dishonors God and devalues the blessing. God *with* us is joy unspeakable and the peace that surpasses understanding.[21] God *for* us is His favor, the X factor between the best we can do and the best God can do. And God *in* us is power, resurrection power.

Every spiritual blessing belongs to us by virtue of what Christ accomplished through His death and resurrection.[22] And when we finally arrive at the end of God's revelation, God's most ancient instinct finds its eternal expression. It's there that we tie the other end of Ariadne's thread to the last blessing in the Bible. The original blessing becomes the eternal blessing:

> Blessed are those who wash their robes, that they may have the right
> to the tree of life and may go through the gates into the city.[23]

In the pages that follow, we'll pull the thread of God's blessing all the way from Genesis to Revelation. My prayer is that this book would be the genesis of God's blessing in your life and a revelation of the bigger blessing He wants you to become to others.

Can I make a suggestion as we begin this journey together?

Don't read this book by yourself. Reading it with a friend or family member has the potential to turn this book into a double blessing. Some books are best read by yourself, but *Double Blessing* is best experienced in community. Reading it with someone else will multiply the blessing.

Part 1

DOUBLE BLESSING

How to Get It

DOUBLE PORTION

Let me inherit a double portion of your spirit.

2 KINGS 2:9

On January 6, 1998, I was sitting in a doctor of ministry class at Regent University in Virginia Beach when I got called out of class to take a phone call. Nothing on earth can psychologically prepare you to hear the life-altering words that you've lost a loved one.

Bob Schmidgall wasn't just my father-in-law; he was a spiritual father. He planted and pastored Calvary Church in Naperville, Illinois, for thirty-one years. It was his example that inspired my dream of pastoring one church for life. He was my mentor, my model for ministry. He wasn't perfect, but there was a unique anointing on his life.

Two days before that phone call, my father-in-law celebrated his fifty-fifth birthday. He was in the prime of life, the prime of ministry. At his annual physical, his physician had told him, "I could drive a Mack truck through your arteries." How could he die from a massive heart attack days later? If you've walked through the valley of the shadow of death, you know it poses questions that are unanswerable on this side of eternity. And while God gives the oil of joy for mourning,[1] our grieving doesn't resolve until we enter a dimension of reality the Bible calls heaven.

The days following his death were an emotional blur, and that's the grace of God. The spirit goes into shock, much like the body. I don't remember much from the days surrounding his death, but there is one moment I will never forget.

After driving from Virginia Beach back to Washington, DC, in record time, Lora and I caught the next flight to Chicago. A few hours but what felt like a lifetime later, we found ourselves at Friedrich-Jones Funeral Home in Naperville, Illinois. It's hard for me to describe what happened next, and I can't explain why I prayed what I prayed. But as I stood at the foot of my father-in-law's casket, I asked God for a double portion of His spirit. I'm not sure I knew exactly what I was asking for, but I knew I needed His anointing if I was going to honor my father-in-law's legacy. So I asked God for a double portion, not unlike the prophet Elisha.

Double Down

Toward the end of his ministry, the prophet Elijah knew his days were numbered. So he said to his apprentice, Elisha, "Tell me, what can I do for you before I am taken from you?"[2] I suppose Elisha could have asked for any number of things, including Elijah's estate. But Elisha made no bones about what he really wanted:

Let me inherit a double portion of your spirit.[3]

Is it any coincidence that Elisha's curriculum vitae includes twenty-eight miracles, exactly twice as many as his prophetic mentor?[4] I think not, but let me flip the script. The true measure of Elijah's success was not the fourteen miracles he had a hand in. It was watching the next generation do things he didn't even dare dream of. Simply put, success is succession. Please don't read that as a platitude. Success is handing the baton to those who come behind us and cheering them on as they run farther and faster than we did.

My undergraduate education began at the University of Chicago. The U of C has produced ninety-eight Nobel laureates, but I'm not sure any of them left as big an imprint on that university as its famed football coach, Amos Alonzo Stagg. Stagg coached the original Monsters of the Midway for four decades, winning two national titles in 1905 and 1913. His brainchildren include the huddle, the onside kick, the T formation, and the forward pass.[5]

Amos Alonzo Stagg invented football as we know it, but that isn't his greatest legacy. When he accepted the invitation to coach, he gave an acceptance speech of sorts to the university president: "After much thought and prayer, I decided that my life can best be used for my Master's service in the position you have offered."[6] Stagg would coach football until the age of ninety-eight, but he didn't just coach his teams. He discipled his players.

After one of his winning seasons, a beat reporter congratulated the coach on a job well done. Instead of passively receiving that compliment, Stagg coached that young reporter. He said in his straightforward manner, "I won't know how good a job I did for twenty years. That's when I'll see how my boys turned out."[7]

As you might imagine, Amos Alonzo Stagg was inducted into the College Football Hall of Fame. What you might not know, however, is that he was inducted as both a player and a coach. But it gets even better. Stagg was inducted into the Basketball Hall of Fame too! In fact, Amos Alonzo Stagg coached football, basketball, *and* baseball at the University of Chicago. He actually turned down six offers to play professional baseball, but he helped a lot of future major leaguers with another one of his inventions—the batting cage![8]

Legacy isn't measured by what we accomplish in our lifetimes. It's measured by our coaching tree, our mentoring chain. It's measured by the fruit we grow on other people's trees. It's measured by the investments we make in others that are still earning compound interest twenty years later. It's measured by every blessing we bestow.

The relationship between Elijah and Elisha prototypes what the double blessing is all about. After receiving Elijah's mantle, Elisha flips the blessing by turning it into twenty-eight miracles for others! In the process, Elisha becomes Elijah's legacy.

Elijah was Elisha's double portion. And Elisha was Elijah's double blessing.

Whose double portion are you? And who is your double blessing?

Hit Your Knees

Under Bob Schmidgall's leadership, Calvary Church grew to become one of the largest churches in America at the time. More significantly, it was one of the most generous mission-giving churches in the country. Of course, he kept that fact concealed as best he could, not wanting the congregation to become self-satisfied with their level of sacrifice! And he and my mother-in-law led the way, often making financial pledges that outpaced their income.

Bob Schmidgall is a difficult portraiture to paint. When he prayed, you felt like there was no way God wouldn't answer! When he preached, it stretched your faith to believe God for bigger things. But the thing that had an impact on so many was the way he went out of his way to serve those in need. If he passed a motorist stranded with a flat tire, there was a very good chance he'd help change it. He often found himself at the hospital at all hours of the night, reading a scripture and offering an encouraging word. When I speak at churches or conferences across the country, I'll occasionally share a story about him. Almost without exception, even two decades after his death, someone from the crowd will catch me and tell me something that Bob Schmidgall did to bless them in a life-changing way.

As I stood at the foot of his casket on the day he died, thoughts and feelings flooded my mind and my heart. But this I believe: God has honored that double-portion prayer in ways I never could have conceived of.

Can I take a little pressure off your prayer life? God's blessings aren't contingent on your ability to combine the twenty-six letters of the English alphabet into some kind of abracadabra. And you definitely don't have to tell God how to do His job! News flash: God does not get nervous! And neither should we! That said, God won't answer 100 percent of the prayers we don't pray. So we do have to ask, as best we can. But we have to do more than that. One of the most common mistakes we make is thinking we can attain the level of success others have achieved without the corresponding sacrifices! Before you envy someone else's success too much or too long, you might want to count the cost. That person's success is the by-product of sacrifices others were not willing to make!

The first thing to give out on my father-in-law's pants were the knees because he spent so much time on them praying. To ask for a double portion of his anointing without hitting my knees like he did would have been disingenuous and dishonoring. The blessing of God is not a substitute for praying like it depends on God or working like it depends on us. It's a supplement. If you want success without sacrifice, good luck with that because that is exactly what you'll need—*luck*. The blessing of God is anything but a good-luck charm. You cannot earn it, but you'll have to work for it. And while it's absolutely free, it'll cost you dearly! If you want a double blessing, be prepared to double down on your work ethic and prayer ethic!

That's why Elijah responded to Elisha's request this way: "You have asked a difficult thing."[9]

Bold Prayers

When my father-in-law passed away, National Community Church was a two-year-old toddler. We numbered fewer than a hundred people, and we wouldn't become a self-supporting church for another year. I wasn't entirely sure National Community Church was going to survive, but I banked on this core belief: *God honors bold prayers because bold prayers honor God.*

When I initially prayed that double-portion prayer, I surmised that it might translate into a church twice the size of Calvary Church. And that would have been a bold prayer back then. But I'm now convinced that a double portion means so much more than "times two"! God has answered that prayer in ways I did not propose and could not have predicted. The double portion I prayed for came through two anointings, without me even knowing. One is a calling to pastor, and the other is a calling to write. While it sometimes feels like I'm holding down two day jobs, I cannot imagine my life without one or the other.

Over the past two decades, National Community Church has grown to the size Calvary Church was when my father-in-law passed away. And I would be surprised if we did not double in size over the next decade. Of course, that's out of my control. We plant and water, but God gives the increase.[10] Pastoring a church in our nation's capital isn't always easy, but I wouldn't want to be anywhere else doing anything else.

I love to preach, but most of my impact is through written words, not spoken ones. Somewhere along the way, I went from being a pastor-author to being an author-pastor. Of course, I'm grateful I get to do both. For the record, I still have some God-sized goals that haven't happened just yet, like the film scripts I've been pitching but striking out on. And I've experienced my fair share of failure. But I genuinely believe that whatever measure of impact I've experienced as a pastor and as an author traces back to that double-portion prayer at the foot of my father-in-law's casket. I hope it honors his legacy and flips the blessing, just like Elisha's double portion.

Prisoners of Hope

The concept of the double blessing has been used and abused by name-it-and-claim-it preachers for longer than I've been alive. I understand the dangers of misinterpretation and misapplication as it relates to God's promises, but we better not throw the blessing out with the bathwater! We must understand what it is and what it isn't. The double blessing is not *health, wealth, and prosperity*. It's not a 200 percent return on every investment either. It's something bigger and better than that.

There are half a dozen "double promises" in Scripture. The prophet Isaiah promised a double portion of joy or prosperity, depending on your translation of choice.[11] The apostle Paul conferred double honor on those who lead well.[12] And as we've just explored, a double portion of Elijah's spirit netted twice as many miracles in the ministry of Elisha. But perhaps the most unique binary blessing in the Bible is declared by the prophet Zechariah:

> Return to your stronghold, O prisoners of hope;
>   today I declare that I will restore to you double.[13]

The prophet Zechariah declared this double blessing to Jewish prisoners of war, but he called them prisoners of hope. Those are polar opposites, are they not? So which is it—prisoners of war or prisoners of hope? That depends on your perspective, doesn't it? If you let your circumstances define the way you see God, you are a prisoner of perspective. Or worse, a prisoner of your past mistakes! But if you let God define the way you see your circumstances, you are a prisoner of hope.

Please don't let anyone name you except God. You are not the labels people put on you. You are who God says you are! You are the apple of God's eye.[14] You are the object of His affection.[15] You are more than a conqueror.[16]

Israel had experienced a bitter defeat at the hands of Babylonians. They were at the mercy of their captors, who had defiled their temple and mocked their

God. But God reminded them of who would have the last laugh. For their pain, He prescribed the promise of double blessing.

The NIV says, "I will restore twice as much to you."

The KJV says, "I will render double unto thee."

The NLT says, "I will repay two blessings for each of your troubles."

We've got to be very careful not to turn biblical principles into quadratic equations. Yes, better is one day in the courts of the Lord than a thousand elsewhere.[17] But I'm not convinced that the psalmist was formulating a one-thousand-to-one ratio. After all, the blessing of God's presence cannot be reduced to hours or minutes any more than to dollars or cents. A day is like a thousand years to God,[18] yet He exists outside our four dimensions of spacetime. So time is immaterial to an eternal God.

That said, let's not underestimate the blessings of God either or ignore the fact that God is the one who promises a double blessing. I recognize that this promise was given to Jewish refugees living in the fifth century BC, but I also believe it belongs to us. Why? Because the God who made the promise is the same yesterday, today, and forever.[19] Because every spiritual blessing is ours in Christ.[20] And because "no matter how many promises God has made, they are 'Yes' in Christ."[21]

You cannot claim the promises of God like a game of Pin the Tail on the Donkey, but every promise has your name on it. Every blessing in the Bible is part and parcel of our spiritual birthright by virtue of what Christ accomplished on the cross. Positioning ourselves for those blessings begins by kneeling at the foot of the cross and ends with us casting our crowns before the throne of God. In between, we flip every blessing.

The Best Is Yet to Come

The book of Job may be the oldest book of the Bible, but it strikes a timeless chord. Everything that was precious to Job—his family, his health, his livelihood—was taken from him. Job didn't just survive those setbacks; he gave God the sacrifice of praise. At his lowest point, he blessed the God who gives and the God who takes away.[22]

At my father-in-law's funeral, I did my best to pull a Job. Fortunately, our friends and family did a better job of consoling us than Job's did consoling him. I'll never forget the person who picked up all our shoes and shined them before the funeral. It was a small act of kindness, but it meant the world to us. And it's those kinds of blessings that I make a mental note of and try to flip.

There was also a word of encouragement that our family held on to. If Bob Schmidgall had a Jonathan, it was Betta Mengistu. And during our darkest days, Uncle Betta's words were a lifeline: "When we have a setback, we do not take a step back, because God is already preparing our comeback." Spoken by anyone else, those words would not have carried the same weight. In fact, they may have had the opposite effect. Spoken by him, they helped us bear the burden of grief.

Hold that thought.

A few years ago, I was part of a panel at a conference with Bob Goff. Bob is one of my favorite people on the planet, and he has a way of saying things that simplifies and amplifies the good news of the gospel. I can't remember the question, but Bob's answer was incredibly encouraging: "The best chapter titles come later."

Maybe you're in a chapter titled "Setback," be that a bitter divorce, a bad decision, or a difficult diagnosis. You can't have a chapter titled "Comeback" without having a prior chapter titled "Setback." That's the story of Job's life, isn't it? The book of Job reads like a tragedy until the last chapter, but God gets the last laugh. The best chapter is the last chapter, and it could be titled "Double Blessing."

> When Job prayed for his friends, the LORD restored his fortunes. In fact, the LORD gave him twice as much as before![23]

Is there someone you need to pray for? Like Job it may be a friend who offended you, or it may be a boss who betrayed you. Not only does the act of forgiveness break the curse of bitterness, but it also invokes the blessing of God. Let forgiveness begin a new chapter in your life!

Now, did you notice the specificity of what God did? It says that the Lord gave him *twice* as much as before. But who's counting, right? I'll tell you who— the God who catches our tears in His bottle.[24] Please don't turn this passage into a formulaic promise, but please know that the Lord doesn't lose track of the things we've suffered.

> The LORD blessed Job in the second half of his life even more than in the beginning. For now he had 14,000 sheep, 6,000 camels, 1,000 teams of oxen, and 1,000 female donkeys.[25]

What I find fascinating about this double blessing is the fact that it's in alignment with old covenant law. If a thief was found guilty of stealing an animal, the price of recompense was paying back double.[26] Why wouldn't that hold true for the thief who comes to steal, kill, and destroy?[27]

If you have experienced heart-wrenching loss like Job, finding a new normal is not easy. It takes time to get back on your feet, and I would exhort you to take your time! If you try to shortcut sorrow, it short-circuits the soul. While I cannot promise that the pain will go away and never come back, the peace of God will help you manage it. And the promises of God will help you overcome it.

When your heart begins to heal, will you be bold enough to believe God for a double blessing? Will you be brave enough to believe that God wants to bless the second half of your life even more than the first half? Remember, a game is never won at halftime. And it's not lost either! Because I believe that the blessings of God overtake obedience,[28] I believe in second-half rallies and fourth-quarter comebacks! And I believe that for you. The question is, do you?

Now let me double back to Zechariah's promise.

I'm partial to *The Message*'s paraphrase: "This very day I'm declaring a double bonus." If you are in relationship with Jesus Christ, there is no double jeopardy. Your sin is forgiven and forgotten. Yet as amazing as that is, it's only half the gospel. Not only is the debt of our sin paid in full, but the righteousness of Christ is also transferred to our account. And, I might add, all of it. If that's not a double bonus, what is? And it includes every spiritual blessing in Christ.

I've lived through chapters titled "Failure," and they're frustrating. My storyline contains "Heartache," and it still hurts. My table of contents includes "Pain" and "Suffering," but there is a God who is working all things together for the good of those who love Him and have been called according to His purpose.[29] And because of that, the best is yet to come!

UMBRELLA BLESSING

All these blessings shall come upon you and overtake
you, if you obey the voice of the LORD your God.

DEUTERONOMY 28:2, ESV

In the west aisle of the north transept of Westminster Abbey, there is a memorial
to a mercurial man named Jonas Hanway. London's iconic abbey is the final
resting place for some of history's most famous poets and politicians and sci-
entists. The who's who includes Queen Elizabeth I, Sir Isaac Newton, Charles
Dickens, and Charles Darwin. The relief honoring Jonas Hanway depicts a man
distributing clothing to children with an inscription that reads,

> The helpless infant nurtured thro' his care, the friendless prostitute
> shelter'd and reform'd, the hopeless youth rescu'd from misery and
> ruin, and train'd to serve and to defend his country, uniting in one
> common strain of gratitude, bear testimony to their benefactor's
> virtues. "THIS was the FRIEND and FATHER of the POOR."[1]

Jonas Hanway made his fortune as a sea captain and merchant. Later in life,
he turned his attention toward philanthropy. Hanway served as both governor
and vice president of Foundling Hospital, a home for the homeless. In the eighteenth century, the word *hospital* was used more generically—it simply indi-
cated that hospitality was offered to families in dire straits or children deserted
by their parents.[2]

But there is something else for which Jonas Hanway is famous. He did what
no Englishman had done before. Jonas Hanway was the first male Londoner to

carry an umbrella. The portable roof, as it was called, was considered an accessory suitable only for women. Two hundred and fifty years ago, real men got wet.

I can picture Jonas Hanway walking the streets of London, singing in the rain under his umbrella. I can also hear coachmen and chimneysweeps hooting and hollering, giving him a hard time! Jonas Hanway may have been the most mocked man of his generation, but he was also the driest.

What does any of that have to do with double blessing?

I like to think of the blessing of God as an umbrella. An umbrella doesn't change the forecast. Life will rain pain, that's for sure. But the blessing of God does provide a covering of sorts, an extra layer of protection against the elements.

Does that umbrella of blessing mean we get to sidestep sickness? No, it does not. How about suffering? Nope. Failure? I'm afraid not. God loves us too much to rob us of the very things that will catalyze our character development. Besides, what makes us think we can be conformed to the image of Christ without being betrayed by Judas, criticized by Pharisees, or tempted by the devil himself?

The blessing of God doesn't mean you won't get wet, but it can keep you singing in the rain like Jonas Hanway. What is that umbrella blessing? It's an extra measure of grace during tough times. It's a song in the night during seasons of sadness. It's the peace that surpasses understanding when life doesn't make sense. It's joy unspeakable when you reach the end of your rope.

Of course, we have to position ourselves under that umbrella of blessing. And I'll show you how. But I like the way Ed Young says this: "We need to get under those things God has put over us so we can get over those things God has put under us."[3]

Habits of Highly Blessed People

In 1406 BC, a blessing was pronounced on God's people from the top of Mount Gerizim. With an elevation of 2,849 feet above sea level, Mount Gerizim was one of the highest peaks in ancient Israel. Why God chose to pronounce this blessing from a mountain peak is a mystery to me, but in the grand scheme of God's plan, I think Mount Gerizim may be as significant as Mount Sinai.

On the summit of Mount Sinai, God met with Moses and inscribed ten commandments on stone tablets. Those commandments create the condition on which the blessing of God is predicated. The blessing of God is *not* carte blanche. All of God's blessings come with a condition that must be met. In this instance, it's plain and simple.

> If you fully obey the LORD your God and carefully follow all his commands I give you today, the LORD your God will set you high above all the nations on earth.[4]

As one of my favorite T-shirts says, "This is not rocket surgery!" There is no better way to position ourselves for God's blessing than good old-fashioned obedience. But did you catch the qualifiers? We must *fully* obey the Lord and *carefully* follow His commands. Instead of looking for loopholes or coming up with cop-outs, we go the extra mile. Please note, fully obeying and carefully following His commands does not denote *legalism*. Legalism is obeying the letter of the law while violating the spirit of the law. It's making human amendments to God's laws, making them harder to obey than they were meant to be! That doesn't honor God. In fact, it dishonors God's original intent. Legalism is behavior modification at best and self-righteousness at worst. That approach does not net God's blessing.

Let me zoom out.

When we submit our lives to Christ, we come under the umbrella of God's blessing. Our covering is Christ crucified, a covering that was foreshadowed as far back as the Garden of Eden. After Adam and Eve ate from the tree of the knowledge of good and evil, God covered their nakedness with clothing made from animal skins. That first sacrifice foreshadowed the final sacrifice on Calvary's cross.

The covering of Christ is prefaced by the Passover as well. On the night that God delivered Israel out of Egypt, He instructed them to smear their doorframes with the blood of the Passover lamb.[5] The blood of the lamb provided a protective covering. Jesus is our Passover Lamb, and it's His blood that breaks the power of canceled sin.[6]

If you are in Christ, you are under God's covering. That's worth celebrating every single day—His mercies are as sure as the sunrise! That said, we have to make a daily decision to stay under the umbrella of God's blessing by walking in obedience. Please read what I'm about to write very carefully, but don't read into it. When we get outside the guardrails of God's good, pleasing, and perfect will as revealed in Scripture, we subject ourselves to the consequences of sin. That isn't a threat. It's a reality check.

If you cheat on your taxes, for example, you are stepping out from under the umbrella of God's blessing. The same is true if you cheat on your spouse. Does God forgive those offenses? If we repent, of course He does! But I cannot promise that the IRS or your spouse will.

It's important, at this juncture, to make a distinction between *penalty* and *consequence*. When you confess your sin, that sin is forgiven and forgotten. The *penalty* for sin was paid in full two thousand years ago, but you still have to live with the *consequences* of your actions.

When we disobey God, we put ourselves in a precarious position. Again, that isn't a threat. And of this I'm sure: God doesn't want fear to dictate our decisions. Perfect love casts out all fear, so we can face the future with holy confidence! That said, you cannot break the law of sowing and reaping any more than you can break the law of gravity. No one can. The law of sowing and reaping will make you or break you, and the pivot point on that seesaw is obedience! Simply put, obedience is *the first habit* of highly blessed people.

Extended Warranty

Just as the blessings of God come with a condition, they also carry a warranty. In contractual law, a warranty protects us against a manufacturer's defect or seller's default. Those warranties come in lots of different varieties with many different riders. There are lifetime warranties, which have no time limit. There are extended warranties, which broaden the umbrella of coverage. But let's be honest—most of us have been burned by the fine print. In my experience, most warranties oversell and underdeliver. But I have some good news: there is no expiration date on the promises of God, and those promises are backed by a God who does not default.

All these blessings shall come upon you and overtake you, if you obey the voice of the LORD your God.[7]

Notice that the condition is repeated for good measure: "If you obey the voice of the LORD your God." I've written a book on how to hear the voice of God, *Whisper*. I won't detail all seven languages outlined in that book, but I will note that the Latin word for "obey" is *obedire*, which means "to give ear." Obedience starts with an ear that is consecrated to Christ. It's tuning in to His frequency and turning up the volume. It's obeying His whispers, even if culture is screaming the exact opposite.

Is the still, small voice of the Holy Spirit the loudest voice in your life?

Now notice the warranty: "All these blessings shall come upon you and overtake you." Have you ever experienced a blessing that seemingly comes out of nowhere? It sneaks up on you from behind? That is the blessing of God overtaking you. As sure as your sin will find you out, the blessings of God will always catch up with long obedience in the same direction![8]

You can google map your latitude and longitude, but I live 5,879 miles from Mount Gerizim. That's an awfully long distance, even as the crow flies. Yet I'm not "out of area." And there are no roaming fees when it comes to blessing. The blessing of God has no borders, no boundaries! The blessings pronounced from the top of Mount Gerizim are as valid today as they were 3,425 years ago. Why? Because God is watching over His word to perform it.[9]

When it comes to making a claim on a warranty, it usually requires several phone calls and too much time on hold, listening to elevator music. God's warranty works in the opposite way. God is the one who comes knocking! Hanani the seer said, "The eyes of the LORD search the whole earth in order to strengthen those whose hearts are fully committed to him."[10] In other words, God is actively looking for opportunities to fulfill His promises!

The psalmist said, "Surely goodness and mercy shall follow me all the days of my life."[11] The word translated *follow* is a Hebrew hunting term.[12] You can turn your back on God. You can run in the opposite direction as fast and as far as you can. You can deny His existence and avoid Him at every turn. But the Hound of Heaven is undeterred. He never stops tracking us because He cannot give up on us. If you turn around, you'll discover that the heavenly Father is right there with arms wide open, ready to bless you and welcome you back home.

With the warranty covered, it's time to pop this umbrella blessing. And an umbrella is only as good as its ribs!

Mandelbrot Set

In fractal geometry, there is a complex set of numbers that produces an infinitely intricate shape when plotted on a plane. It's called a Mandelbrot set, after the founder of fractal geometry, Benoit Mandelbrot.[13] Clouds and coastlines are classic examples of this endless complexity. Any detail can be magnified to reveal even more detail, ad infinitum.

The blessings of God are a Mandelbrot set. They aren't one size fits all. Each blessing is custom fitted to your complexity and, I might add, your personality. Take the mercy of God, for example. The mercy God has shown you is as unique as your fingerprint. The writer of Lamentations said that God's mercies are *new* every morning.[14] The Hebrew word for "new" doesn't just mean "again and again." It means "different." In other words, today's mercy is different from yesterday's mercy, which is different from the mercy of the day before that.

If you want to fully appreciate God's mercy, take out a calculator. Multiply your age by 365 days; then add the number of days since your last birthday. The total number of days you've been alive is synonymous with the different strains of mercy you have been shown. Each day's mercy is a never-to-be-repeated miracle. The day my father-in-law was ushered into eternity, he had experienced 20,077 daily strains of mercy.

Let me push this envelope a little further.

There never has been and never will be anyone like you, but that isn't a testament to you. It's a testament to the God who created you. And the significance of that is this: no one can worship God *like you* or *for you*. When we sing a song like "Great Is Thy Faithfulness," we may be singing the *same words,* but we are singing *a very different song.* God has been faithful to me in thousands of different ways. When I sing of His faithfulness, I'm singing out of my unique experiences. And so are you. If you don't sing, the person next to you might not miss your voice, but God will. In fact, you are holding out on God. Why? Because your praise is irreplaceable! Like our praise that is uniquely offered to God, God's promises are uniquely fitted to us.

The blessing pronounced from the top of Mount Gerizim is a fractal blessing. By my count, this umbrella blessing contains at least seventeen distinct subblessings. It covers the gamut of human experience—relational, occupational, financial, emotional, generational, and spiritual. It reads a little bit like comprehensive insurance coverage! Because I don't want to shortchange this blessing, I've included it in its entirety. Don't just read this blessing. Take a few moments to meditate on it, letting this blessing seep into your spirit. It might even be worth memorizing!

> You will be blessed in the city and blessed in the country.
> The fruit of your womb will be blessed, and the crops of your land
>   and the young of your livestock—the calves of your herds and
>   the lambs of your flocks.
> Your basket and your kneading trough will be blessed.
> You will be blessed when you come in and blessed when you go out.

> The Lord will grant that the enemies who rise up against you will be
> defeated before you. They will come at you from one direction but flee
> from you in seven.
>   The Lord will send a blessing on your barns and on everything you
> put your hand to. The Lord your God will bless you in the land he is
> giving you.
>   The Lord will establish you as his holy people, as he promised you
> on oath, if you keep the commands of the Lord your God and walk in
> obedience to him. Then all the peoples on earth will see that you are
> called by the name of the Lord, and they will fear you. The Lord will
> grant you abundant prosperity—in the fruit of your womb, the young
> of your livestock and the crops of your ground—in the land he swore to
> your ancestors to give you.
>   The Lord will open the heavens, the storehouse of his bounty, to
> send rain on your land in season and to bless all the work of your hands.
> You will lend to many nations but will borrow from none. The Lord will

make you the head, not the tail. If you pay attention to the commands
of the LORD your God that I give you this day and carefully follow them,
you will always be at the top, never at the bottom.[15]

According to rabbinic tradition, every word of Scripture has seventy faces
and six hundred thousand meanings.[16] The Word of God—every word—is ka-
leidoscopic. You cannot dive its depth nor summit its height. And that's certainly true of this umbrella blessing.

Seventy Faces

Before I turn the kaleidoscope on this umbrella blessing, let me remind you that
bad things happen to good people. Again, an umbrella does not guarantee we
won't get wet. The algorithm of the Almighty includes free will, and free will is
a free radical. I might also point out that good things happen to bad people.
That's part and parcel of God's prevenient grace. In the words of Jesus, God
"makes his sun rise on the evil and on the good, and sends rain on the just and
on the unjust."[17]

According to the twenty-fifth canon passed by the Second Council of Or-
ange in AD 529, the grace of God is the genesis of all good.[18] We can't even take
credit for our good works because the genesis of those good works is the grace
of God.

The blessing of God doesn't mean that you'll win every case, win every
contract, or win every election. It doesn't mean that you'll end the season unde-
feated or uninjured or that someone won't add insult to that injury! But the
blessing of God can help you perform to the best of your God-given ability—
and beyond. And that's true no matter what you do.

If blessing had a first name, I would call it Favor.

If blessing had a last name, I would call it Anointing.

God wants to help you do what you do in a way that sanctifies you and
glorifies Him. How does God do that? By giving us things to do that are hu-
manly impossible! Why? So that when God does them, we can't take the credit!

The favor of God is the X factor. And His anointing is the difference between
the best you can do and the best God can do. It's gifting beyond natural ability

and provision beyond human resource. It's also wisdom beyond knowledge, which I call "God ideas." And I'd rather have one God idea than a thousand good ideas! Good ideas are good, but God ideas change the course of history!

Your Weak Hand

The umbrella blessing is all-inclusive, all-encompassing. It says, "Wherever you go and whatever you do, you will be blessed." But let me zoom in on one sub-blessing because it's a microcosm of the whole blessing.

> The LORD will send a blessing on your barns and on everything you
> put your hand to.[19]

If you don't have a barn, you're out of luck. I'm kidding, of course. This blessing has agricultural undertones because that's whom the blessing was originally bestowed on. But you can fill in the blank with whatever it is that you do. God wants to bless your home, your office, your organization, and your church.

I've prayed this blessing on professional athletes, elected officials, and heart surgeons. I've prayed it on teachers and lawyers and entrepreneurs. No matter what you do, God wants to help you do it in a way that makes people praise God. We all have bad days, and no one bats a thousand at the plate. But the attitude with which we approach our work should shift the atmosphere! And excellence honors God.

I don't think God is guaranteeing a Midas touch, where everything we touch turns to gold. None of us is exempt from the ten-thousand-hour rule.[20] We've got to grow in our giftings by trial and error. We'll win some and lose some along the way! But the work of our hands should somehow bear God's blessing, whether that's a little extra love or a little extra excellence.

Dorothy Sayers said, "No crooked table legs or ill-fitting drawers ever, I dare swear, came out of the carpenter's shop at Nazareth."[21] Jesus crafted furniture the way He treated people—with great care. It doesn't matter whether you work a white-collar or blue-collar or no-collar job; it's our utmost for His highest. Excellence invokes a blessing, and blessing evokes excellence. You could even call *excellence* a habit of highly blessed people.

When I was in graduate school, I took an occupational assessment that showed a low aptitude for writing. In other words, "Whatever you do, don't write books!" I felt called to write, but I knew that writing was not my natural gifting. Fortunately, God doesn't call the qualified; He qualifies the called.

Without the help of the Holy Spirit, I'm below average! That's why I take my shoes off when I write. It's my way of acknowledging that I'm on holy ground. It's my way of asking God for a writing anointing. When I start typing, what I'm really doing is worshipping God with the twenty-six letters of the English alphabet. I'm taking every thought captive and making it obedient to Christ with a keyboard. Now, your employer might not be too happy if you started showing up to meetings barefoot. But is there a unique way for you to acknowledge that you are fulfilling God's calling? Is there a unique way to acknowledge that the boardroom or classroom or locker room is holy ground?

God wants to use you at your point of greatest giftedness, no doubt. He's the one who gave you those gifts in the first place! But God also wants to use you at your point of weakness. Why? Because it's in our weaknesses that His power is made perfect.[22] He doesn't just anoint our strong hands. He anoints our weak hands too! And when He does, there is a keen awareness that God is working in us and through us in a way that is beyond what we could ask or imagine!

Multiplication Anointing

In the fall of 2006, I was speaking at a conference in Baltimore with Tommy Barnett. Tommy and his son Matthew cofounded the Los Angeles Dream Center. Tommy shared about the providential purchase of the Queen of Angels Hospital, a 360,000-square-foot building that sits on 8.8 acres of prime real estate overlooking US Route 101. The owners turned down more lucrative offers from major Hollywood studios and sold it to the Dream Center for pennies on the dollar. It now ministers to fifty thousand people every month through hundreds of need-meeting ministries. It was the Los Angeles Dream Center that inspired our DC Dream Center, and Matthew Barnett was kind enough to cast the vision to our congregation.

After sharing his testimony of God's favor, Tommy Barnett gave an altar call that changed the trajectory of my life. He invited to the altar anyone who wanted what he called a *multiplication anointing*. I had never heard the phrase before, and I even wondered whether it was biblical. But if Tommy Barnett was throwing down that mantle like Elijah, I was picking it up like Elisha! And, of course, I've since discovered just how biblical it is! In fact, it's part of the fabric of the original blessing: "Be fruitful and multiply."[23]

The Hebrew word translated "multiply" is *rabah*. It means "to make much," "to make numerous," and "to make great."[24] It can be translated "greater," as in "They will do even greater things than these."[25] It can be translated "abundantly," as in "far more abundantly than all that we ask or think."[26] In one of His parables, Jesus pointed out that good soil produces a thirty, sixty, or hundredfold return.[27] That's the goal, isn't it? Stewardship is giving God a good return on His investment.

Now let me go back to that altar where I prayed for a multiplication anointing.

I was days away from the release of my first book, *In a Pit with a Lion on a Snowy Day*. Honestly, the statistics surrounding book sales are awfully sobering for first-time authors. The average U.S. nonfiction book is now selling less than 250 copies per year and less than 3,000 copies over its lifetime.[28] I mustered all the faith I could manage and prayed for a multiplication anointing on that book. My whispered number? I felt a little foolish even asking, but I prayed that it would sell twenty-five thousand copies. I may not have thought of it this way then, but I was opening my umbrella. I was invoking the original blessing that God had pronounced in the Garden of Eden. That kind of prayer doesn't guarantee a specific sales number. Truth be told, we often aim too low! That book has now exceeded expectations by half a million copies, and my only explanation is the multiplication anointing.

If your goal is to multiply sales for selfish purposes, God won't bless it. But if your motives are pure, God has blessings in categories you cannot conceive of. Does the multiplication anointing need to be coupled with a work ethic? Absolutely! God doesn't bless lack of effort any more than lack of integrity. If you want the umbrella blessing, you have to break a sweat and burn some calories. You might even lose a little sleep! I can tell you this: writing a book requires me to set my alarm very early in the morning. I'm up and at it before the sun rises. During my writing season, it's long days that are mentally, emotionally, and spiritually exhausting. But the blessing of God means that the whole is greater than the sum of the parts. Why? Because God multiplies our efforts with His anointing!

The umbrella blessing makes this promise: "The LORD will grant you abundant prosperity—in the fruit of your womb, the young of your livestock and the crops of your ground."[29] Since multiplication is one of the overarching storylines of Scripture, it shouldn't come as a surprise that it's the subplot of this umbrella blessing. Simply put, the blessing of God *is* a multiplication anointing.

What does God want to multiply? Anything that is good or right or pure or just. He wants to multiply the gifts of the Spirit and the fruit of the Spirit. He wants to multiply your time, talent, and treasure for His glory and for your good. But what God does for us is never just for us! God wants to bless your family to the third and fourth generations. He wants to multiply His blessing on your life so it spills over onto your neighbors and coworkers.

We think right here, right now. But God is thinking nations and generations! And I promise you this: *His vision for your life is bigger and better than yours!* That's what the umbrella blessing is all about. And that multiplication anointing is yours for the asking!

Consider this your altar call.

THE X FACTOR

No good thing does [God] withhold
from those who walk uprightly.

PSALM 84:11, ESV

During his celebrated career as a composer, George Frideric Handel wrote forty-two operas, twenty-nine oratorios, and 120 cantatas. Of Handel, Ludwig van Beethoven said, "To him I bow the knee."[1] Handel certainly ranks as one of history's greatest composers, but he hit a point of diminishing return later in life. At age fifty-six, Handel was past his composing prime. He was depressed. He was in debt. And a stroke hindered the use of his right hand. Handel was struggling to stay musically relevant, which is rather ironic given the fact that he was about to score one of history's most iconic pieces of music.

On August 22, 1741, George Frideric Handel started composing. He would not leave his home for three weeks. In fact, he rarely left his composing chair. Twenty-one days later, Handel emerged from his writing room with a 259-page masterpiece called *Messiah*. The opening act prophetically points to the coming Messiah. The middle act is Handel's commentary on the passion of Christ. The final act celebrates the risen Savior, who "shall reign forever and ever." Finally Handel inked three letters on the last page, *SDG—soli Deo gloria*—"To God alone be the glory!"

That's the backstory, but here's the rest of the story.

Messiah debuted as an Easter offering at the Great Music Hall in Dublin, Ireland, on April 13, 1742.[2] The music mesmerized its listeners, but it accomplished so much more than that. It wasn't just a concert; it was a benefit concert. That inaugural performance raised £400—$86,000 in today's dollars![3] And that £400 was used to free 142 men from debtors' prison. That is what qualifies *Messiah* as a double blessing. The first blessing is beautiful music that inspires the soul. The second blessing? Setting 142 captives free!

Of course, that's just the firstfruits of what was destined to become perhaps the most performed piece of music in Western history. In his will, George Frideric Handel left a full score of *Messiah* to Foundling Hospital. Remember the umbrella-wielding Jonas Hanway? Well, Handel funded the hospital where Hanway served as governor from 1758 to 1772. All proceeds from that piece of music were used to further its Matthew 25 mission of feeding the hungry, housing the homeless, and caring for the sick.

What is the double blessing?

The first blessing is using our God-given time and talent to make a difference in the world. For Handel, that meant making music that stirs the soul. The second blessing is using the treasure that our time and talent produces, typically in the form of a paycheck, to generously bless others.

Time, Talent, Treasure

As a pastor, I've seen a lot of offering buckets passed in a lot of church services. But I have yet to see someone get up out of their seat, stand in the bucket, and attempt to pass it. That would probably break the bucket and seem a little strange. But that's precisely what we're doing when we give back to God, isn't it? The person giving that money traded their time and talent for that treasure. For some, it's minimum wage earned by the sweat of their brows. For others, it's their creative ideas that earn commissions. Either way, it's not just cold, hard cash we're donating. It's the time and talent we traded for that treasure! When you place something in an offering bucket, you put part of yourself in there with it. Of course, that equation works two ways.

It takes about five hundred volunteers to pull off a dozen services at seven campuses on any given weekend at National Community Church. On average, our volunteers serve about three hours on a weekend. Do the math, and that adds up to 1,500 hours volunteered. If you multiply that number by the median hourly pay rate in DC, that's $49,500 of time donated week in and week out. Of course, that doesn't include our outreach ministries or mission trips. Our dream team at the DC Dream Center volunteered 16,000 hours this past year, loving and serving and mentoring kids in Ward 7, an underserved and underresourced neighborhood in our nation's capital. That adds up to a $528,000 donation but multiplies into so much more.

Remember the old adage "Time is money"? It's true in more ways than one! You traded your time for the balance in your bank account. For many of us, that's nine to five, Monday to Friday. And whether you're an accountant or an administrative assistant, an educator or a rideshare driver, you traded your talent for that treasure too. That's what makes your gift so valuable. Or maybe I should say "invaluable." You may give the same amount of money as someone else, but your gift is unique. Why? Because it was *your* time and *your* talent that earned it.

George Frideric Handel traded twenty-one days of time for *Messiah*. Of course, he also traded years of playing scales and decades of composing cantatas. Then he used the treasure that piece of music produced to bless those who needed it most. That's what the double blessing is. That's what the double blessing does. And it's as unique as you are!

Handel wasn't a musician who followed Christ; he was a Christ follower who made music. That sequence is as significant as seeking *first* the kingdom of God. And I hope it's true of you, no matter what you do. Music was Handel's passion, but the gospel was his mission. And Handel's music served a dual purpose. He stewarded his God-given talent as a musician to write anointed oratorios, but he also leveraged the treasure it produced to become a double blessing—a blessing to those who listened to his music, a blessing to those who benefited from his generosity.

"*Messiah* has fed the hungry, clothed the naked, fostered the orphan . . . more than any other single musical production," notes one of Handel's biographers. Another wrote, "Perhaps the works of no other composer have so largely contributed to the relief of human suffering."[4]

To that I say, hallelujah.

Double Bottom Line

In the 1950s, there was a game show called *The $64,000 Question*. You probably have not seen the show, but I bet you've heard the idiom. "A $64,000 question" refers to a critical question. It's often the most important yet most difficult question to answer. Why? Because the answer hinges on factors that cannot be forecasted.

Let me pose a $64,000 question: Does the success of *Messiah* have anything to do with the fact that it debuted at a benefit concert or that the concert's proceeds were bequeathed to Foundling Hospital? I know there are those who would argue that *correlation doesn't equal causation*. And while I understand that logical fallacy, it's trumped by a theological conviction. If God knows that you're going to honor Him with the outcome, I believe He is delighted to doubly bless. Sure, the success of *Messiah* has a lot to do with the musical score. But there is another factor at play, an X factor.

Can I tell you why God has blessed our coffeehouse on Capitol Hill? It's more than our honey lavender latte, even though I must say, it's delicious. And while our coffeehouse sits one block from Union Station and kitty-corner to the Securities and Exchange Commission, it's more than just location, location, location.

Why, then? I believe it's because Ebenezers Coffeehouse gives every penny of profit to kingdom causes. What is there not to bless?

Our coffee doesn't just taste good; it does good, and it feels good. Why? Because it's coffee with a cause! More than $1.2 million in net profits have funded dozens of causes that are near and dear to the heart of God. We also leverage Ebenezers for the Living Room, a ministry to our friends experiencing homelessness. We have a core conviction as a church: *God will bless us in proportion to how we give to missions and care for the poor in our city.* If we invest our time, talent, and treasure in things that are near and dear to the heart of God, I'm not worried about our bottom line! Why? Because God's got our back.

Ebenezers Coffeehouse has been voted the number one coffeehouse in Washington, DC, multiple times, against pretty stiff competition. Again, some might consider this correlation without causation. That said, I honestly believe that God has blessed our coffeehouse because He knows that the buck doesn't stop with us, literally! The X factor is the favor of God, and the favor of God is the by-product of flipping the blessing with every cup of coffee we serve.

We have a double bottom line at Ebenezers. Like any business, we want to generate a net profit while employing best business practices. We love five-star reviews, and we know that product quality and customer service are a huge part of that equation. But net profit isn't our end goal. There is a second bottom line when you do business as mission. Our ultimate goal is to give it all away!

If you cultivate a double-blessing mindset that is focused on flipping every blessing, you better buckle your seat belt. Why? Because God is going to open the windows of heaven and pour out more blessing than you can contain. Am I talking about only material blessings? Of course not. Giving produces joy, and more joy is just what the world needs!

When you flip the blessing, it takes the pressure off you and puts the ball in God's court. It enables you to live with holy anticipation, waiting to see what God does next.

Full Blessing

Let me go back to Handel's *Messiah* and the $64,000 question. Does the benefit concert or the bequeathment to Foundling Hospital have anything to do with the longevity and popularity of *Messiah*? Here's my take. If God knows that you won't hoard the £400 blessing, He won't withhold His favor.

No good thing does he withhold
from those who walk uprightly.[5]

Do you remember getting your first paycheck? I still remember the excitement as I opened that envelope, but I experienced quite a letdown. Why? Well, I was making only $5.25 an hour to begin with. Then I discovered something called withholding tax. Those are the taxes withheld by your employer and sent directly to the government. Let's just say that my first paycheck wasn't all that I had imagined it would be!

I've got some very good news, but first, a word of caution. God doesn't bless cheating, and that includes cheating on your taxes! Capeesh? If you want to posture yourself for God's blessing, integrity is on par with humility. It's so tempting to take shortcuts and cut corners, isn't it? Especially when no one is watching. But if you compromise your integrity, you short-circuit God's blessing.

The good news? If we operate with integrity, there is no withholding tax on the blessings of God. And that's the goal, isn't it? To live in such a way that God is able to give us His full blessing—*blessings beyond our ability to ask or imagine*. Don't settle for anything less or anything else.

If you have to compromise your integrity for an opportunity, it's not an opportunity. That's called temptation. Don't sacrifice the favor of God for the promotion of man. Just as the first will be last and the last will be first, sometimes what seems like a step backward proves to be a giant leap forward. Eventually, integrity will catapult you far beyond maneuvering or manipulating. Integrity is staying in the lane of blessing, even when you feel like changing lanes. Trust me—integrity is the fast pass to blessing.

If you don't hold out on God, He is not going to hold out on you. If you give God the glory, there is no good thing He will withhold. Why? He's a good, good Father!

Which of you, if your son asks for bread, will give him a stone? Or if he asks for a fish, will give him a snake? If you, then, though you are evil, know how to give good gifts to your children, how much more will your Father in heaven give good gifts to those who ask him![6]

One fun footnote: I was depressed when I discovered that withholding tax, but my mourning turned to dancing a few months later when I got a letter from the IRS with a tax refund. I made so little money that they gave it all back! Just like that after-the-fact refund, blessings that are the by-product of integrity have a way of boomeranging months and years and decades later!

The Drop Box

Along with our coffeehouse, we also own and operate a movie theater on Capitol Hill. The Miracle is a second-run theater, but we host quite a few red carpet and prerelease screenings. One of the most memorable was the documentary film *Emanuel*. The movie tells the story of unfathomable forgiveness for the man who went on a race-motivated, hate-filled shooting spree in Charleston, South Carolina, on the evening of June 17, 2015. When the credits rolled, I was speechless. There is a unique anointing on the film and on its director, Brian Ivie.

In 2011, Brian was a rising junior at USC's School of Cinematic Arts. He read an article in the *Los Angeles Times* about a pastor in Seoul, South Korea, who built a drop box for abandoned babies. That pastor has cared for more than six hundred unwanted babies, most of whom were abandoned because of deformities or disabilities.

As Brian read that article, a thought shot across his synapses: *If I don't do anything about this, if I don't tell this story, everyone's going to forget.*[7] Call that what you want, but I call it a God idea. But it's only an idea until you do something about it. You have to take the thought captive and make it obedient to Christ.[8] How do you do that? With time, talent, and treasure. With blood, sweat, and tears.

Brian sent an email to Pastor Lee, the Korean pastor. He recruited a team of eleven students to shoot the film. He raised $65,000 to fund it. Then he slept on the floor of the orphanage for three months while shooting the film. While making that documentary, Brian Ivie put his faith in Christ because of the way that Korean pastor loved the least of these. When everything was said and done, Brian produced an award-winning documentary called *The Drop Box*.

Back to *Emanuel.* As with any film, it's not easy to find funding. I've been shopping a few films myself for longer than I'd like! Not long after our screening, Steph Curry and Viola Davis stepped in as executive producers of that film. That movie is one of the most powerful I've seen, and I recommend you see it.

Can I tell you why I believe God has blessed the films Brian has produced with both funding and awards? It's the heart behind the films that touch on themes near and dear to the heart of God. But there is one more thing. Brian Ivie is pulling a Handel with *Emanuel.* How? It's a benefit film. If you watch the film, it will bless your soul. But it will do more than that. It's a double blessing because the profits from the film go to those who lost loved ones in that tragic shooting.

To that I say, go thou and do likewise!

Mad Skillz

At the very end of his life, Moses pronounced blessings on the twelve tribes of Israel. One of my favorite blessings was pronounced on the Levites: "Bless all his skills, LORD, and be pleased with the work of his hands."[9]

As someone who has had a dozen surgeries, I've prayed this blessing on more than a few surgeons. I certainly wanted a surgeon who graduated from med school and got good grades too. But I make no apologies for praying God's anointing on their skills!

I know this is slang, but the anointing of God turns our skills into skillz—mad skillz.

It's the X factor that adds the z to the nth degree! I've prayed this blessing on NFL quarterbacks, corporate executives, and cabinet members. I've even blessed our baristas at Ebenezers Coffeehouse! No matter what you do, God wants to anoint you to do it.

"If it falls to your lot to be a street sweeper," said Dr. Martin Luther King Jr., "sweep streets like Michelangelo painted pictures, sweep streets like Beethoven composed music. . . . Sweep streets like Shakespeare wrote poetry. Sweep streets so well that all the hosts of heaven and earth will have to pause and say: 'Here lived a great street sweeper who swept his job well.'"[10]

The Cambridge dictionary defines *X factor* as "a quality that you cannot describe that makes someone very special."[11] The Oxford dictionary defines it as "a variable in a given situation that could have the most significant impact on the outcome."[12]

In this deathbed blessing, Moses blessed Joseph with "the favor of him who dwelt in the burning bush."[13] I know we don't get to pick and choose the blessings of God like answers on a multiple choice test or options at a potluck dinner. The truth? All the blessings of God belong to us! If you belong to Christ, you are Abraham's seed and heir to His covenant blessings.[14]

I'm not entirely sure what this favor entails, but I know I want it. And not unlike the multiplication anointing, I know I need it. Something happened at the burning bush that turned a stammering shepherd into one of the greatest leaders the world has ever known. The burning bush represents the blessing of favor. It gave Moses the courage to confront Pharaoh and say, "Let my people go."[15] It was the X factor that turned his staff into a snake, parted the Red Sea, and provided manna every morning.

Don't miss the subtext of this blessing. When Moses pronounced this blessing on Joseph, what was he doing? He was flipping the blessing! He knew that

Joseph needed a revelation of I AM as much as he did. Again, the blessing is God—God with us, God for us, God in us.

Would you be bold enough to ask God for "the favor of him who dwelt in the burning bush"? To ask God for the X factor? And not just thirty times or sixty times, but one hundred times. You have not because you ask not.[16]

Of course, with great blessing comes great responsibility. The blessing usually comes with a Pharaoh to confront and a people to deliver. It won't make your life easier, but it will help you do hard things. And God will accomplish things you won't be able to take credit for!

THE AVOGADRO CONSTANT

The LORD bless you
and keep you.

NUMBERS 6:24

How many atoms do you think are in a drop of water?

That is the question Bob DeMoss asked me at an otherwise-ordinary break-fast meeting. After putting his finger on the end of the straw in his water glass to create a little suction, he pulled it out of the glass and released one droplet on his index finger. Then Bob asked that question: "How many atoms do you think are in that one drop of water?"

Go ahead. Take a guess.

A drop of water is awfully small, about five one-hundredths of a milliliter. But it felt like a trick question, so I decided to go big or go home. I thought it might be as many as a million, but I guessed a billion, just to be safe. That's when Bob leaned over the table and said, "There are five quintillion atoms in that one drop of water."

I had no reason not to trust Bob, but I had just met Bob. And I found that astronomical number a little hard to believe! So I did some research, and sure enough! An Italian scientist, Amedeo Avogadro, calculated the number of mol-ecules in one mole of substance. It's called the Avogadro constant, and it adds up to 6.022×10^{23}.[1] So Bob's estimate may have actually been on the conservative side!

My point? A drop of water is not as simple as it seems. In fact, it's more complex than we can imagine. What's true of water is true of you, and it's true of God's blessings too. Now you know why a single drop of water graces the cover of this book! It represents God's blessings, the atoms of which add up to even more than the Avogadro constant. And the ripple effect it creates is the double blessing.

The Sixfold Blessing

The centerpiece of the priestly blessing is the Hebrew word *barak*. If you put that word under a linguistic microscope, you discover six basic meanings. Each of those six meanings is a subblessing, an Avogadro constant unto itself.

While the Israelites were wandering in the wilderness, God instructed Aaron to pronounce a priestly blessing on the people. What makes this particular blessing unique is that it contains the very words of God. We must be careful not to turn this invocation into an incantation, but we must not underestimate the prophetic power of these words either.

> The LORD bless you
>   and keep you;
> the LORD make his face shine on you
>   and be gracious to you;
> the LORD turn his face toward you
>   and give you peace.[2]

The genesis of the military salute is debatable, but one theory suggests that it originated with knights who raised their visors.[3] It was the medieval way of showing friendly intentions by showing one's face. In that respect, it's reminiscent of this priestly blessing. God raises His visor, so to speak. He turns His face toward us. Our peace is found in His posture toward us—God with us, God for us, God in us. Raising one's visor was a medieval way of revealing one's identity. Isn't that what God does when He reveals Himself as "I AM WHO I AM" at the burning bush?[4]

To receive that blessing, you must raise your visor too. God won't bless whom you *pretend* to be! Your disguises may fool everyone else, but they deflect the blessing of God. You know whom God is able to bless? Those who have the humility and courage to be themselves, without pretense. It's another habit of highly blessed people! God sees right through our masks anyway, but He wants us to lift our visors. The net result of this blessing? Intimacy with the almighty God.

A salute is a gesture of respect. Generally speaking, it's subordinates who salute superiors. In God's kingdom, it's superiors who salute subordinates. The greatest of all is the servant of all, and Jesus sets the precedent.

The first meaning of the Hebrew word *barak* is "to salute."

The second meaning is "to kneel down."

If you want to bless little children, you have to get down on their level. When you get down on all fours, it levels the playing field and changes the game. Isn't that what God did in Bethlehem? God most high became God most nigh. The God who saluted Moses at the burning bush kneeled down in a manger. God doesn't just pronounce hygienic blessings from on high. He touches lepers, celebrates Samaritans, and eats with sinners.

The third meaning is "to kiss on the mouth."

I wish this were as simple as it sounds, but we live in an age of adulterated affection and exploited power. Pure love and true power are hard to find and even harder to trust. Why? Because so many have been betrayed by a kiss and that false kiss feels like a curse. To those who steal the innocence of others, Jesus spoke in no uncertain terms: "It would be better for them to have a large millstone hung around their neck and to be drowned in the depths of the sea."[5] Why such strong words? Because God is love and He hates anything that perverts its purity.

I'm afraid we've forgotten what pure love and true power look like, so let me repaint an old picture. It looks like the sinless Son of God carrying a three-hundred-pound cross down the Via Dolorosa for everyone else's sin and then forgiving the ones who nailed Him to it. For the record, Jesus Himself was betrayed by a kiss. That betrayal pierced His soul, just like the cat-o'-nine-tails that ripped into His back, the crown of thorns that cut into His forehead, and the nine-inch spikes that nailed Him to the cross.

If you've been on the wrong side of a false kiss, few things are harder to forgive. But forgiveness is the only thing that will set you free. I know you cannot forget, but with God's help you can turn the page. God's kiss may not erase the memory, but His blessing is bestowed with a fatherly affection that forgives all. And it's more than that. The original language hints at mouth-to-mouth resuscitation. Just as God breathed into the dust and formed Adam, the blessing of God is the fifth force that animates us.[6] It's in Him that "we live and move and have our being."[7] His blessing is our second wind, our second chance.

Do you know why God wants to bless you beyond what you can ask or imagine? Because God loves you beyond what you could ask or imagine!

The Power of the Tongue

When I was in seminary, I spoke to a gathering of men at a drug-rehabilitation program. I met a man who had made some mistakes that contributed to his addictions. He had gotten out from under the umbrella of blessing and paid the price in rehab. But I felt tremendous empathy for him when he shared his backstory. He told me what his dad told him every time he made a mistake as a child: "What the hell—you stupid?"

Imagine those words ringing in your ears. It was obvious by the tears in his eyes how deeply those words cut into his soul. They echoed loud and long. I'm not blaming the father for this man's mistakes, but they were more than careless words. They were a curse that left an open wound. Is it any wonder his son made some stupid decisions? He was simply living up to—or down to—his father's words.

Death and life are in the power of the tongue.[8]

We all know the old adage "Sticks and stones may break my bones, but words will never harm me." And we all know that's not true! Our words don't just carry weight; they have the power to rewrite narratives. A curse can turn a comedy into a tragedy, but blessing can flip the script the other way.

During a fragile time in my teenage years, I was given the gift of life-giving words. I was kneeling at an altar when a missionary put a hand on my shoulder and started praying over me. Then his prayer turned prophetic: "God is going to use you in a great way." It was only one sentence, but I've held on to those words through thick and thin. And I've tried to flip that blessing by speaking life-giving words to others.

That brings us to the fourth meaning of the Hebrew word *barak:* "to speak words of excellence about." And it deserves a little extra attention.

One of the most powerful blessings you can bestow on another person is well-timed words. Remember the woman who broke open her alabaster jar of perfume and anointed Jesus? Remember the way the Pharisees and the disciples criticized her? Jesus counteracted their criticism with the gift of life-giving words: "Wherever the gospel is preached throughout the world, what she has done will also be told, in memory of her."[9] Can you imagine the way those words buoyed her spirit the rest of her life? Those are the kinds of words you have tattooed on your body or inscribed on your tombstone! Jesus blessed her with prophetic words, and they were fulfilled one more time with your reading of them!

As children of God and followers of Christ, we assume the mantle of the Old Testament priests who administered the blessing. You are part of that royal priesthood.[10] So that lot falls to us! It's our job to declare God's praises and pronounce God's blessings! Let's fulfill our priestly duty, but let's not *overspiritualize* blessing and cursing. These are not compartmentalized biblical concepts. Blessing and cursing are two very different ways of life, two very different ways of treating people.[11]

If the transcript of your life were read aloud, what would your words reveal? How do you talk about people when they aren't present? Do you berate them or brag about them behind their backs? How do you talk to people when they're present? Do you put them down, or do you look them in the eye and compliment them to their faces?

I have a three-inch-thick file that is filled with kind notes and thoughtful letters that I've received from readers of my books and from people I have the privilege of pastoring. Why do I keep them? Because every word of encouragement is a keepsake! Life-giving words are to the spirit what oxygen is to the lungs!

Whose words are in your file?

And whose files will you fill?

Like apples of gold in settings of silver,
  so is a word skillfully spoken.[12]

A number of years ago, I hiked the Inca Trail to Machu Picchu. When we got to Dead Woman's Pass, I had a throbbing headache caused by oxygen deprivation. At that elevation, the atmosphere has 37 percent less oxygen. Fortunately, our guide pulled out a can of pure oxygen. As I inhaled, the headache went away. Life-giving words are pure oxygen. There are a lot of headaches and heartaches caused by a lack of life-giving words. And there might be 37 percent less oxygen in the atmosphere where I live in Washington, DC. But the right words at the right time can change the game. They can even change a life!

Bloodline

Does it come as any surprise that the Enemy of our souls is called the Father of Lies and the Accuser of the Brethren? He speaks lies that can suck the life out of us. And his accusations are a sucker punch that can knock the wind out of us. How do we overcome his lies and his accusations? According to the writer of Revelation, we overcome them "by the blood of the Lamb and by the word of [our] testimony."[13] At first glance, one of those things is not like the other! Right? I would not put my testimony on par with the precious blood of Christ, but it's one key to overcoming the Enemy.

Your testimony has the power to set other people free! How? Well, if God did it for you, He can do it for them. And if God did it before, He can do it again. A testimony is a prophetic blessing! It is the seedbed where faith takes root and bears fruit. Now let me flip that overcoming coin:

> It was not with perishable things such as silver or gold that you were
> redeemed from the empty way of life handed down to you from your
> ancestors, but with the precious blood of Christ, a lamb without blemish
> or defect.[14]

The blood of Christ cancels the curse of sin, breaks the yoke of bondage, pays the ransom for our redemption, guarantees the promises of God, and signs the new covenant on the dotted line.

It is our redemption.[15]

It is our forgiveness.[16]

It is our confidence.[17]

It is our purification.[18]

It is our healing.[19]

It is our life.[20]

In horse racing, it's not uncommon to bet based on bloodlines. In case you care, virtually all the world's five hundred thousand thoroughbred racehorses descend from twenty-eight ancestors born in the eighteenth and nineteenth centuries. According to one genetic study, 95 percent of male thoroughbreds can be traced back to one superstud stallion.[21] Pedigree is a big deal when it comes to horses, and the same could be said of us.

One of the songs I put on repeat this past year is "No Longer Slaves" by Bethel Music. I love the line "Your blood flows through my veins."[22] The old hymn says it this way:

> There is a fountain filled with blood
> Drawn from Immanuel's veins;
> And sinners, plunged beneath that flood,
> Lose all their guilty stains.[23]

As a child of God, you are His bloodline! That is our birthright. That is our blessing.

The fifth meaning of the Hebrew word *barak* is "to make peace." The blessing was announced by angels to shepherds outside Bethlehem: "On earth peace, goodwill toward men!"[24] That peace treaty was signed by the blood of Christ, sealed by the Holy Spirit, and delivered by an empty tomb!

Live Long and Prosper

The sixth meaning of the Hebrew word *barak* is "to cause to prosper."

If you've been blessed financially, give credit where credit is due. It is God "who gives [us] the ability to produce wealth."[25] It is God who enriches us so that we "can be generous on every occasion."[26] Because of the havoc wreaked by the so-called prosperity gospel, we tend to throw this blessing out with the bathwater. That's a mistake on par with false humility. At its core, the blessing of God has undertones of productivity and overtones of prosperity. The problem isn't misinterpretation; it's misapplication. Remember, God doesn't bless us to raise our standard of living. God blesses us to raise our standard of giving.

Before pronouncing the sixfold blessing, Jewish priests would extend their arms and form the Hebrew letter *shin* with both hands. *Shin* is the first letter in the Hebrew word *shalom,* which means "peace and harmony" or "prosperity and tranquility." It's also used idiomatically as both a greeting and a goodbye.[27] *Shin* also stands for *Shaddai,* the name by which God was known to Abraham, Isaac, and Jacob. God self-identifies as El Shaddai when He established His covenant with Jacob, which is a reassertion of the original blessing: "I am El-Shaddai—'God Almighty.' Be fruitful and multiply."[28]

Here's a fun fact for *Star Trek* fans. Leonard Nimoy, who played the role of Spock, got the idea for the Vulcan salute from his Orthodox Jewish upbringing. He used one hand instead of two, but the Vulcan greeting—"Live long and prosper"—is an abbreviated version of the priestly blessing.[29]

This ancient blessing has your name on it. Again, it's not meant to be an abracadabra that we mindlessly verbalize like some magical incantation. But it is a potent invocation. Don't just read this blessing; receive it:

> The LORD bless you
>   and keep you;
> the LORD make his face shine on you
>   and be gracious to you;
> the LORD turn his face toward you
>   and give you peace.[30]

GOD IN THE HANDS
OF ANGRY PEOPLE

May the LORD smile on you
and be gracious to you.

NUMBERS 6:25, NLT

On July 8, 1741, Jonathan Edwards preached a sermon that might rank as the most famous sermon in American history. It's credited with catalyzing the Great Awakening, but I wonder whether it has done more long-term harm than short-term good. Even if you didn't grow up in church, you probably bumped into the title at some point—"Sinners in the Hands of an Angry God." I take issue with that title. I also take issue with the tone.

Before you brand me a heretic, let me say that Jonathan Edwards's writings have profoundly influenced my life in a positive way. Edwards was a brilliant academic, enrolling at Yale College when he was twelve and serving as Princeton's third president. He was a prolific author and devoted pastor. And his progeny is pretty impressive. A few names you may recognize include his grandson Aaron Burr, who dueled Alexander Hamilton; his third great-grandson Frank Nelson Doubleday, who founded the publishing company by the same last name; and his third great-granddaughter First Lady Edith Roosevelt, wife of Teddy Roosevelt. One more for good measure: Aaron Rodgers, quarterback of the Green Bay Packers, is Edwards's second cousin nine times removed, but I digress![1]

Jonathan Edwards left quite the legacy, but in my humble opinion, his most famous sermon missed the mark. And the standard I'm applying to Jonathan Edwards should be applied to me—and everyone else for that matter. I consistently say to our congregation, "As soon as I'm omniscient, I will let you know, but I would not hold your breath." I also add, "Don't take my word for it." My word is not the gospel. The gospel is the gospel. When it comes to faith and practice, the Bible is our final authority. If what I say doesn't line up with Scripture, call me on the carpet.

I'm all for tough sermons on tough topics because tough love demands it. But those tough words must never betray the heart of our heavenly Father. I have no issue with the first word in the title: *sinners*. That's exactly what we are—sinners in need of a savior. "All have sinned and fall short of the glory of God."[2] I do, however, take issue with the last two words: *angry God*.

Does God get angry? You better believe it. And it's critically important that we understand what triggers God's anger. King Solomon gave us a laundry list: "These six things the LORD hates, yes, seven are an abomination to Him: a proud look, a lying tongue, hands that shed innocent blood, a heart that devises wicked plans, feet that are swift in running to evil, a false witness who speaks lies, and one who sows discord among brethren."[3] Yes, God hates those things. But the question is, why? The answer: He hates those things because He loves us!

The prophet Malachi added one more thing to Solomon's laundry list: divorce.[4] Considering the fact that half of marriages end in divorce, we better not misinterpret what God means. God hates divorce, but does He hate divorcées? Of course not! God hates divorce because of the pain it causes and the way it splinters family trees. That's why Jesus said, "What God has joined together, let no one separate."[5] God hates divorce because the marriage covenant is sacred. But if you're going through a divorce, I hope you know that God doesn't love you any less. In fact, He couldn't love you any more! God is with you. God is for you. And God is going to get you through this!

The Heart of God

I say "Amen" to most of Edwards's message "Sinners in the Hands of an Angry God." But I take issue with this little snippet:

The God that holds you over the pit of Hell, much as one holds a spider, or some loathsome insect, over the fire, abhors you, and is dreadfully provoked; his wrath toward you burns like fire; he looks upon you as worthy of nothing else, but to be cast into the fire; he is of purer eyes than to bear to have you in his sight; you are ten thousand times so abominable in his eyes as the most hateful venomous serpent is in ours.[6]

I recognize that Edwards lived in a very different day and age, but dang! Is it just me or does that seem like a scare tactic? Yes, the fear of God is the beginning of wisdom.[7] But when it comes to repentance, this is not the approach God takes. It's His kindness that leads us to repentance.[8] When God wants us to change, He shows us kindness. If that doesn't work? He shows us even more kindness!

I have no doubt that we grossly underestimate the holiness of God. And for the record, I couldn't care less about being politically correct. What I'm advocating for is biblical correctness. Any theology that starts with original sin, not original blessing, is false theology. And it betrays the heart of our heavenly Father.

I know far too many people—and you do too—who have been beaten over the head by Bible-believing Christians who belie the heart of God with their lack of love. They project their own imperfections onto God, and He becomes "God in the Hands of Angry People." The result is way too many people rejecting God for all the wrong reasons! They reject God for who He's *not*. They reject a reflection of people who project their imperfections onto God.

Let me take a risk right here and put a little twist on the priestly blessing by trying to translate it into emojis. Emoji isn't an exact language, but there is a reason we use emojis when we want to convey a little extra emotion.

"The LORD bless you" is a smiling face with smiling eyes, and I might add a Vulcan salute, praise hands, and fist bump up front. "The LORD . . . keep you" is a hugging face with a flexed bicep. "The LORD make his face shine on you" is a sun with a face and a face throwing a kiss. "Be gracious to you" is the winking face and a thumbs-up. "The LORD turn his face toward you" is a smiling face with heart-shaped eyes. "The LORD . . . give you peace" is a party popper, a handclap, confetti, and a cupcake, unless you're gluten intolerant. Finally, I'd throw in some fireworks for good measure.

My seminary professors are either rolling over in their graves right now or rolling-on-the-floor-laughing emoji. I don't want to denigrate or depreciate this priestly blessing in any form or fashion, but I do want to bring the blessing down to earth a little bit. The blessing isn't an abstraction. It's as tangible and relatable as a baby wrapped in swaddling clothes.

Let me set the record straight. God does not loathe you (angry-face emoji). Without a revelation of God's love, you'll relate to Him out of fear rather than affection. And that is as far as you can get from the heart of God.

Warmer, Warmer

When I was a kid, we used to play a game with my grandma called Hide the Thimble. I have no idea whether my grandma made that game up or whether others have played it. My grandma would hide one of her sewing thimbles, and the grandchildren would search all over the house trying to find it. If we were getting farther and farther away from the thimble, she would call us back by saying, "Colder, colder." If we were getting closer and closer, she would coach us on by saying, "Warmer, warmer." And when we got really close to finding that thimble, my grandma would raise the pitch in her voice and say, "Hotter, hotter." This is what children did before video games! We played Hide the Thimble, and we loved it.

If your God is angry at you, you're getting colder, colder.

If your God loves you, you're getting warmer, warmer.

A. W. Tozer said, "What comes into our minds when we think about God is the most important thing about us."[9] So let me ask the question, What comes to mind? Is there an angry expression on His face? Or does the heavenly Father have smile lines around His eyes? Is He recoiling with arms crossed? Or is He reaching out to you with arms wide open?

Can I tell you who you are? You are not a spider that God loathes—that's for sure!

You are the apple of God's eye.[10]

You are the object of His affection.[11]

You are sought after.[12]

Don't let anyone label you any other way! Don't label yourself any other way!

The key to a healthy and holy identity is believing that you are who God says you are. Believing yourself to be anything less than who God says isn't doing anybody any favors, including you. It's called false humility, and false humility is just as dangerous and damaging as pride.

Can I tell you who God is and what God thinks of you?

In Job, He is bragging about you behind your back.[13]

In Romans, He is interceding for you at the right hand of the Father.[14]

In Psalms, His mercy and goodness follow you all the days of your life.[15]

In Exodus, His faithfulness is unfailing.[16]

In Jeremiah, His kindness is unending.[17]

In Song of Songs, His love is unrelenting.[18]

In Zephaniah, He is rejoicing over you with singing.[19]

Why am I citing a sermon from the eighteenth century and calling it on the carpet? Because its words cast a long shadow on the heart of God. And nothing is more important than discerning God's heart toward you. Yes, God *gets* angry. But He's not an angry God. And there is a big difference! Simply put, "God is love."[20] Yes, His love mandates His anger toward those things that are outside His good, pleasing, and perfect will. But there is nothing that can separate us from the love of God. In fact, nothing you do can make Him love you any less! Why? Because God's love is *not* reactive. The love of God is the most proactive, most powerful force on earth.

Rejecting the God Who Isn't

In her memoir, *Living with a Wild God*, Barbara Ehrenreich shares the story of how her family foreclosed on God. In the late nineteenth century, her great-great-great grandfather was on his deathbed. His daughter, Barbara's great-grandmother, sent for their priest to administer last rites. The priest sent word that he would come for no less than twenty-five dollars. That's when Barbara's great-grandmother Mamie McLaughlin renounced God.[21]

On one level, it's hard to blame Mamie. And it's easy to play Monday Morning Theologian a hundred years later. But instead of rejecting God, maybe

Mamie should have rejected the priest? The priest's unwillingness to pronounce a blessing backfired and turned into a multigenerational curse. Then Mamie made the mistake that so many of us make when someone we love or trust lets us down—we give up on God. I know how disappointing that can be, but if you project human failings onto God, you end up with "God in the Hands of Angry People." It's not God's fault, unless you blame Him for giving us free will.

A few years ago, I heard Eric Metaxas speak at the National Prayer Breakfast in Washington, DC. It's hard not to be a little distracted by the who's who in the room, but Eric arrested my attention when he said, "Everything I had rejected about God was actually not God." Then he pushed the envelope a little further: "It was just dead religion. . . . It was people who go to church and do not show the love of Jesus . . . people who don't practice what they preach, people who are indifferent to the poor and suffering. . . . I had rejected that, but guess what? Jesus had also rejected that. . . . Jesus was and is the enemy of dead religion."[22]

Many people who reject God aren't really rejecting God but are rejecting religion without knowing it. They are rejecting a misrepresentation of who God is. They aren't rejecting God for who He *is*. They are actually rejecting God for who He *isn't*. My advice? Go ahead and reject who God isn't—the misrepresentations, the mischaracterizations. But don't stop there. Go on a quest to rediscover who God really is.

I have a theory: *if you don't love God, it's because you don't know God.* I hope that doesn't come across as condescending, but if you really knew the God of blessing, it would be impossible to resist His unconditional, unrelenting love.

Let me remind you of the latitude and longitude of God's blessing.

At Bethlehem, He is God *with* us.

At Calvary, He is God *for* us.

At Pentecost, He is God *in* us.

I hope you've experienced God in all three ways at all three places! If you know God is *with* you no matter what, you can get through anything! If you know God is *for* you, you can overcome every obstacle in your way! And if you know God is *in* you, nothing can stop you. That is *the* blessing—God with us, God for us, God in us!

Naming Rights

One of the highest honors God has conferred on the human race is naming rights. He let Adam name the animals, which had to be a ton of fun for both Adam and God. Some of those names have made spelling bees awfully entertaining! My favorite? It's a toss-up between the *Wunderpus photogenicus* and the tasselled wobbegong. God also gives parents the privilege of naming their children. Of course, it's a placeholder. Our true names will be revealed by God when we enter eternity.[23] In the meantime, I'm Mark.

After the priestly prayer, God put His name on His people:

They will put my name on the Israelites, and I will bless them.[24]

There are more than four hundred names for God in Scripture, and each one reveals a unique dimension of His character. He is *Jehovah Nissi,* God our Banner; *Jehovah Rapha,* God our Healer; and *Jehovah Jireh,* God our Provider.[25] By putting the name of God on the people, the priest was endowing them and enduing them with God's character. Not unlike a notary who authorizes or a notable who endorses, God put His name on His people.

Hold that thought.

When Diana Nyad was nine years old, she stood on a beach in Fort Lauderdale, Florida, and asked her mom an innocent question: "Where is Cuba?" Her mom pointed toward the horizon and said, "It's right over there. You can't see it but it's so close, you could almost swim there."[26]

Twenty years later, in 1978, Diana Nyad would attempt to swim from Cuba to Florida. She swam seventy-eight miles in forty-two hours, but strong winds stopped her short of her goal. The dream of becoming the first person to swim across the straits of Florida would then lie dormant for more than three decades. At age sixty, Diana figured it was now or never. Her second attempt to swim from Cuba to Florida fell short because of an asthma attack. Her third attempt failed because she was stung by two Portuguese man-of-wars. And her fourth attempt ended with nine jellyfish stings.

Then, on the morning of August 31, 2013, Diana Nyad would make one last attempt. Almost fifty-three hours and 110 miles later, Diana Nyad swam ashore in Key West.[27] Her tongue was terribly swollen, but she managed three messages: "One is, we should never, ever give up. Two is, you are never too old to chase your dream. And three is, it looks like a solitary sport but it takes a team."[28] Without her team of thirty-five people, including doctors, meteorologists, family, and friends, Diana would not have fulfilled her destiny.

How did Diana Nyad do what no one had done before? How did she endure the physical and mental punishment? And why did she refuse to give up, even after four failed attempts? Motivation is incredibly complicated, and I don't want to oversimplify. But I think it goes back to something that happened on her fifth birthday.

Her father, Aristotle Nyad, called Diana into his den and said in his thick Greek accent, "I have been waiting so very long for this day. Now you are five. Today is the day you are ready to understand the most significant thing I will ever tell you." Aristotle opened an unabridged dictionary on his desk and pointed to her name. He said, "Tomorrow you will go to your little preschool and you will ask your little friends if their names are in the dictionary. They will tell you no. You are the only one, darling. You are the special one."

Then Aristotle pointed to the page and said, "Your name is Nyad. First definition, from Greek mythology, the nymphs that swam in the lakes, oceans, rivers, and fountains to protect the waters for the gods. Listen to me, darling, because now is coming the most important part. Next definition, a girl or woman champion swimmer. Darling, this is your destiny!"[29]

How did Diana do what no one had done before? The short answer: Aristotle Nyad put his name on her! His blessing was her beacon. When the sharks circled and the jellyfish stung, when dehydration and hallucinations set in—she prevailed because of the words her father had spoken over her fifty-nine years earlier. That is the power of the blessing!

Just as Aristotle Nyad opened the unabridged dictionary, we open the Bible. Scripture is our script, giving us new names and new narratives. It's also our musical score. The priestly blessing is customarily chanted by Jewish parents over their children every night. By the time a child turns thirteen, they've been blessed 4,745 times! And singing it helps lock the lyrics into the child's soul.

Our names are inscribed in the Book of Life, just as Diana's name was in the dictionary. Your name is both a birthright and a blessing. But its true destiny and its true identity will not be revealed until we meet God face to face. That eternal blessing will unravel every mystery.

Blessing Rituals

A few decades ago, archaeologists found two silver scrolls in a Jewish burial chamber near the Old City of Jerusalem. The priestly blessing was inscribed on them, and they are believed to be the oldest biblical texts in existence.[30] The scrolls were ancient amulets, inspired by the instructions given in Deuteronomy:

> These commandments that I give you today are to be on your hearts.
> Impress them on your children. Talk about them when you sit at home
> and when you walk along the road, when you lie down and when you
> get up. Tie them as symbols on your hands and bind them on your
> foreheads. Write them on the doorframes of your houses and on your
> gates.[31]

The Jewish people are ingenious when it comes to ritual reminders of God's blessings, surrounding themselves with tokens of the Torah. Scrolls called mezuzahs were affixed to their doorframes but not just the front door. The mezuzah was fastened to every door except bathrooms and closets! You couldn't go anywhere in your own home without a ritual reminder: "Hear, O Israel: The LORD our God, the LORD is one."[32]

I can't help but think of the sign placed outside the Notre Dame locker room by Coach Lou Holtz: "Play Like a Champion Today." Immortalized by the cult classic *Rudy*, it's tradition for every player on the Fighting Irish to tap the sign on the way out of the locker room.

Observant Jews also wore a set of black leather boxes called tefillin on their arms, hands, fingers, or foreheads. Like every religious ritual, the tefillin could easily be reduced to lucky charms. But the word itself derives from the Aramaic word *palal*, which means "to pray with pleading."[33]

Tattooed

A few years ago, I spoke at a men's conference with Brian "Head" Welch, the Grammy-award-winning guitarist for the heavy-metal band Korn. Between our sessions I interviewed him and decided to go off-script with a question. Brian is pretty tatted up; in fact, he's running out of real estate! I knew some of his tattoos were BC, before Christ. But I was curious about the ones that were AD. So I threw Brian a softball: "Tell us the backstory behind some of your tattoos."

Brian said that the most painful tattoos were the ones on his eyelids. Shocking! One eyelid was tattooed with *shekhinah,* while the other eyelid was tattooed with *kabod.* Both are Hebrew for different dimensions of "the glory of God."[34] Then he talked about a verse tattooed on his neck, Matthew 11:28:

> Come to Me, all who are weary and heavy-laden, and I will give you rest.[35]

After making millions of dollars achieving the highest levels of success in the music industry, Brian bottomed out. He was depressed to the point of being suicidal. He turned to drugs and alcohol. Brian said his life was an absolute mess when his realtor sent him a seemingly random email at four o'clock one morning. Brian hadn't gone to bed yet, so he read the email. The realtor explained to Brian that he felt led to send him a verse of Scripture, specifically Matthew 11:28. Brian read it, and the rest is history. He decided to take Jesus up on His offer. Thirteen years later, he's a totally different person. You don't have to be around Brian very long to sense the peace that surpasses understanding that guards his heart and his mind.

The forgiveness of God is tattooed on his heart.

The love of God is tattooed on his soul.

And, of course, the glory of God is tattooed on his eyelids!

I don't think you have to visit your local tattoo parlor, but ritual reminders of God's blessings are mission critical. Over the years I have surrounded myself with spiritual mementos. A picture of a cow pasture in Alexandria, Minnesota, where I felt called to ministry sits behind my desk. An old metal sign from one of the miraculous pieces of property we have purchased hangs on my wall. I've got an old liquor bottle from the crack house we turned into Ebenezers Coffee-house. Some of those mementos would seem insignificant to others, like my ticket to Super Bowl XLV, but even that has a backstory of blessing.

In the second half of *Double Blessing*, we'll explore the importance of taking inventory of your blessings so you can flip them. Suffice it to say, you've got to establish blessing rituals that fit your spiritual rhythm. If you're a parent, it might be a bedtime or breakfast blessing.

When our children were younger, I turned Luke 2:52 into a blessing that I prayed over them almost every day: "May you grow in wisdom and stature and in favor with God and with man." Figure out what God wants you to do and what works for you; then put it into practice. You may not see an immediate return on investment, but those blessings will gain weight. Don't be surprised if they inspire your children fifty-nine years from now!

FIGHT FOR IT

I will not let you go unless you bless me.

GENESIS 32:26

Shortly after the outbreak of World War II, Finland was invaded by the Soviet Union. The Soviet army was three times larger, had thirty times as many airplanes, and had a hundred times as many tanks.[1] Yet despite being overwhelmingly outnumbered, Finland emerged from the Winter War victorious.

The outcome of military conflicts is typically determined by tangibles like troops and tanks, but in this instance, a difficult-to-define intangible may have won the war. In a *New York Times* feature article on the Finnish people, the author credited what he considered to be the least common denominator in the article's title, "Sisu: A Word That Explains Finland."

The Finns have something they call sisu. It is a compound of bravado and bravery, of ferocity and tenacity, of the ability to keep fighting after most people would have quit, and to fight with the will to win. The Finns translate sisu as "the Finnish spirit" but it is a much more gutful word than that.[2]

The essence of the Finnish army was encapsulated by that single word: *sisu*. That word also epitomized the Finnish athletes who dominated the world of long-distance running in the 1940s. The *Times* article extrapolated: "A typical Finn is an obstinate sort of fellow who believes in getting the better of bad fortune by proving that he can stand worse."[3]

There are moments in life, often when all seems lost, when what you need is some *sisu*. The persistent widow whom Jesus celebrated in one of His parables was Jewish, not Finnish, but she had *sisu*. She would not quit in her quest for justice.[4] She had what I would call a sanctified stubborn streak. Folks like that don't take no for an answer, but they don't take yes for an answer either. Why? Because they're always believing God for something bigger, something better!

I don't believe in bad luck. Sure, bad things happen to good people. Occasionally those bad things are compounded by even worse timing. That said, what we call "bad luck" is often the by-product of bad decisions or bad habits. Sometimes the outcomes are self-inflicted. Sometimes we're the innocent bystanders. Either way, fixating on the *cause*, which we cannot control, is often counterproductive. Instead, we need to focus on the *effect*, which we can control, and redouble our efforts to do something about it.

We cannot keep bad things from happening, but we're still response-able for our reactions. Life will knock you down, but you have a choice to make. You can stay down. Or like a Finnish soldier or Jewish widow, you can get back up with even more determination to fight for what you believe. A little *sisu* can go a long way.

Choose Your Battles Wisely

Lora and I used to have a little saying taped to our bathroom mirror: "Choose your battles wisely." There are some battles you need to bow out of. They aren't worth your time or energy. Then there are battles you cannot afford to surrender. You've got to figure out what battlefield you're willing to die on, then take your stand.

What does any of that have to do with the blessing of God?

I would be doing a disservice to double blessing if I didn't address a few common misconceptions about the blessing of God. Some people treat the blessing like a lottery ticket, hoping they'll get lucky. Of course, that's nothing more than a well-camouflaged get-rich-quick scheme. Others trivialize the blessing by turning it into some sort of magic trick. They reduce God to a formula: *if you do X, God will do Y.* The problem with this is that God is predictably unpredictable!

The blessing of God is not good luck; it's hard work. The blessing of God is not a magic trick; it's long obedience in the same direction. And while we're on the subject, it's not a dog or pony show either. God is not impressed with religious showboating. Praying in *King James* English doesn't make it any more effective, I promise *thee* that.

The blessing of God cannot be earned any more than our salvation. It's part of the package deal procured at Calvary's cross. If you are in Christ, every blessing in the Bible belongs to you.[5] But once you've been on the receiving end of God's grace, you want to give God everything you've got. One-quarter of that equation is loving God with all your strength, which equates to blood, sweat, and tears. I might even add calories to the mix.

The French chemist Louis Pasteur is famous for saying, "Fortune favors the prepared mind."[6] In the same spirit, God blesses those who are willing to break a sweat for what they believe in. You can't just pray like it depends on God. You also have to work like it depends on you. The blessing of God doesn't just fall into our laps. Yes, God "gave" the Israelites the Promised Land. But that didn't mean that the giants in the land threw up the white flag.

Joshua didn't just fight the battle of Jericho. He fought at least thirteen battles, defeating thirty-one kings in the process. Those kings did not surrender without a fight. And when the people of God had finally won the Promised Land, the fields didn't just yield their crops without the Israelites having to plant. They had to plow fields and dig wells by the sweat of their brows. Very rarely are the blessings of God served on silver platters. We have to work for them—and sometimes fight for them with some *sisu*.

Nice Name

There is a cryptic encounter in the book of Genesis that makes a fascinating case study when it comes to getting God's blessing. Jacob was on his way back home to get reconciled with his brother, the same brother from whom he had stolen both the birthright and the family blessing. After sending his family and his possessions across the Jabbok River, Jacob experienced what would prove to be the defining moment of his life.

Jacob was left alone, and a man wrestled with him till daybreak. When the man saw that he could not overpower him, he touched the socket of Jacob's hip so that his hip was wrenched as he wrestled with the man. Then the man said, "Let me go, for it is daybreak."

But Jacob replied, "I will not let you go unless you bless me."

The man asked him, "What is your name?"

"Jacob," he answered.

Then the man said, "Your name will no longer be Jacob, but Israel, because you have struggled with God and with humans and have overcome."

Jacob said, "Please tell me your name."

But he replied, "Why do you ask my name?" Then he blessed him there.

So Jacob called the place Peniel, saying, "It is because I saw God face to face, and yet my life was spared."

The sun rose above him as he passed Peniel, and he was limping because of his hip.[7]

Bible scholars aren't entirely sure whom Jacob wrestled with. Some argue that it was an angel, while others point to it as a preincarnate appearance of Christ. I lean toward taking Jacob at face value when he said, "I saw God face to face."[8]

To fully appreciate this episode in Jacob's life, including the name change, a little backstory is necessary. When he was born, Jacob was grasping the ankle of his older brother, Esau. And his parents named him accordingly. The literal meaning of Jacob's name is "one who grabs heels," and that's fine. But the figurative meaning is "one who deceives."[9] Really? That's the best you can come up with, Isaac and Rebekah? Lora and I don't claim to be the best parents on the planet, but we knew better than to name any of our children Liar, Cheater, and Deceiver.

In Jewish culture, naming a child is a prophetic exercise. A name is the beginning of a narrative, and unfortunately, Isaac and Rebekah gave Jacob something to live down to. Yet despite his many mistakes, Jacob had a redeeming quality. Not unlike the Finnish people, Jacob had *sisu*. And it's evidenced in this ancient cage fight.

If I were Jacob, I may have thrown in the towel the second I saw who it was that I had to wrestle. And I probably would have cried uncle long before Jacob's hip pointer injury. What kept Jacob in the ring? The only answer I can come up with is this: Jacob valued the blessing above all else. He wasn't just willing to fight for it. I think he was willing to die for it.

Again, the blessing of God is a gift from God. You cannot earn it, per se. But are you willing to risk life and limb for it? Are you willing to pull an all-nighter for it? Are you willing to go to the mat and get back up for it?

With all his faults, Jacob accurately estimated the value of the blessing! And whether we're consciously aware of it or not, we long for the blessing as much as he did. In her wonderful book *The Promise of Blessing*, Kate Patterson noted that the Jewish people understood the "concrete advantages" of the blessing. It wasn't just pie in the sky by and by. "That's why Old Testament people longed for blessing," said Patterson, "even more than 21st century people long for success."[10] Maybe those two things are one and the same!

Our hardest-fought battles often result in our hardest-earned lessons, the kind of lessons you never forget. Jacob's unwillingness to let go of God until God blessed him proves to be the tipping point, the turning point of his life. It doesn't just change his trajectory—God changes his name! Jacob becomes Israel, and the rest is history!

Go and Get Your Scars

According to legend, when the knights of the Round Table returned to King Arthur's court after battle, they were carefully examined. If their bodies did not bear any battle scars, they were sent back into battle with an exhortation: "Go and get your scars!"

When I survey Scripture, the people I admire most are the most scarred. It's not hard to imagine David and his mighty men comparing battle scars while sharing the backstories behind them. Paul's Wikipedia page includes a long list of life-threatening incidents that must have left some physical evidence of the pain and suffering he survived. In fact, he said, "I bear on my body the scars that show I belong to Jesus."[11] And then there's Jesus Himself, who set the standard. And it's not just His nail-pierced hands and feet. His back was tattooed by a Roman whip, while a crown of thorns left its permanent imprint on His forehead.

Please do everything within your power to avoid self-inflicted injuries, but you cannot sidestep the bumps and bruises inflicted by bad bosses or painful losses. But those scars, earned in pursuit of blessing, may prove to be your greatest source of pride!

In his book, *Just Mercy*, Bryan Stevenson documents his efforts to fight systemic injustice in the criminal justice system. I was moved to tears more than once, but one story struck a unique chord. While sharing his story at a small African American church in Alabama, Bryan noticed an older black gentleman in a wheelchair who was making intense eye contact during his talk. Afterward the man cornered Bryan and asked him a question he didn't know how to answer: "Do you know what you're doing?" Bryan wasn't sure how to answer, so the man asked that question again! Then he revealed the answer to his rhetorical question: "You're beating the drum for justice!"

The old man pulled Bryan in close, leaned his head down, and said, "You see this scar at the top of my head? I got that scar in Greene County, Alabama, trying to register to vote in 1964." Still holding on to Bryan, he said, "You see this scar on the side of my head?" He turned his head, revealing a four-inch scar. He said, "I got that scar in Mississippi demanding civil rights." The man then lowered his head once more, revealing a mark at the base of his skull. "You see that mark? I got that bruise in Birmingham after the Children's Crusade."

The old man tightened his grip on Bryan's arm and said, "People think these are my scars, cuts, and bruises." With tears in his eyes, he said, "These aren't my scars, cuts, and bruises. These are my medals of honor."[12]

Remember the umbrella blessing? Just as it doesn't mean you won't get wet, it doesn't mean you won't get hurt! Even if your cause is a righteous one! After his wrestling match with God, Jacob walked with a limp the rest of his life. While painful, that limp was a constant reminder of God's blessing! And the same can be true of your scars, your hurts, your bumps, and your bruises.

Can I let you in on a little secret?

I don't trust leaders who don't limp! A leader who has all the answers isn't answering the tough questions. And a leader who has it all together all the time is faking it. I know—we'd rather walk on water! But the problem with that is this: no one can follow you! If you want to build trust, don't just share your success stories. When you authentically share your failure stories, it builds trust and increases empathy. People will follow a leader like that, a leader who limps with a blessing limp, all the way to the ends of the earth. Isn't that exactly what the disciples did? Actually they followed Jesus further than that. Eleven of the twelve followed Him to their deaths!

Leading with a Limp

I've had the joy and privilege of leading National Community Church for more than two decades. And I can honestly say that I wouldn't want to be anyplace else doing anything else. However, if you have led anything for any length of time, you know that there is wear and tear that produces bumps and bruises!

Let me share a few hard-earned lessons I've learned along the way.

First, *keep a sense of humor.*

The happiest, healthiest, and holiest people on the planet are those who laugh at themselves the most. The words *humility* and *humor* come from the same Latin root. Etymologically, they are cousins. Of course, keeping a sense of humor in tough situations isn't any easier than keeping your wits about you.

When Ronald Reagan was inaugurated on January 20, 1981, he was the oldest president ever elected. Four years later, his age was even more of an issue. But Ronald Reagan managed to disarm his political opponents by poking fun at himself. "When I go in for a physical now," said Reagan, "they no longer ask me how old I am, they just carbon-date me."[13] During a presidential debate in 1984, Reagan didn't shy away from the age issue. He flipped the script on those who thought he was too old to run, saying, "I will not make age an issue of this campaign. I am not going to exploit, for political purposes, my opponent's youth and inexperience."[14] Even Walter Mondale, his political opponent, could not help but laugh! When all else fails, try to keep a sense of humor!

Second, *keep a sense of perspective.*

One way to keep our sense of perspective is by counting our blessings! And while this may sound somewhat perverse, another way is by reminding ourselves of how it could be worse! Psychologists call it a downward counterfactual. This fictitious letter penned by a college student to her parents is a good example:

Dear Mom and Dad,

I have so much to tell you. Because of the fire in my dorm set off by student riots, I experienced temporary lung damage and had to go to the hospital. While I was there, I fell in love with an orderly, and we have moved in together. I dropped out of school when I found out I was pregnant, and he got fired because of his drinking. So we're going to move to Alaska, where we might get married after the birth of our baby.

Your loving daughter.

P.S. None of this really happened, but I did flunk my chemistry class and wanted to keep it in perspective.

One of the best ways to keep our sense of perspective is by prophesying our praise. It's not just praising God for what He has *already done,* past tense. It's praising God, by faith, for what He *will do,* future tense. Instead of focusing on your circumstances, it's declaring the character of God, the promises of God. Simply put, prophesy is declaring what will happen in the future. You can prophesy fear, prophesy doubt, prophesy pain. Or you can prophesy praise! It's refusing to let what's wrong with us keep us from worshipping what's right about God. When we prophesy our praise, we regain perspective by recalibrating our spirit.

Third, *say what needs to be said.*

I live in a city that sometimes spins the facts and puts a positive face on falsehood. That's not every politician, mind you. But it's a few too many! The irony is that most people can see right through our smoke screens! You know what people really appreciate? Good old-fashioned authenticity! Especially when it's coupled with humility! The blessing is never a bluff. It doesn't scratch itching ears that need a talking-to.[15] The blessing is full of grace and full of truth—*grace* means "I'll love you no matter what"; *truth* means "I'll be honest with you no matter what." Don't internalize; verbalize. But make sure you speak the truth in love! That means we don't say things to simply get them off our chests. Rather, we're caring enough to confront.

Fourth, *you control what you control.*

It's much easier to *act* like a Christian than it is to *react* like one! You cannot control how people treat you, but you can always control how you treat them. I've made some difficult decisions as a leader, decisions that not everyone has agreed with. And that comes with the territory, right? Leaders get to make the decisions no one else wants to, and that means we're the lightning rods for people's complaints. Or worse, we're their punching bags! But I refuse to react! Sure, I'll confront people if I don't agree with their tone or their tactics. But I made a resolution long ago that I will do my level best to make sure everyone I encounter feels *loved* and *heard* and *blessed*.

Proverbs 19:11 says, "It is to one's glory to overlook an offense." In other words, make it your goal to be *unoffendable*! That certainly doesn't mean you become someone's punching bag, but it does mean turning the other cheek! When you take offense, you start playing defense with your life. You write people off who tick you off. You let skepticism and cynicism seep into your soul. If you don't deal with it, taking offense festers in your spirit until it turns into bitterness. And bitterness doesn't just rob us of our joy; it steals the blessing.

Fifth, *it's okay to not be okay.*

If you look at a US president's portrait *before* and *after* they took office, it usually looks like they have aged far more than the four or eight years they spent in office! Leadership takes a toll, and so does life. I've had seasons that have stretched me past what I thought was my emotional or physical breaking point. I would liken it to one too many reps on the bench press. Without a spotter, you're left with two options: roll the bar down your body or tip the bar until the weights fall off. Both options are embarrassing, and that's how our weaknesses make us feel. But it's those weaknesses that make us more relatable and likable!

To be honest, I walk with more of a limp every year I lead. And that's okay. I wish I could tell you that leadership gets easier with time, but in my experience it does not. The stakes only get higher! But just like Jacob, the limp reminds us of what we've gone through to get the blessing!

Sixth, *the blessings of God will complicate your life.*

This simple revelation changed the way I live, the way I lead. Sin will complicate your life in ways it should not be complicated. The blessings of God will complicate your life in ways it should be complicated.

When Lora and I got married, it complicated our lives. Praise God for a quarter century of complications! We have three complications named Parker,

Summer, and Josiah, and I cannot imagine my life without them! The larger the organization you lead, the more complicated it gets. The more money you make, the more complicated your taxes are. I didn't know it at the time, but when I prayed that double portion prayer at the foot of my father-in-law's casket, I was asking God to complicate my life times two! And I praise God for answering that prayer. If you ask me to pray that God would make your life easier, I won't do it. I pray that God would complicate your life in ways that only He can—with double blessing!

Do you remember the reward for good work in the Parable of the Talents? It wasn't extra vacation time or an early retirement. The reward for good work was *more* work. That's how it works in God's kingdom. If we're being honest, many of our prayers revolve around personal comfort. I'd advocate the opposite! If you're feeling courageous, try this prayer: *Lord, complicate my life!*

A Bowl of Stew

Let me double back to Jacob one last time.

This is a book about *how to get the blessing*, but I would be remiss if I didn't disclose the many ways in which we can lose it as well. That list is as long as the begats in the Bible, which are full of cautionary tales. For Samson, it was selling his secret for a one-night stand. For Judas, it was thirty pieces of silver. And then there's Esau, who sold his birthright to Jacob for a bowl of stew!

It's easy to sentence Samson for his lack of self-control, but what is your siren call? It's easy to condemn Judas for selling out, but what is your price point? It's easy to accuse Esau of short-sightedness, but what is your Achilles' heel?

Sin is the epitome of poor judgment. More often than not, sin is meeting a *legitimate need* in an *illegitimate way*. Sin is sneaky that way! And we have no alibi, save the cross of Jesus Christ. Sin is not worth the price we have to pay, and we know that, yet we do it. The question, of course, is, why? There is no easy answer to that question, but if we don't value God's blessing above all else, we sell our souls for a cheap substitute. For Samson, it was sex. For Judas, it was money. For Esau, it was food. Not much has changed, has it?

While we're on the subject of sin, attempting to *not sin by not sinning* is a losing battle. You need a vision that is bigger and better than the bowl of stew you're tempted by! Then, and only then, will you see sin for what it really is—settling for less than God's best. The blessing of God is the hidden treasure,[16] the pearl of great price,[17] the crown of glory that never fades away.[18]

There is a difference between God's *will* and God's *way*. God's will is as explicit as the Ten Commandments inscribed on stone tablets. God's ways? They are strange and mysterious.[19] Did you know that you can do the will of God and God can oppose your actions? That sounds sacrilegious, right? But if you do the will of God in a spirit of pride, God cannot bless it. Why? Because "God opposes the proud."[20] That's a scary proposition, isn't it?

Moses wanted to deliver his people from the injustice of slavery, which was the will of God. But he went about it the wrong way. He tried to expedite God's plan by killing an Egyptian taskmaster, thereby delaying God's deliverance by forty years!

If you want to experience God's full blessing, you have to do God's will God's way! And please be careful not to equate *your way* with *the way*. In the words of Oswald Chambers, "Never make a principle out of your experience; let God be as original with other people as He is with you."[21] Again, God's blessing is as unique as your fingerprint.

Don't settle for a bowl of stew.

Hold out for God's best, God's blessing.

It's worth the wrestling match!

BLESSINGS IN DISGUISE

What are you, mighty mountain? Before
Zerubbabel you will become level ground.
Then he will bring out the capstone to shouts
of "God bless it! God bless it!"

ZECHARIAH 4:7

"I am now the most miserable man living."

The man who uttered those words also alleged, "If what I feel were equally distributed to the whole human family, there would not be one cheerful face on earth." And his self-prognosis wasn't any more optimistic than his self-diagnosis: "Whether I shall ever be better I can not tell; I awfully forbode I shall not."[1]

Maybe you've been there, done that?

Few biographies begin with less opportunity or more adversity. Life in rural America in the early nineteenth century wasn't easy to begin with, but he was born into abject poverty. His mother, whom he adored, died when he was just nine years old. In the aftermath of that loss, he and his twelve-year-old sister were abandoned by their father for seven months. When their father returned with his new bride, their new stepmother found them living like animals. The boy's father believed that time spent in school was doubly wasted: it wasn't just a waste of his son's time; it also robbed him of his son's manual labor. When his father caught him reading a book, it was not beyond him to destroy the book and whip his son.

When he reached the age of majority and was free to leave his family, he bundled his few earthly possessions, threw them over his shoulder, and headed west to get as far away from his past as he could. Of course, miles don't erase memories. He was already marked by what one colleague described as a "mysterious and profound melancholy."[2]

The trend line of his adult years wasn't much different from his childhood. He suffered heartbreak when his first love died. An attempt at business ended in bankruptcy. And his foray into politics was met with defeat, not once or twice but half a dozen times.

Despite all those personal challenges and professional setbacks, Abraham Lincoln would eventually win the highest office in the land and become one of the most beloved and revered presidents in American history. I would argue that it wasn't *despite* those challenges and setbacks; it was *because* of them. It's past challenges that uniquely prepare us for future opportunities. Who better to lead this country through a civil war than a man who had to overcome so many obstacles?

Seasons of Suffering

God grows us up spiritually in a hundred different ways, but the most effective method may be allowing us to endure situations that demand the character we need to cultivate. Could He deliver us from those difficult situations? Of course He could, but He loves us too much to short-circuit our sanctification. God doesn't always deliver us *from* our difficulties, but He does deliver us *through* them.

The best way to cultivate patience is to be put in a situation that demands it, lots of it. How about courage? Well, it's not the absence of fear—that's for sure! What about love? There is no greater opportunity to exercise the love of God than to be surrounded by enemies. Mercy? You can't exercise forgiveness if you've never been wronged. And if you need more patience, courage, love, or mercy? Don't be surprised if you find yourself in a situation that demands even more of it.

I'm not suggesting that God proactively puts us in those situations, but He often allows them because they're part of our maturation process. Again, the umbrella blessing is not an immunity card. It's not a get-out-of-jail-free card either. We're still subject to the law of sowing and reaping. And we still live in a fallen world, which means we'll experience our fair share of pain and suffering.

Plus, God is not a helicopter parent. Just like Joseph, Esther, David, and Daniel, we will experience personal setbacks and seasons of suffering. The good news? It will be for our good and God's glory.

The last thing I want to do is make light of the difficulties you've endured. I actually want to validate them. It seems like every news cycle these days brings new allegations of sexual harassment or sexual abuse. If you've been the victim of that kind of abuse, it's not just news. Those stories trigger memories that trigger emotions that are incredibly painful. If you've experienced the heartache of miscarriage, a baby's cry can pull your heartstrings and produce profound sadness. If you've walked through a difficult divorce or gotten a grim diagnosis from a doctor, it feels like a thousand-pound weight sitting squarely on your shoulders.

I don't know what challenge you're facing, but I do know that God's grace is sufficient. That grace can be experienced in a thousand different ways. Sometimes it's manifested through thoughtful friends and wise counselors. Sometimes it's a day at the beach or a mountain hike. And, of course, it's a relationship with the God who will never leave us or forsake us.[3] He's the God who gives beauty for ashes, the oil of joy for mourning, and the garment of praise for the spirit of heaviness.[4] How do I know this? Because Scripture says it, and I've experienced it. I've walked through the valley of the shadow of death more than once, and I've seen God redeem unbearable pain and unimaginable suffering. I've also watched God turn some of the worst days of my life into some of the best.

Before Any Great Achievement

In 1853, Charles Spurgeon was installed as the pastor of New Park Street Chapel. It was the largest church in London, and Spurgeon was only nineteen years old. Charles Spurgeon pastored the church for thirty-eight years, and during his tenure, it would become the largest church in the world. Known as the prince of preachers, his sermons were recorded by stenographers who sold them for a penny apiece. Fun fact? When I graduated from Bible college, my graduation gift was an eighty-six-volume set of Spurgeon's sermons!

Along with preaching four to ten times per week, Spurgeon authored 150 books. He also founded a pastors' college, opened an orphanage, served as editor-in-chief of a monthly magazine, and oversaw sixty-six charities![5] I wonder what he did in his spare time!

On March 18, 1861, exactly two weeks after Abraham Lincoln moved into the White House, Spurgeon's congregation moved into the newly constructed Metropolitan Tabernacle.[6] Was Spurgeon excited? I'm sure he was. But there is one more thing you should know about Charles Spurgeon. Like Lincoln, he suffered from depression much of his life. And it's the timing of those depressive episodes that I find both intriguing and instructive. In Spurgeon's own words,

> Before any great achievement, some measure of the same depression is very usual. . . . Such was my experience when I first became a pastor in London. My success appalled me; and the thought of the career which it seemed to open up, so far from elating me, cast me into the lowest depth, out of which I uttered my *miserere* and found no room for a *gloria in excelsis.* Who was I that I should continue to lead so great a multitude? I would betake me to my village obscurity, or emigrate to America, and find a solitary nest in the backwoods, where I might be sufficient for the things which would be demanded of me. It was just then that the curtain was rising upon my life-work. . . . This depression comes over me whenever the Lord is preparing a larger blessing for my ministry.[7]

I discovered Spurgeon's confession when I felt a lot like he did. I was feeling absolutely overwhelmed as we embarked on a real-estate development that I knew would take many years and many millions of dollars. I'm certainly not complaining. Honestly, I wouldn't have had it any other way! But I'd be lying if I said I didn't struggle with doubt and discouragement and depression at times. My guess is that I'm not alone!

I was recently at a multicultural gathering of pastors in DC, and one of those pastors was brave enough to share about his bout with depression. I followed it up by asking whether any of the other pastors in the room were struggling with depression. By my count, half the hands shot up! Can I tell you why we need to confess our faults and foibles to one another? To remind ourselves that we're not alone! I don't think each of those hands represents a major depressive episode by technical DSM-V standards,[8] but they aren't shadowboxing either! If you're wrestling with depression, don't try to tough it out. Seek out some help!

There are seasons in life when darkness sets it and we're tempted to call it quits on a marriage or a dream or even a relationship with God. Sometimes the most spiritual thing you can do is just hang in there a little longer. A new day is going to dawn, and with it, the mercies of God. In my experience, internal struggles and external opposition are often indicators that you're on the brink of a breakthrough. Maybe, just maybe, God is breaking ground for a bigger blessing!

It's Always Darkest Before Dawn

In 1650, an English theologian named Thomas Fuller wrote a religious travelogue in which he said, "It is always darkest just before the day dawneth."[9] Over time that idea became an axiom: *things often seem to be at their worst right before they get better!*

There are seasons in life when we're not sure how to get to the other side of our issues. In fact, we're not sure there is another side! Sometimes it's a season of transition. You move to a new place, and you lose your bearings a little bit. You feel lost and lonely. Sometimes it's a season of grieving. When you experience loss, the compass needle spins as you try to orient toward a new normal. Sometimes it's a season of life, like a quarter-life or midlife crisis. When you evaluate your current status, it doesn't measure up to the expectations you had ten or twenty years ago. And, of course, sometimes it's a season of depression, as it was for Charles Spurgeon and Abraham Lincoln.

If you find yourself in one of those seasons, you need to know that we have a High Priest who is able to sympathize with our weaknesses.[10] Jesus didn't just carry a three-hundred-pound cross; He carried the full weight of the world's sin on His sinless shoulders. By doing so, He defeated sin and death. He also broke the curse that was as old as Eden!

> Christ redeemed us from the curse of the law by becoming a curse for us, for it is written: "Cursed is everyone who is hung on a pole." He

redeemed us in order that the blessing given to Abraham might come to
the Gentiles through Christ Jesus.[11]

The cross was a symbol of shame, a token of torture. There is no greater injustice in human history than the Son of God being crucified by His creation!
But God flipped the curse by becoming the curse, thereby turning the cross into
a universal symbol of love and hope and forgiveness!

God Bless It

In 536 BC, a remnant of Jewish refugees returned to Jerusalem and began rebuilding the temple that Nebuchadnezzar had destroyed. Not long after laying
the foundation, that rebuilding project was put on pause for nearly fifteen years.[12]
If you've ever had a dream detoured or delayed, you know how discouraging a
dream deferred can be. But it's often when we're just about to give up that God
shows up. At the eleventh hour, God resurrected the dream and called Zerubbabel to begin rebuilding with these words:

> What are you, mighty mountain? Before Zerubbabel you will become
> level ground. Then he will bring out the capstone to shouts of "God
> bless it! God bless it!"[13]

The odds were against Zerubbabel because of overwhelming opposition.
But opposition isn't cause for concern. Quite the opposite. If you aren't experiencing any opposition, it might mean you're maintaining the status quo and not
making much of a difference. Is opposition fun? Not at all! But I've learned a few
lessons about opposition over the years.

First of all, *you cannot please all the people all the time!* The diffusion-of-
innovation theory suggests that 16 percent of every human bell curve consists of
"resisters." It doesn't matter whether your name is Moses and you come down
from Mount Sinai with stone tablets inscribed by the finger of God, 16 percent
of the people still won't be buying what you're selling. In the words of Abraham
Lincoln, "You can please some of the people all of the time, you can please all of

the people some of the time, but you can't please all of the people all of the time."[14] Such is life and leadership.

Second, *the blessings of God don't always seem like blessings at the beginning!* Did you notice what the people shout when everything is said and done? They shout, "God bless it! God bless it!" Someday, we'll thank God for the prayers He didn't answer as much as the ones He did. Why? Because we ask for things that would short-circuit the plans and purposes God is working in our lives! In the same sense, someday we'll thank God for the challenges we've faced as much or more than those we've avoided. We may feel like cursing them up front, but at the end of the day, we'll see them for what they are—blessings in disguise!

I don't like opposition any more than anyone else, but a third lesson I've learned is this: *opposition can have a refining effect on vision.* Don't dismiss criticism out of hand. Listen to those criticisms because, right or wrong, they might reveal red flags. Sure, some of those criticisms represent the resisters! But it would behoove you to not only listen to those concerns but to proactively beat them to the punch by answering them authentically. Whatever you do, don't pretend to have all the answers! Remember, people don't trust leaders who have it all figured out. They trust leaders who walk with a limp.

If you don't let opposition get the best of you, you'll get the best of it. It'll make you into a bigger person, a better person. And therein lies the blessing! It's the mountains we overcome that make us who we are! The inclination is to curse the mountains in our path or try to avoid them altogether, but we don't know enough at that point to recognize whether the obstacle is a blessing or a curse. Sometimes what we believe to be a blessing is really a curse in disguise, and vice versa. Don't be too quick to curse the challenges you face, because God may be preparing you for something bigger, something better!

The Obstacle Is the Way

In AD 170, Marcus Aurelius waxed eloquent on the topic of turning obstacles upside down and inside out. The last of the Five Good Emperors wrote these immortal words: "The impediment to action advances action. What stands in the way becomes the way."[15] Simply put, *the obstacle is the way*.[16] That's more than philosophical jujitsu or seeing the silver lining. Every time I experience adversity, I remind myself that God is increasing my capacity.

In 2017, I ran the Chicago Marathon to celebrate God healing my asthma after forty years of suffering from it. I learned a lot of lessons through that experience. At the top of the list? To run 26.2 miles, you've got to push your physical limits by setting stretch goals. And that involves a great deal of pain. At first, a three-mile run seemed like a stretch. By the end of my training, I ran three miles on my rest-and-recovery day! That could be said of every distance I eventually trained at, save the marathon itself.

Life is like that, isn't it? When we experience stress, it stretches us. God is increasing our capacity to make difficult decisions or handle tough situations. I used to think that *stressed* and *blessed* were at odds with each other. And we've got to work hard to eliminate unhealthy stress that causes distress. But stress, properly managed, is a catalyst for growth. It may seem like an oxymoron, but you can be *stressed and blessed*. As you grow in God's grace, the things that stressed you out ten years ago will seem like a walk in the park. The obstacles you overcome get grafted into your testimony. And every testimony is a prophecy![17] God did it before, and He can do it again!

Sometimes our worst days prove to be God's greatest gift. I don't say that glibly. I say that as someone who spent two days on a respirator after emergency surgery for ruptured intestines. I have a fourteen-inch scar down the middle of my abdomen to show for it. The day I almost died—July 23, 2000—certainly ranks as one of the worst days of my life. I would never want to go through those surgeries again, but I wouldn't trade the lessons learned for anything in the world. What doesn't kill you really does make you stronger!

I used to be a little self-conscious when I took off my shirt because my scar was big enough to "scare the children." But over time, I began to see that battle scar as a medal of honor. Truth be told, it makes me look like I have a six-pack. Well, at least a two-pack. Every scar tells a story of pain, but scars are also evidence of obstacles overcome. And it's those scars that God will use to help others heal. Remember doubting Thomas? His doubt met its match in the nail-scarred hands of Jesus!

Flip the Curse

I'm not sure what obstacles you face. I'm sure some of them seem like unscalable mountains, and it's awfully tempting to try to go around them. My advice? Go through them, with God's grace. And when God gets you to the other side, the mountain will have become a level path. The obstacle will have become the way!

Part of positioning ourselves for blessing is spotting blessings in disguise! It's seeing opportunity where others see obstacles. That may sound like nothing more than a good pep talk or TED talk, but it's good theology! What did Joseph do to his brothers who faked his death and sold him into slavery? He didn't curse them. He gave them *shin*. Like the Jewish priests who raised their hands and pronounced a blessing on the people of God, Joseph blessed his brothers through his pain. And his words reveal a double-blessing mindset: "You intended to harm me, but God intended it for good to accomplish what is now being done, the saving of many lives."[18]

If you curse those who cause you pain, it only compounds the problem. I know it's hard not to, but it was a posture of blessing that reconciled Joseph's relationship with his brothers. And it has the power to do the same for you! Nothing turns the page or turns the table like a blessing.

Joseph endured thirteen years of pain and suffering, including a false accusation that landed him in prison. There must have been moments when Joseph felt cursed, right? But through all the injustice, he didn't play the victim. God was writing a long redemption story, and Joseph finally connects the dots. His enslavement and imprisonment were blessings in disguise, were they not? I'm not calling them *good*. Both involved tragic circumstances and tremendous suffering. But God used those circumstances to position Joseph in Pharaoh's administration, which ultimately saved two nations from famine!

That isn't the first time or the last time God flipped the curse. Notice what God said to Judah and Israel through the prophet Zechariah:

> Among the other nations, Judah and Israel became symbols of a
> cursed nation. But no longer! Now I will rescue you and make you
> both a symbol and a source of blessing.[19]

God wants to turn you into a *symbol* of blessing, but that isn't the ultimate goal. If we turn the blessing of God into a pseudo status symbol, the blessing becomes a curse because of pride. The goal? To become a *source* of blessing! Yes, that means leveraging our time, talent, and treasure for others. But it also means leveraging our pain for another's gain.

Flip the Pain

The easiest way to flip the blessing is to inventory the gifts God has given us, then return the favor in kind. But there is a far more difficult way to flip the blessing, a backflip of sorts. It's inventorying our pain and suffering, then leveraging those hurts to help others heal. That, of course, is much easier said than done.

When we experience pain, it's very difficult to think about anything else, anyone else. It's hard not to wallow in sorrow, playing the victim. That doesn't give others the right to play judge and jury by patronizing our pain. After all, the way each of us processes pain is as unique as our personalities. The timeline is too. That means giving margin to those who are mourning. Don't disappear on them, but give them room to grieve in their own unique way!

I've walked through enough unimaginable tragedies with people I pastor to know that the only way out of our pain is to leverage it for someone else's gain. Flipping our pain doesn't just redeem it. It functions as a painkiller. And it often translates into someone else's miracle!

Isn't that what Abraham Lincoln did? It was his personal pain and suffering that enabled him to endure a civil war. He leveraged lessons learned through tough times. He exercised character cultivated in the crucible. That's what great leaders do, and no one did it better than Jesus.

For the joy that was set before Him, Jesus endured the cross.[20] His pain is our gain. His shame is our salvation. His suffering sets us free.

Are you leveraging your pain for another's gain?

Bookend Blessings

One of the false assumptions many people make is that God cannot use them because of their brokenness. Quite the contrary! God cannot use you until you are broken! Of all the psalms, Psalm 51 may be the most cathartic. King David had committed adultery with Bathsheba and killed her husband to cover it up. He's a broken man. From the depths of that brokenness, he writes these words:

> My sacrifice, O God, is a broken spirit;
>> a broken and contrite heart
>> you, God, will not despise.[21]

It's the broken places where God's grace seeps into the crevices. It's the broken places where God uses us to help others heal. It's the broken places where God is breaking ground for a bigger blessing.

There is an ancient Japanese art form called *kintsugi* that repairs broken pieces of pottery by filling the cracks with a lacquer made from powdered gold. The dysfunctions are not disguised. The cracks are celebrated with golden seams. It's those cracks that give the repaired pottery its unique character! As you count your blessings, don't forget the broken places, the broken pieces!

Like plants that miraculously manage to grow through the cracks in concrete, the blessings of God are irrepressible. His blessings have a way of surfacing here, there, and everywhere! But it takes a good eye to spot blessings in disguise.

Let me double back to Joseph. The story ends with a double blessing—two nations saved from famine. That doesn't right every wrong that Joseph endured, but it does redeem them!

There is a second double blessing that is far more subtle but no less significant. Joseph learned the importance of blessing from his father, Jacob—the same Jacob who wrestled with God. I can picture Jacob limping all the way from Canaan to Egypt, leaning on his walking stick. The most surprising moment of Jacob's life—and perhaps the greatest moment—was discovering that the son he thought was dead and buried was alive and well. Even more amazing, Joseph was Pharaoh's second-in-command. Jacob knew enough to know that this kind of promotion can come from only God, a by-product of blessing. Imagine the wellspring of emotions that both Joseph and Jacob must have experienced that day!

What happens next is easily overlooked, but it's a substantial subplot.

"Joseph brought in his father, Jacob, and presented him to Pharaoh. And Jacob blessed Pharaoh."[22] What did Jacob do? Jacob *blessed* Pharaoh. That's what people who have been blessed by God do! They flip the blessing they fought for! But Jacob doesn't just bless Pharaoh coming in, he blesses Pharaoh going out. "Jacob blessed Pharaoh again before leaving his court."[23] Jacob pronounced a double blessing on Pharaoh!

What if we bookended every encounter the same way Jacob did? What if we blessed people at *hello* and blessed them again at *goodbye*? I have a hunch that more appointments would turn into divine appointments! I bet we'd find favor with a few more Pharaohs too!

LIVING IN WIDE-EYED WONDER

Every day I will bless you.

PSALM 145:2, ESV

On September 5, 1977, the *Voyager 1* space probe was launched from Cape Canaveral aboard a Titan-Centaur rocket. It has been speeding through space at an average speed of thirty-eight thousand miles per hour ever since, almost a million miles per day. *Voyager 1* is the first spacecraft to travel beyond the heliopause into interstellar space, and NASA continuously calculates its distance from Earth.[1] As of this writing, *Voyager 1* is 13,490,006,617 miles from Earth and counting.

That is pretty amazing, isn't it? But not as amazing as you.

The *Voyager 1* will run out of gas, so to speak, around the year 2025. At that point, it will have traveled more than fifteen billion miles! But guess what? That is less than half the length of the DNA strand in your body if it were stretched end to end. The cumulative DNA in all the cells in your body is about twice the diameter of the solar system![2]

In the words of the psalmist, you are "fearfully and wonderfully made."[3] If you are near someone you love right now, why don't you just remind them by saying, "You're amazing!" After all, their genetic fingerprints are as unique as yours!

According to one estimate, there are thirty-seven sextillion chemical reactions happening in the human body at any given time.[4] You are digesting food, regenerating cells, purifying toxins, catalyzing enzymes, producing hormones, and converting stored energy from fat to blood sugar.

Of course, none of this is a testament to you. It's a testament to the God who created you. But when was the last time you thanked God for any of those microscopic miracles? I bet it was the last time something went wrong! The health of the human body isn't something to be taken for granted; it's something to praise God for. The blessing pronounced by the apostle John isn't as simple as it seems:

> Beloved, I pray that you may prosper in all things and be in health,
> just as your soul prospers.[5]

By my count, praising God for good health adds up to at least thirty-seven sextillion blessings! Not to mention the five quarts of blood that travel through one hundred thousand miles of arteries, veins, and capillaries or the 550 liters of pure oxygen we inhale via twenty-three thousand breaths every single day.

The English author G. K. Chesterton once stated that his ultimate goal in life was to take nothing for granted[6]—not a sunrise, not a flower, not a laugh. I love that life goal. And if we could pull it off, it would produce praise without ceasing!

Favorite Things

Can you name this tune?

> Raindrops on roses and whiskers on kittens
> Bright copper kettles and warm woolen mittens

Written by Richard Rodgers and sung by Julie Andrews, "My Favorite Things" is one of the most popular songs in *The Sound of Music*. The modest melody is rivaled only by the humble lyrics. What I love about the song is that it's the simple pleasures that produce such profound joy. As we grow older, it's easy to forget our favorite things, isn't it? Over time we take them for granted. The goal of gratitude is to appreciate them even more!

The English poet Elizabeth Barrett Browning said,

Earth's crammed with heaven,

And every common bush afire with God:

But only he who sees, takes off his shoes;

The rest sit round it, and pluck blackberries.[7]

Don't pluck blackberries without praising God! Or strawberries or blueberries for that matter! Maybe that's one dimension of what Jesus meant when He told us to "behold the birds"[8] and "consider the lilies."[9]

For the record, ornithologists have identified at least eighteen thousand species of birds.[10] If you're into bird-watching, that'll keep you busy for quite some time! In fact, if you were able to behold a new bird every day, it would take fifty years minus a few days to spot them all. And while there are only ninety species of lilies,[11] no two are exactly alike! Few flowers are more spectacular than the Easter lily, tiger lily, or stargazer!

Cynicism sucks the mysterious out of the mundane, while skepticism sucks the miraculous out of it. And the soul suffers. Worship does the exact opposite! Living in wide-eyed wonder is recapturing our childlike curiosity. It's seeing the mystery and the miracle in every single moment. "Worship is transcendent wonder," said the Scottish philosopher Thomas Carlyle. "Wonder for which there is now no limit or measure; that is worship."[12]

According to the science of bioacoustics, millions of infrasonic and ultrasonic songs are being sung all the time. Most of them are inaudible to the human ear because our range of hearing is relatively small, between twenty and twenty thousand hertz. But according to the eminent etymologist Lewis Thomas, if we could perceive creation's collective chorus—the singing of seabirds, the rhythmical drumming of mollusks, and the harmonics of hovering flies—that song might literally lift us off our feet.[13] Juxtapose that with this:

Then I heard every creature in heaven and on earth and under the earth

and in the sea. They sang.[14]

This revelation is not future-tense prophecy; it's present-tense reality! And it's not just good theology; it's good science.

Did you know that whale songs can travel up to ten thousand miles underwater? Or that Eastern meadowlarks sing up to a hundred different songs?[15] Or that supersensitive sound instruments have discovered that earthworms make faint staccato notes? Or that the electron shell of the carbon atom produces the same harmonic scale as the Gregorian chant?

No wonder the ancient Greek philosopher Pythagoras said, "A stone is frozen music."[16] If we fail to praise God, the stones will sing our solo.[17] And "the trees of the field will clap their hands"![18]

A Tree Is a Tree Is a Tree

In 2009, a tree researcher named Dr. Martin Gossner sprayed the oldest tree in the Bavarian Forest National Park with an insecticide called pyrethrum. All the organisms that were living on or in the bark of that tree fell to the earth. Dr. Gossner collected 2,041 insects, organisms, and animals belonging to 257 different species.[19] A tree, you see, is not just a tree.

Dendrologists like Dr. Gossner are discovering that trees communicate and form community in ways we've been unaware of. If a giraffe starts eating an African acacia tree, the tree releases a chemical into the air that signals a threat. That same species of tree nearby detects that scent and begins producing toxic chemicals before the giraffe reaches them. They don't communicate in words, but they have their own sophisticated language. And they form community—a wood-wide web, if you will—through their root systems and microorganisms in the soil that share nutrients.[20]

That is nothing short of a miracle, bless God.

To grow its trunk, a beech tree needs as much sugar and cellulose as a 2.5-acre wheat field can produce, and it'll take 150 years for that trunk to reach its full girth.[21] During its 400-year life span, sixty reproductive cycles will produce 30,000 beechnuts. Of the 1.8 million beechnuts it produces during its lifetime, just one of them will become a full-grown beech tree.[22] So a beech tree isn't just one in a million; you've got to add eight hundred thousand to that million.

Every day during the summer months, one square mile of forest releases about twenty-nine tons of oxygen into the air. You and I each breathe in about two pounds per day, so one square mile of forest produces enough oxygen for about ten thousand people.[23] Put that in your pipe, but maybe don't smoke it.

When was the last time you hugged a tree? Or at least said thanks? A tree is more complicated than the naked eye allows us to see. It's an ecosystem unto itself, just like everything and everyone else. The psalmist said, "The earth is the LORD's, and everything in it."[24] God doesn't just own the cattle on a thousand hills;[25] He owns the hills. He owns everything on them and under them and the airspace over them.

According to rabbinic tradition, when a person goes out in springtime and sees a tree blooming, he or she should bless it by saying, "Blessed be He who has His world lack nothing, having created in it comely creatures and beautiful trees, so that human beings may enjoy them."[26] When we eat an apple or apricot or avocado, we feel like we're winning the gratitude game if we thank God for the fruit itself, right? Have you ever thanked God for the tree it grew on? Or blessed it?

We've already delineated the blessing of complexity. Simply put, the blessings of God will complicate your life and make it more complex. Those are holy complications! Let me flip that coin and drill down on the complexity of blessing.

One Hundred Blessings

Did you know that an observant Jew says a bare minimum of one hundred blessings per day? Those blessings cover the gamut of human experience. They offer a blessing before they eat, like many of us. But they also offer blessings during the meal for different tastes and smells. And after the meal is over—you guessed it—they offer a bookend blessing. Observant Jews bless God for a new day, a new article of clothing, and a new experience. And whenever they experience something pleasurable, it translates into praise. On that note, when was the last time you blessed God after having sex with your spouse? It was His idea after all. Don't rob Him of praise. In fact, praise Him more often!

What impresses me most about Orthodox Judaism is the way they nuance blessings. For example, they don't simply praise God for rainfall. In the words of Rabbi Judah, "We give thanks unto You for every rain drop You caused to fall on us."[27] Given the fact that there are 90,921 drops in a gallon of water, that's a lot to be thankful for! And remember, each drop is made up of more than five quintillion atoms!

If one smelled freshly baked bread, a blessing was to be recited: "Blessed be He who created this bread."[28] They would bless God after eating it as well, but smell and taste are double blessings. According to rabbinic tradition, "A man should taste nothing before he utters a blessing."[29]

One of my favorite blessings is zoological: "On seeing an elephant, a tailless ape, or a long-tailed ape, one should say, 'Blessed be He who makes strange creatures.'"[30] I don't know why they singled out those particular animals, but have you ever seen the backside of a baboon? Don't tell me God doesn't have a sense of humor!

Now let me ask the obvious question: Why one hundred blessings?

During the days of King David, a devastating plague is said to have claimed the lives of a hundred Israelites every single day. That's when a council of Jewish rabbis prescribed the practice of reciting one hundred blessings per day to counteract the plague. According to tradition, the plague stopped immediately.[31] I can't promise that gratitude will cure whatever ails you, but it's a good start. And it's where the double blessing begins.

According to the Talmud, if you enjoy something without saying a blessing, it's as if you have stolen it. "A man embezzles from God when he makes use of this world without uttering a blessing."[32] How many little blessings have you shoplifted? How many big blessings make you guilty of grand larceny? The way we make restitution is by recognizing that every good and perfect gift comes from God. Anything less is embezzlement.

The Gratitude Challenge

A few years ago, I issued a gratitude challenge to our congregation. The challenge? Thank God for the things you typically take for granted. The gratitude challenge requires an extra measure of mindfulness, revealing just how much we take for granted.

A physician in our congregation took the gratitude challenge quite seriously and literally, attempting to thank God for the many miracles that were happening in her body at any given moment. As she left church, she started praising God: *Thank You, God, for aerobic respiration. Thank You for mitochondria, which right now are creating ATP. Thank You for ATP. Thank You for glycolysis. Thank You for pyruvate.* If you have to look up *pyruvate,* you aren't alone! And you might want to keep that dictionary handy.

By the time she got home, she was thanking God for each of our amino acids: *Thank You, God, for glycine. Thank You for leucine. And isoleucine. And tryptophan. And for the fact that all organisms that form amino acids have the same chirality so that my body can reuse the nutrients and cellular building blocks of the food I break down.*

She prayed while she took a walk outside, thanking Him for bones and ligaments and tendons. She also thanked Him that she somehow never took an anatomy course in college, because otherwise she would have felt compelled to thank Him for each bone by name, which would have definitely set her back even more on her quest to get through most of the miracles she was receiving at that moment. She spent the day praying without ceasing! She literally didn't stop and just consciously kept listing things she was thankful for.

As she listened to music, she thanked Him for her ear's cochlea. While she made dinner, she thanked Him for xylem in the plants she was preparing. She spent a lot of time thanking Him for the molecular properties of water. She thanked Him for the bacteria in her colon that help her digest food. She thanked Him for genetic recombination that made developing and cultivating cotton plants possible for the jeans she was wearing. By the time the sun set and it got dark at nine o'clock, she thought God got amused with the futility of her trying to thank Him for everything. The Spirit finally hushed her, saying, *You can stop now.*

Needless to say, she won the gratitude challenge hands down! And while some may think this exercise borders on overkill, maybe that's because we underappreciate God's attention to detail. Let me push the gratitude envelope a little further. I try to live by a little maxim: "Whatever you don't turn into praise turns into pride." And there are no exceptions, which means there is no alternative. One of the simplest ways to position ourselves for future blessings is by praising God for past blessings! In fact, we're not ready for the next blessing until we have adequately thanked God for the last one!

The Art of Gratitude

The Batterson family has four values: gratitude, humility, generosity, and courage. Those values are the cardinal points on our compass, and they are not unrelated. Generosity rises or falls to the level of our gratitude. And gratitude is both an art and a science.

A wide variety of well-substantiated studies have found that gratitude increases patience, decreases depression, replenishes willpower, and reduces stress.[33] It doesn't just lengthen life; it improves the quality of life. And if you want a good night's sleep, don't count sheep. Count your blessings!

The science of gratitude is pretty straightforward, but putting it into practice is an art form. Not only is experimenting with new ways of expressing gratitude advisable, but it's also biblical. Isn't that what the psalmist advocates? "Sing to the LORD a new song."[34] God doesn't just want to be worshipped out of left-brain memory; He wants to be worshipped out of right-brain imagination. Finding new words and new ways to worship God is part and parcel of living in wide-eyed wonder. That said, I still haven't come up with a better way of staying positive than the good old-fashioned gratitude journal. Lora and I have each kept a gratitude journal for the better part of a decade. My journal is multipurpose. It's my prayer journal, gratitude journal, and dream journal. After all, it's the answered prayers and fulfilled dreams that translate into gratitude anyway. I'm just getting a head start.

Several years ago, Lora and I were inspired by Ann Voskamp's wonderful book *One Thousand Gifts*. We decided to start numbering our gratitudes every year with the goal of hitting a thousand. I usually fall short of a thousand, but I end up with a lot more than I would have otherwise! Numbering our gratitudes may be the most practical way to count our blessings, naming them one by one.[35] But it's more than just a best practice; it's the baseline of obedience. The apostle Paul said, "Rejoice always, pray continually, give thanks in all circumstances."[36] That's easier said than done, but jotting down what I'm grateful for every day is like a gratitude alarm reminding me that His mercies are new every single morning.[37]

Do you remember the ten lepers that Jesus healed? All ten were healed of leprosy, but only one of them was healed of a much worse ailment—ingratitude.

One of them, when he saw that he was healed, came back to Jesus, shouting, "Praise God!" He fell to the ground at Jesus' feet, thanking him for what he had done. This man was a Samaritan.[38]

Gratitude is a pilgrimage back to the foot of the cross. It's giving thanks and giving glory to God.

Flipping the blessing is giving unto others as God has given unto us, but radical generosity starts with profound gratitude for every good and perfect gift.

Let me double back to the gratitude challenge and give you a few guardrails. First, *buy a journal.* I like unlined journals because I can doodle, but you choose what works for you. Second, *write down three gratitudes every day.* Why three? Because one or two is too easy! And you may not be ready to identify a hundred blessings every day just yet! Third, *do it for forty consecutive days.* There is nothing magical about forty days, but there is something biblical about it. Plus, it's long enough to establish a gratitude habit. The goal isn't forty days of gratitude; it's a double-blessing mindset that lasts a lifetime. Fourth, *recruit a friend to do it with you.* Taking the challenge with someone you love will make it far more meaningful, and it will also keep you accountable.

Why is it so important to keep a gratitude journal? It's the way we take inventory of the blessings of God. Then, and only then, are we able to flip those blessings, which we'll focus on in the second half of this book. But let me push the envelope even a little further.

Most of us are good at praising God for the big things, but we fail to praise God for the little things. And we're good at praising God after the fact, but not a second before. Gratitude is thanking God *after* He does it, and that's great. But faith is next-level gratitude. Faith is thanking God *before* He does it. It's prophesying your praise!

Partial Miracles

Since I was a young child, I've suffered with severe asthma. In fact, my earliest memory is an asthma attack. There were not forty days in forty years that I did not have to take my inhaler, and I took it multiple times a day. I slept with it under my pillow and played basketball with it in my sock. I never went anywhere without my inhaler. It was my constant companion, my crutch. Then on July 2, 2016, God did an unimaginable miracle.

We kicked off a series at National Community Church titled Mountains Move, and I challenged our church to pray the bravest prayer. By *bravest prayer,* I meant the prayer you've prayed a hundred times that God hasn't answered yet or the most impossible miracle you could believe God for. Either way, the bravest prayer for me was that God would heal my asthma. And God did just that. I have not touched an inhaler from that day to this day, and I praise God by keeping track of the days! But let me share the backstory because I think it's a piece of this miraculous puzzle.

There is a two-part miracle in the Gospels that I find fascinating and encouraging.[39] Jesus laid hands on a blind man, and this man experienced a *partial* miracle. His sight was restored, but people looked like trees walking. So he was still myopic—let's call it 20/100. That is where many of us doubt God instead of praising God for a partial miracle. We give up because we didn't get the whole miracle, but some miracles happen in stages! Those are the moments when we need to double down in prayer!

If you want to experience the whole miracle, try praising God for partial miracles! What's a partial miracle? It's a small step in the right direction! In this instance, it's going from legally blind to 20/100. Too often we withhold our praise for partial miracles, and then we wonder why the full miracle never happens. Why not praise God every step of the way, even if it's two steps forward and one step back!

About a month before God healed my asthma, I climbed Cadillac Mountain on Mount Desert Island in Maine. It's certainly not the tallest mountain I've ever climbed, but I managed to do so without the use of my inhaler. For me, that was miraculous! In fact, I went four days without my inhaler, which may have been the longest span of my life at that point. I actually wondered if the Lord had healed me, but then I had to take a puff of my inhaler on day five. Was that discouraging? Absolutely! But instead of bemoaning the fact that I had to take my inhaler on day five, I decided to praise God that I went four days without it. I shared that partial miracle with our congregation a few weeks before challenging them to pray the bravest prayer. In retrospect, I believe that publicly praising God for that partial miracle was one small step—one giant leap—toward the double blessing of two healed lungs.

Whole miracle or partial miracle, bless God.

God Bless You

In the first half of this book, we've focused on *how to get* the blessing.

We've explored the habits of highly blessed people—humility, integrity, generosity, creativity, and praising God for partial miracles. We've discussed ways of positioning ourselves for blessing, not the least of which involves praying like it depends on God and working like it depends on us. God won't bless a lack of effort any more than a lack of gratitude. Obedience is the baseline of blessing, but it takes some tenacity too! It may even involve a wrestling match with God, as it did for Jacob.

Before we flip the blessing and focus on *how to give it,* let me share one final footnote.

"God bless you."

It's a common courtesy when someone sneezes, and we say it instinctively. But that blessing, like so many others, has lost much of its original meaning. We know not what we say!

In the sixth century, the greatest threat to humankind was the bubonic plague. It is estimated that this disease killed as many as one hundred million Europeans.[40]

Sneezing was one of the plague's telltale symptoms. As such, Pope Gregory ordered that anyone who sneezed be blessed immediately.[41] It's easy to look back across fourteen hundred years of history and dismiss this practice as slightly superstitious. But what else were they to do? It would be thirteen hundred years before Louis Pasteur demonstrated that disease is caused by harmful microbes we cannot see with the naked eye.[42]

On that note, medicine is one of God's great blessings. As someone whose life has been saved several times via medical intervention, I'm grateful for modern medicine and the doctors who practice it. Given all my surgical procedures, I'm also grateful for anesthetics and analgesics! God's blessings come in a wide variety of forms, including pill form. Sure, it's pharmaceutical companies that produce pills. But who provided the raw materials?

If we aren't careful, invocations like "God bless you" can become empty incantations. But instead of dismissing them as meaningless rituals, perhaps we need to rediscover their original intent—and reimagine ways of putting them into meaningful practice. Instead of trivializing what is sacred, we must sanctify what seems trivial.

Remember the mezuzah? The ritual reminder of God's blessing affixed to Jewish doorposts? I like Leonard Sweet's take: "To mezuzah our universe is to create sacred space and sacred rituals wherever we go."[43] It starts with a sneeze, but when you live with wide-eyed wonder, it encompasses absolutely everything on God's green earth!

The only way to *get the blessing* is to see the blessing, including well-disguised blessings like brokenness. Once you see it, you have to seize it. How? First, by thanking God for it. But gratitude must translate into generosity. Once you get the blessing, the only way to keep it is to give it away! That's incredibly counterintuitive, but that's how blessings become double blessings. It's time to flip the coin and flip the blessing.

Part 2

DOUBLE BLESSING

How to Give It

THE LAW OF MEASURES

Whoever can be trusted with very little can also
be trusted with much.

LUKE 16:10

In August 1996, National Community Church was just getting off the ground.
It was a memorable month for a myriad of reasons, not the least of which were the
lack of people and lack of money! Half of our original core group were students
who happened to be on summer break. And it was August recess, which meant
our Hill staffers were on vacation. The low point was the weekend thirteen people
showed up, and we may have included Father, Son, and Holy Spirit in that count.
Our total church income was $2,000 that month, and it cost $1,600 to rent the
DC public school where we met. That left $400 for our salaries and all other ex-
penses. Did I mention we were living in the nation's capital, where the cost of
living ranks right near the top? To say that we were in survival mode would be an
understatement, but that is often when God shows up and shows off.

During those dog days of summer, I discerned two distinct impressions.
The first was that our church needed to start giving to missions, which we'll
double back to in a minute. The second was a prompting to pray a perimeter
around Capitol Hill while reading this promise from the book of Joshua:

I will give you every place where you set your foot, as I promised Moses.[1]

It's impossible to put a price tag on the promptings of God, but amortized
over twenty-three years, that 4.7-mile prayer walk has netted six properties for
National Community Church. The combined value will surpass $100 million

when we're done developing them, and I know that's a big number, but God's vision for His church is bigger than ours! And *God has blessings for us in categories we cannot conceive of.* Of course, it's our job to steward those blessings by flipping them for others!

Don't despise the day of small beginnings! If you do little things like they're big things, God has a way of doing big things like they're little things! And the net worth of those properties goes way beyond a balance sheet. Our goal is bigger than simply building a church. We want to be a bigger blessing to our city. In fact, we want to solve our city's problems for it. We want to change statistics right here, right now. And we want to do things that will make a difference a hundred years from now. It's impossible to appraise the eternal value of changed lives because each one is invaluable and irreplaceable, but these property miracles have translated into a lot of people miracles!

For the record, I was *not* praying for property when I prayed that circle. That thought never crossed my mind. As I circled Capitol Hill, I was praying for people. I was praying that God's kingdom would come, that's God's will would be done in the nation's capital as it is in heaven. That said, the Promised Land was *land.* Properly stewarded, those properties are helping us advance God's kingdom and become a bigger blessing to our city. And the fact that the addresses we now own are right on that prayer circle is no coincidence. Each one is a real-estate miracle in its own right, and I'll share some of those double-blessing backstories with you.

The other August impression was less distinct—but no less significant— than the prompting to pray a perimeter. I felt like God wanted us to begin giving to missions, but we weren't even close to being a self-supporting church. How can you give what you don't have? But instead of rationalizing away that revelation, we decided to circle a promise:

> Give, and it will given to you. A good measure, pressed down, shaken together and running over, will be poured into your lap. For with the measure you use, it will be measured to you.[2]

By faith, we made our first $50 investment in missions. That may not seem like much now, but we had to give it before we could second-guess it. That $50 check represented a quantum leap of faith, and God honored it according to His promise. The very next month, our monthly giving tripled from $2,000 to $6,000, and we have never looked back.

Now let me say a few things before we go any further.

First, don't get distracted by anything that detracts from the ultimate importance of the Great Commandment and the Great Commission. In the grand scheme of things, money is immaterial. It is nothing more than a means to a much greater end—to carry out our kingdom calling. That said, money issues are heart issues. God does not need your money—I promise you that. But He wants your heart, and He cannot have one without the other! Jesus said, "Where your treasure is, there your heart will be also."[3]

Second, my prayer for you is that you would grow in the grace of giving.[4] Gratitude is the genesis of generosity, but I hope the second half of this book is a revelation. Again, I don't believe that God owed us that triple blessing because we took a fifty-dollar step of faith. But I do believe that we could have missed out on all that God had in store for us if we had withheld that fifty dollars. God is not a get-rich-quick scheme, but He loves to bless those who He knows will flip the blessing. And I'm confident of this: *you cannot outgive God*. Of course, it sure is fun trying!

Fifty-Dollar Faith

During our first five years as a church, we didn't have a lot of money to give to missions. But we gave what little we had, and the law of measures continues to catch up with us! Since 2001, as of this writing, our congregation, composed largely of single twentysomethings, has invested $19,391,647 in kingdom causes. We've also taken 228 mission trips around the world. The sun doesn't set on our missionary family around the globe, and we're doing our level best to make a difference on the home front. NCC resettles 65 percent of refugees in the DC area—helping them furnish apartments, find employment, and acclimate to America. We served six thousand meals to our friends experiencing homelessness last year, helping some of them find a place to live. And our DC Dream Center is discipling and mentoring hundreds of kids in an underserved part of our city.

God has done immeasurably more than we could have asked or imagined back in August 1996. And we're just getting started. We want to *grow more* so we can *give more*! But here's my point: Stewardship doesn't start with millions of dollars. The double blessing starts with fifty-dollar faith!

> If you are faithful in little things, you will be faithful in large ones.[5]

I know people—and you do too—who say they'll be more generous once they have more money. I'm not buying what they're selling! You may think it's easier to tithe on a lot of money, but it's a mirage. If you don't tithe on George Washington, Abraham Lincoln, and Alexander Hamilton, you won't give a Benjamin Franklin! Quit fooling yourself. Quit making excuses. And start exercising fifty-dollar faith! Generosity starts right here, right now. Don't wait until you have enough, because enough will never be enough. Give God the first fifty, and see what happens!

An Abundance Mentality

In the Parable of the Talents, Jesus called the servant who buried his talent in the ground *wicked*.[6] That seems a little extreme, doesn't it? The servant was simply protecting what he already had. But there is another word for that: *greed.* Not only does that decision reveal a lack of trust; it also reveals a scarcity mentality.

A scarcity mentality operates out of fear rather than faith, and it nets greed rather than gratitude. It's playing not to lose, which is why it's satisfied with breaking even. A scarcity mentality would never give up five loaves and two fish, which is why it never experiences miracles of multiplication. A scarcity mentality thinks in terms of addition and subtraction, so $5 + 2 = 7$. If you allow a scarcity mentality to take root, you become like the servant who buried his talent in the ground. You become a cul-de-sac of blessing, and the blessing dead-ends with you. Simply put, enough is never enough.

An abundance mentality, on the other hand, recognizes that it's all *from*

God and it's all *for* God. That's the beginning of double blessing. It's understanding that every good and perfect gift comes from God,[7] which means we
don't own anything. In fact, anything you think you own probably owns you!
Even your talent is on loan from God. God is the one who gives us the ability to
produce wealth.[8]

What God does for us is never just for us. It's ultimately for others! Like the
feeding of the five thousand, 5 + 2 = 5,000 R12. Miraculously, there was more
food left over than they started with.[9] That's what happens when you take what
you have in your hands and put it into the hands of God. People with an abundance mentality don't direct deposit God's blessings into a savings account; they
open a brokerage account and reinvest the dividends in others! They don't just
love to give; they live to give.

Start Small

I love the way Jesus celebrated unsung heroes like the little boy who gave five
loaves and two fish. He did the same with the widow who gave two coins.

> While Jesus was in the Temple, he watched the rich people dropping
> their gifts in the collection box. Then a poor widow came by and
> dropped in two small coins.[10]

Can you picture these rich people dropping their coins from the high dive?
They were all about making a splash! Then along comes this widow who dis-
creetly dropped two small coins in the box.

In the seventeenth century, around the time the King James Version was
published, the smallest coin in circulation was the mite. So that was the denomi-
nation chosen by translators of the KJV. In our economy, it would be two pennies. But the smallest and least valuable coin in first-century Judea was the
lepton. Its diameter was the size of a pencil eraser, and it was worth about six
minutes of an average day's wage.[11] Add these two coins, and this woman gave
the equivalent of twelve minutes of time. That seems like so little, yet it was her
generosity that Jesus celebrated.

"I tell you the truth," Jesus said, "this poor widow has given more than all the rest of them. For they have given a tiny part of their surplus, but she, poor as she is, has given everything she has."[12]

The value of a gift isn't determined by *how much you give*. The true value is a function of *how much you keep*. This woman gave so little, yet she gave so much.

Like many nonprofits, National Community Church has coordinated a number of giving campaigns over the years. While those initiatives set numeric targets according to financial best practices, the real goal is for everyone who participates to simply grow in the grace of giving. I don't want to diminish the significance of large gifts. We're beyond grateful to have been on the receiving end of many miraculous ones, but the most meaningful gifts aren't always the largest ones. It's often the smallest gifts that represent the biggest sacrifice, like the widow who gave her two coins.

When Lora and I pray about the part God wants us to play in that kind of campaign, we use two guardrails to guide our giving.

First, we want to *stretch our faith*. In other words, we want our gift to represent more time and talent and treasure than we currently have. Like a stretch goal, we want our generosity to push us past previous limits.

Second, we want it to *involve a measure of sacrifice*. Like a good workout, giving doesn't feel good until it hurts a little! You have to break down the muscle for it to grow stronger, and that includes the giving muscle. Frankly, we want our family to feel the effect. That way, we're all in it together.

For nearly a decade, I was a proud member of the Junky Car Club. Yes, it is a real club. In fact, it used to put out a calendar and I was Mr. August one year. For the record, that's the full extent of my male-modeling career! I didn't join the club because we couldn't afford a new car. I joined because I knew an old car would cost less, meaning we could give more to the kingdom causes we care about. Please understand, this doesn't even qualify as a sacrifice by first-century standards! But Lora and I wanted our kids to see our values in action. Driving a twentieth-century Honda with 220,000 miles on it gave us more margin to give. The only reason I stopped driving that car is that someone gave us a new car. Well, *new* by my old Honda's standards. It was half the age with about half the miles, from an entirely different century! Of course, that new ride gave us an opportunity to flip the blessing!

Reverse Tithe

Many years ago, I read a biography about the life and legacy of J. C. Penney, the founder of the department store by the same name. The *C* in *J. C.* stood for *Cash*—no kidding. But that wasn't the motivation behind his entrepreneurial endeavors that resulted in sixteen hundred department stores bearing his name. The son of a Baptist preacher, J. C. Penney was motivated by the Golden Rule. His very first store was named Golden Rule Store, and he titled his autobiography *Fifty Years with the Golden Rule*.[13]

During the Great Depression, Penney sank into his own depression. Times were tough, and Penney found himself on the brink of bankruptcy and the brink of divorce. He even contemplated ending his own life. That crisis landed Penney in a sanatorium in 1932, but it was there that he found his way back to God. Wandering those lonely corridors early one morning, he heard a hymn from his childhood:

Be not dismayed whate'er betide
God will take care of you
All you need he will provide
God will take care of you[14]

J. C. Penney followed the sound of that song into the sanatorium chapel, where doctors and nurses were worshipping God. Then one of the sanatorium staff read the words of Jesus: "Come to me, all you who are weary and burdened, and I will give you rest."[15] Not unlike Brian "Head" Welch, whose story I have already shared, J. C. Penney found rest in those very same words![16] And the rest is history.

J. C. Penney lived until the age of ninety-five, and his life is a testament to the power of double blessing. When he died in 1971, his empire of department stores had become America's second largest retailer behind Sears with annual revenues of $4.1 billion.[17] But Penney used his net worth to add value to others, earning an interesting moniker: the Man with a Thousand Partners. His integrity and generosity affected many millions more, including me. By the end of his life, J. C. Penney was reverse tithing—he was living off 10 percent and giving 90 percent of his income back to God. I know—giving away 90 percent of your income sounds a lot easier when we're talking about billions of dollars! But it always starts with fifty-dollar faith!

Start Here

When Lora and I got married, we made a decision that we could never not tithe. Has it always been easy? No! Especially in August 1996! But we never questioned that decision because it was a predecision. And God has honored it in some strange and mysterious ways! We began our journey of generosity by giving God a 10 percent tithe, but when I read Penney's biography, I knew that wasn't the end goal.

Lora and I had no idea *how* we'd get there, but we set a stretch goal of someday doing the same as J. C. Penney. That was a turning point, a tipping point for us. We stopped setting *getting goals* and started setting *giving goals,* which I'll detail in a later chapter. But that shift in focus was like the tiny rudder that turns a ship. It changed the trajectory of our lives, reorienting us toward double blessing.

It was difficult in the early years of church planting because I didn't make a full-time salary for many years. In fact, I worked two jobs for several years just to make ends meet. But when I started writing, my books turned into more of a double blessing than I would have imagined. I don't write for royalties—and never have. I write because I'm called by God, and my prayer is that my books would change the trajectory of readers' lives just as J. C. Penney's biography did mine. That said, we have found tremendous joy in leveraging book royalties for kingdom causes!

If you want to have twice as much fun, try giving God a double tithe. Or if you have the capacity to do so, go fifty-fifty. It may take some time to get to that giving percentage, and make sure you do it for the right reasons. But I can promise you this: *the more you give away, the more you'll enjoy what you keep!* If you double tithe, you'll experience *double joy.*

Again, I know that some of the numbers and percentages I'm sharing may seem unattainable from where you stand right now. And your next step may be getting out of debt. But don't let what you cannot do keep you from doing what you can. Start with two coins or twelve minutes!

Lora and I grew up in a church whose heartbeat was missions, and the giving vehicle was called a faith promise. As the name suggests, it was a promise based on faith. In Old Testament terms, it was a freewill offering. In other words, it was a gift over and above the 10 percent tithe. It wasn't based on budgeting, as much as it was the by-product of prayer. I made my first faith promise as a seventeen-year-old in high school, and while I can't remember the exact amount, it could not have been much given the fact that I was making minimum wage! But like anything, growing in the grace of giving is about baby steps. That faith promise represents one of my first steps of financial faith, and it taught me to trust God.

Now let me fast-forward about ten years into our church-planting journey.

In 2005, Lora and I introduced the faith promise to our congregation. Whenever we engage in any kind of generosity initiative, Lora and I want to lead the way and go first. It would be disingenuous to ask people to stretch their faith or make a sacrifice beyond what we're willing to do! We made the largest pledge of our lives, putting us in a position where God would have to provide way beyond our budget. A few months after making that faith promise, I signed my first book contract, and I don't believe those are unrelated incidents.

Since I was a first-time author, the advance wasn't huge. But it was more than enough to make our faith promise seem small. Seeing my first book on a bookshelf in a bookstore was an unforgettable experience, but we found just as much joy in writing that check to fulfill our faith promise.

Dream big.

Start small.

Here we go!

SEED THE CLOUDS

Whoever watches the wind will not plant;
whoever looks at the clouds will not reap.

ECCLESIASTES 11:4

In the 1940s, a series of clandestine experiments was conducted for the United States military at a research lab in Schenectady, New York. A collaboration between General Electric and the US Air Force, Project Cirrus was the first attempt to modify a hurricane via human intervention.[1] The research was spearheaded by an academic odd couple.

Irving Langmuir was a Nobel Prize–winning chemist. His assistant, Vincent Schaefer, was a high school dropout with a knack for DIY projects. And their common bond was a love of skiing. In fact, Schaefer was the president of the Schenectady Wintersports Club, of which the Nobel laureate, Langmuir, was a member. During the winter months, they would often climb New Hampshire's Mount Washington, conduct weather experiments at the research station on its summit, then ski back down the mountain.

During one such ascent, Irving Langmuir noticed a cluster of clouds hovering near the summit. Despite the number of clouds, he noted that they produced only a few snowflakes. "Look, Vince," said Langmuir. "With all these clouds everywhere, there's only a flake here and a flake there. Why? I think we ought to do some more studies on that."[2]

Vincent Schaefer went back to the lab and requisitioned a GE freezer that he retrofitted with black velvet. After chilling the freezer to ten degrees below the freezing point of water, Schaefer breathed into the box and created a cloud. Because cold air is heavier than warm air, that man-made cloud hovered in the makeshift freezer. Then Schaefer tried seeding the cloud, much like one seeds the ground. He tried to produce snow by implanting different substances, without much success.

As winter turned to spring and spring turned to summer, it became increasingly difficult to keep the freezer freezing. One fateful July day, it was so hot that Schaefer decided to add dry ice. When he threw the solid carbon dioxide into the freezer, the cloud transformed into snow crystals. Vince Schaefer had nucleated the cloud and made it snow!

Schaefer couldn't wait to scale the experiment and take it out into nature, but a mild autumn delayed their field tests until mid-November. When temperatures finally fell to freezing, he purchased six pounds of crushed dry ice, rented a single-propeller airplane, and flew it into a cumulus cloud. When he seeded that cloud with the dry ice, eyewitnesses on the ground said the cloud seemed to explode. The snow it produced was visible forty miles away!

An assistant editor at the *GE Monogram* announced, "Schaefer made it snow this afternoon over Pittsfield! Next week he walks on water."[3]

Go, Set, Ready

The science of seeding clouds may be a twentieth-century breakthrough, but the theology of seeding clouds is as ancient as Ecclesiastes. There is one verse in particular that I prescribe to procrastinators and perfectionists because it changed the trajectory of my life:

> Whoever watches the wind will not plant;
>> whoever looks at the clouds will not reap.[4]

If you wait until you're ready, you'll be waiting the rest of your life. I wasn't ready to get married. Is anyone? Lora and I weren't ready to have children. Who is? I wasn't ready to pastor a church at twenty-five. We weren't ready to invest in missions, launch a second campus, open a coffeehouse, or build out a city block into a prototype campus, child-development center, and mixed-use marketplace.

Yes, you need to pray like there's no tomorrow. But you also have to plan like there is one! God doesn't bless a lack of planning any more than a lack of praying. That said, the planets will never be perfectly aligned. At some point, you've got to quit making excuses. You have to pick up the plow and start seeding the soil. Or in this case, the clouds!

We have a little mantra at NCC: "Go, set, ready!" That may sound backward, but that's the sequence of faith. Yes, faith is following in the footsteps of Jesus. But faith also goes *first,* and it doesn't matter whether anyone else follows suit. Faith is the willingness to go it *alone.*

Every double blessing traces its origins back to a single step of faith. It was true of the fifty-dollar check we wrote to missions. It was true of the 4.7-mile prayer walk around Capitol Hill. And it's true of you.

What step of faith do you need to take? No more excuses! No more delays! Delayed obedience is disobedience! But if you take that one small step, don't be surprised if it turns into a double blessing.

A Dream Deferred

I felt called to write when I was twenty-two years old but it took thirteen years for me to write my first book. In retrospect, I'm glad I didn't write a book at twenty-two, because I probably would have had to write a book at twenty-three to retract what I said at twenty-two. With each passing year, however, I got more and more frustrated. My birthday became an annual reminder of a dream deferred.

As my thirty-fifth birthday approached, I was reading the book of Ecclesiastes. When I got to the fourth verse in the eleventh chapter, it pushed me over the edge. I decided to seed the cloud by self-imposing a forty-day deadline. I was bound and determined *not* to turn thirty-five without a book to show for it. The net result was a self-published book titled *ID: The True You.* Is it the best book I've written? No, it is not. I actually tried to take it out of circulation, but once a book is on Amazon, it's forever!

That book sold only 3,641 copies, and my first royalty check was $110.43. But I didn't write that book for anyone but me and, of course, as an act of obedience to the One who had called me to write. Writing that book was my way of proving to myself that I could do it. It also proved to be the seedbed for future books. Three of the chapter titles would become future book titles—*In a Pit with a Lion on a Snowy Day, Wild Goose Chase,* and *Soulprint.*

At some point, you've got to stop watching clouds. The technical term is *nephelococcygia,* in case you care. If you have a dream that is gathering dust, you need to seed the clouds with a step of faith. The last two words of Mark's gospel are "signs following."[5] We wish they were "signs preceding," right? It would be so much easier! We also wish the Lord's Prayer said, "Give us this *year* our *yearly* bread." Why? Because then we wouldn't have to trust God on a daily basis! God loves us too much to short-circuit our daily dependence on Him with too much of anything.

I have no doubt that God is preparing good works in advance.[6] But more often than not, we've got to take a step of faith in the direction of that good work. It would have been much easier for the disciples to stay in the comfortable confines of Jerusalem, right? But they obeyed the Great Commission, which called them to step out in faith and preach the Resurrection everywhere they went. The net result? Signs followed.

Wouldn't it be so much easier if God would pave the way with signs preceding? Rather than confirming the proclamation of the gospel after the fact? According to human logic, it would be. But that would rob us of the opportunity to participate in the miracle by exercising our faith, wouldn't it? Sure, God does many miracles in advance. But more often than not, we have to seed the clouds just like the first-century disciples did.

The counterintuitive command God gives Joshua before the parting of the Jordan River is a great example of "Go, set, ready":

> Tell the priests who carry the ark of the covenant: "When you reach
> the edge of the Jordan's waters, go and stand in the river."[7]

We want God to part the river before we step into it. Why? So our shoes don't get wet. We want God to go first so it doesn't require any faith. But this is where so many of us get stuck spiritually. We're waiting for God to part the waters, while God is waiting for us to step into the river! Seeding the clouds is taking a step of faith and getting your feet wet, but let me back up one step.

Writing History

We'll explore several different ways of seeding the clouds, but it all starts with prayer. Prayer is the way we write history before it happens. It's the difference between *letting* things happen and *making* things happen. It's the difference between *us fighting for God* and *God fighting for us*!

Remember when the prophet Elijah announced to King Ahab that he heard the sound of a mighty rainstorm?[8] That had to sound a little silly. There hadn't been a drop of rain in three and a half years, and there wasn't a cloud in the sky. But prophets walk to the beat of a different drummer because they hear with spiritual ears.

> Elijah climbed to the top of Mount Carmel and bowed low to the ground and prayed with his face between his knees.[9]

I don't want to read too much into Elijah's prayer posture, but this was no perfunctory prayer: "God is great; God is good; let us thank Him for our food." This was a contending prayer. It's not just praying *for;* it's praying *through.* Elijah is doubling down by doubling over. It's reminiscent of the first-century sage Honi the Circle Maker, who knelt in the circle he had drawn in the sand and prayed to God, "Sovereign Lord, I swear before your great name that I will not leave this circle until You have mercy on Your children."

I pray in a lot of different postures, but generally speaking, I pace when I pray. That's due in part to multiple knee surgeries from my basketball-playing days that make it a little bit tougher to kneel. But when I need to intercede, I hit my knees! God certainly cares more about the posture of your heart than the position of your body. And He can hear you whether you're standing up or kneeling down. But I choose to kneel because it's a form of humility and a sign of surrender. There are, however, situations where I feel like kneeling isn't enough so I fall flat on my face before God. At NCC, we call it "sucking carpet."[10] I know that sounds a little strange, but it's not unlike Elijah praying in this fetal position. And I think it comes close to the kind of intensity with which Elijah was interceding to end this drought. His unwavering faith is evidenced by the fact that he kept sending his servant to look toward the sea for any sign of rain.

The Seventh Time

Even when there is no visual evidence of God at work, I promise you, God is watching over His word to perform it.[11] The God who began a good work will carry it to completion.[12] Of course, He'll do so on His terms and His timeline.

Finally the seventh time, his servant told him, "I saw a little cloud about the size of a man's hand rising from the sea."[13]

Every so often we'll do a forty-day prayer challenge at National Community Church. The day we began our most recent challenge is the same day that an NCCer interviewed for a job at the Office of Management and Budget (OMB). And that interview was only after two months of phone interviews, security checks, and reference checks!

It was a long, frustrating process, but I love what Jessica did. She seeded the clouds by circling the New Executive Office Building (NEOB) once a day for seven days, sort of like the Israelites who circled the city of Jericho. On day seven, she decided to circle seven times but discovered that Secret Service had blocked off Pennsylvania Avenue because a foreign head of state was visiting. That detour meant a much bigger circle—in fact, twelve times the original distance!

In Jessica's own words, "After fourteen kilometers, three hours, some refreshing rain, and a few sideways glances from Secret Service, I finished. I felt humbled, empowered, and exhausted. I began that circle at 3:34 p.m. on March 6. Twenty-three hours later, at 2:39 p.m. on March 7, I received a phone call from the director offering me the job!"[14]

What was Jessica doing, besides getting good exercise? She was seeding the clouds! Our prayers certainly have to be aligned with the will of God and the glory of God or it's a nonstarter. But if they are, you might want to have an umbrella handy!

I love the insight Jessica shared at the end of her email: "Pastor Mark, that prayer walk was one of the most humbling things I have done. The thing I learned is that God didn't need me to circle those blocks seven times in order to break down a wall around OMB. He needed me to circle those blocks seven times to break down a wall within me, to bring me to a place of humility and total dependence upon Him, and to prepare me for the next step of faith, little or big."[15]

At this juncture, let me break down the double blessing a little further. The first step of faith for Jessica was applying for her dream job in the first place! I know that sounds simple, but most of us aim too low or settle for our second choice. The second step was an interview. The third and fourth steps involved reference checks and security checks. My point? Miracles often start in mundane and menial ways! But that's how we get skin in the game. And while it's in process, don't forget to praise God for partial miracles!

Skin in the Game

Just like Jessica who circled NEOB and the Israelites who circled Jericho, we circled a crack house on Capitol Hill for five years before turning it into Ebenezers Coffeehouse. First we seeded the clouds with prayer, but it was an $85 step of faith that parted the waters.

Lora and I were at an auction for our children's school on Capitol Hill. National Community Church was still trying to find its footing, and Lora and I were barely making ends meet. In part, because of the tuition we were paying to the school whose auction we were attending!

One of the items up for auction was a three-inch-thick binder donated by the Capitol Hill Restoration Society. It contained the zoning codes for new construction on Capitol Hill, zoning codes I knew we'd need to know backward and forward if we were to build a coffeehouse. One minor detail—we didn't even own the property yet! Wouldn't it be wise to wait until we got it under contract before buying that book? Besides, the opening bid of $85 was a big deal back then. We didn't have money to waste, but I felt the Holy Spirit prompting me to take a step of faith. We won the bid on that book, and it now sits in a special place in my office as a reminder to seed the clouds by stepping into the river.

Faith is not a numbers game, but sometimes it can be measured in dollars.

If you aren't willing to risk $85 on your God-given dream, you might not be ready for it. Seeding the clouds means putting skin in the game! That could be investing in yourself by furthering your education. It could be the cost of dinner on a first date. One way or the other, you have to put your money where your dream is.

At flood tide, the Jordan River was about a mile wide. The Promised Land must have seemed so close yet so far! Maybe you feel the same way about a dream God has given you. Let me remind you that the miracle isn't really a mile away! It's one step away!

You are one decision away from a totally different life. It will certainly involve a measure of faith and a measure of sacrifice. And you definitely have to get your feet wet. But if you take the first step, God will take it from there.

Remember the snowstorm over Pittsfield? According to Langmuir, a pellet of dry ice the size of a pea was capable of producing several tons of snow![16] Don't get paralyzed by the size of your dream. Sow a seed, and see what God does! You might just reap a double blessing. Said another way, you might have to *give it* before you *get it*.

Sow a Seed

When I wrote my first published book, *In a Pit with a Lion on a Snowy Day*, I decided to offer a free copy to any church planter who wanted one. I thought it was a unique way to give back to my church-planting tribe, but I was a little surprised by the response. Church planters like free books!

We ended up giving away hundreds of copies before we sold one. Even with my author's discount, we lost money before we made money! But looking in the rearview mirror, I think we were doing exactly what the writer of Ecclesiastes advocated:

Sow your seed in the morning,
    and at evening let your hands not be idle,
for you do not know which will succeed,
    whether this or that,
    or whether both will do equally well.[17]

Remember the secret to the double blessing? You get it by giving it. That dimension of the double blessing deserves double emphasis: *you don't wait to give it until you get it.* You give it *first* as an expression of faith. That is the principle we were practicing when we offered those books for free ninety-nine.

I know the idea of sowing a seed has been used and abused by some false teachers, but that doesn't make it any less true if properly applied. It's also not a money-back guarantee. There will be false negatives and false positives. But sometimes you have to sow a seed at your point of need. One reason is that it takes your eyes off your problems! When you focus on others, it puts your problems in perspective. And don't be surprised if a blessing comes out of nowhere.

When we gave those books away, we had no idea how many copies *In a Pit with a Lion on a Snowy Day* would sell. Like every first-time author, I was keenly aware of the fact that 97 percent of books don't sell five thousand copies. It was a calculated risk, but I knew it was the right thing to do regardless!

We didn't seed those books so that the church planters who received a copy would purchase the book in bulk—I promise you that. But that is exactly what happened. Over the years, more than a few of those church planters have used the book for small groups, a church-wide series, or even as a giveaway to guests. I have no way of calculating the return on investment, but it has sold more than a thousandfold what we gave away!

A decade later, that book continues to defy gravity. The bell curve for most books takes a nosedive after the first year or two, but *In a Pit with a Lion on a Snowy Day* is the gift that keeps on giving. Simply put, God has blessed that book beyond my ability to write or my publisher's ability to market. Why? I have two working theories.

First, I'm grateful for the team of intercessors who pray that God would put my books in the right hands at the right time. To me, a book sold is not a book sold. It's a prayer answered.

Second, if God knows you're willing to give something away, He'll give it His full blessing. Having learned that lesson with my first book, Lora and I gift a free copy of every book I write, right before it releases, to everyone who attends our church. Why would we make our church family buy it? But it seems like the more books we give away, the more copies we sell.

Few things seed the cloud of God's blessing more effectively than generosity.

Blessing is a by-product of generosity, but when we flip the blessing, it flips the coin. Generosity becomes the by-product of blessing. Again, God doesn't bless us to raise our standard of living. God blesses us to raise our standard of giving. Generosity starts and sustains the double blessing.

We seed the clouds with faith.

We seed the clouds with prayer.

We seed the clouds with generosity.

Gaining Momentum

In Newtonian mechanics, momentum is the product of mass times velocity: $p = mv$. If generosity is mass in that equation, then positivity is velocity. And it's not just the power of positive thinking. Positivity is keeping our eyes fixed on Jesus, the author and perfecter of our faith.[18] It puts more stock in the promises of God than the opinions of people, especially self-proclaimed experts.

I recently had coffee with a Major League Baseball hitting coach whose team happened to be in town to play the Washington Nationals. I asked him, "What is the greatest challenge you're facing right now?" They had a six-game losing streak coming into the series. So his answer didn't really surprise me: "The greatest challenge is maintaining positivity."

Positivity and negativity don't just affect a hitter's mindset in the batter's box. Those attitudes affect the culture in the clubhouse. And they aren't just attitudinal issues; they're spiritual matters.

Remember the twelve spies who scouted the Promised Land? Ten of them brought back a bad report, and that report spread so quickly that it infected the entire nation with negativity. Stop and think about it: it was ten negative people who kept an entire nation out of the Promised Land and cost them forty years! Only two of them, Joshua and Caleb, stayed positive! And because of their positivity, they inherited the blessing.[19]

We begin every staff meeting at NCC by sharing wins. Why? Well, it reminds us of *why* we're doing what we're doing. It also seeds the clouds by celebrating what we want to see more of. Your attitude, positive or negative, makes a difference! And it doesn't just invoke God's blessing. It increases the velocity of God's kingdom by spreading God's love.

A Stake in the Ground

In the classic film *Far and Away*, Tom Cruise and Nicole Kidman play Irish immigrants, Joseph and Shannon, who seek their destiny in the Oklahoma Territory during the Land Run of 1893. Riding a rather unruly horse, Joseph giddyups to his piece of promised land and drives his stake into the ground. That stake in the ground represents his hopes and dreams and the love of his life, Shannon.

There are moments in life when you have to drive your stake into the ground, and it becomes the battlefield you're willing to die on. That's what Caleb does forty-five years after spying out the promised land. He stakes claim to Hebron with these William Wallace–like words: "Now give me this hill country that the LORD promised me that day"![20]

According to Jewish tradition, when Caleb entered the Promised Land with the other spies, he broke off from the group and visited Hebron. It was there that Abraham had been buried more than four hundred years before. We aren't sure what happened while he was there, but I have to wonder whether Caleb put a stake in the ground. It's almost as if he swore on his ancestor's grave that he would be back, even if it was the last thing he did. Caleb would eventually conquer Hebron, reclaiming that sacred site. But he did more than that. He seeded the clouds for King David. Over four hundred years later, David was crowned king in the city Caleb had conquered, and David made it his first capital.

You aren't seeding the clouds just for you. You are seeding them for future generations! What God does for us is never just for us! It's always for the third and fourth generations. We think right here, right now. But God is thinking nations and generations!

Is there a promise you need to stake claim to? A blessing you are believing God for? A miracle you cannot afford to give up on? Put a stake in the ground for you and your children and your children's children.

I've already shared about how God healed my asthma after forty years and hundreds of prayers. And I've shared about how I ran the Chicago Marathon to celebrate that miracle. But let me share one more thing. I'll never forget the day I threw away my inhalers. For the record, I don't recommend doing what I did without consulting your physician first. Was it scary? So scary! For forty years, I never went anywhere without one. And for the record, I didn't throw them away until fifty days after God healed me. But throwing away my inhalers was putting a stake in the ground, and God has honored it ever since.

I know that many of my stories revolve around pastoring and writing, but that's who I am and what I do. So I'll share one more testimony. Right before releasing my sixth book, *The Circle Maker,* Lora and I felt like we needed to seed the clouds by creating a foundation. Honestly, it seemed a little silly at the time. The book I wrote right before *The Circle Maker* didn't sell many copies, but I had a holy hunch that God was going to bless that book beyond what I could ask or imagine. And I wanted us to be in a position to flip the blessing. At that point, Lora and I were already double tithing on book royalties. But we decided to up the ante and go fifty-fifty. Creating that 501(c)(3) nonprofit was our way of putting a stake in the ground, and God honored it.

For me, writing is a double blessing. The first blessing is the joy and privilege of writing words that change the trajectory of people's lives. The second blessing is using those royalties to fund kingdom causes we care about. Honestly, I'm not sure which yields more joy. And I'm glad I don't have to choose! Doing both is the double blessing.

I don't want to give the impression that I have overcome greed. I promise you, I have not. Not by any stretch of the imagination! And please understand that our journey of generosity has taken many twists and turns, including a few wrong turns. It has also taken us many years to up the ante and become a bigger blessing to others.

Can I remind you that outcomes are out of your control? But inputs are not. You cannot control the clouds, but you can seed them with your prayers! You can also seed them with generosity and positivity. It honestly doesn't matter how much or how little you make. Our culture mistakenly measures worth by net worth, but God does not. His measure? Faith, but not just any kind of faith. "Faith as *small* as a mustard seed."[21]

Plant that seed, and see what God does!

OPPORTUNITY COST

It is more blessed to give than to receive.

ACTS 20:35

In 2008, four students set out to revolutionize an industry that was as old as Benjamin Franklin's bifocals. They had no expertise in eyewear. They were neck-deep in student loans. And more than a few friends called them crazy. But they couldn't get over how much it cost to buy a pair of glasses! They thought it was ridiculous, and they were bound and determined to do something about it. Their idea was pretty simple: *offer fashionable frames at a fraction of the price, and do so online.* A decade later, Warby Parker was a billion-dollar business! Adam Grant wrote about Warby Parker in his book *Originals,* explaining he was offered the opportunity to invest. Sadly, he declined. In his words, "It was the worst financial decision I've ever made."[1]

In the world of economics, there are two kinds of cost—an actual cost and an opportunity cost. An *actual cost* is an expenditure. It shows up on your balance sheet as a liability, and it's relatively easy to account for. An *opportunity cost* is a hidden cost. It's the loss of potential gain, often because of indecision or inaction. Enter Adam Grant. Failing to invest in Warby Parker did not cost him a single penny in terms of *actual cost*—no harm, no foul. But it cost him millions of dollars in terms of *opportunity cost*—nothing ventured, nothing gained.

Don't begin until you count the cost.[2]

Jesus spoke those words in the context of a construction project, but they are true of a thousand things. When it comes to counting the cost, most people fail to realize that it's a two-sided coin. Most of us are pretty good at counting the actual cost. Counting opportunity cost? Not so much. Why? Because opportunity cost involves scenario planning and systems thinking. And when you try to account for the future, there are far more variables at play. Spiritually speaking, counting opportunity cost is a moral calculation that involves a measure of faith. And few things are more critical when it comes to your future.

You can do nothing wrong and still do nothing right. Goodness is not the absence of badness. That is a glass-half-empty gospel. Faithfulness is *not* holding the fort. It's playing offense, which is the opposite of playing it safe. As Christ followers, we should be more known for what we're *for* than what we're *against*. Sure, you can maintain the status quo and there will be no net loss. There is no actual cost. But the opportunity cost is staggering.

If you stay in the boat, you'll never walk on water!

If you stay in the boat, you'll miss out on the miracle!

Potential is God's gift to you. What you do with it is your gift back to God. And that goes for every blessing as well.

Count the Cost

One of the most unique corporate takeovers in American history took place on January 15, 1955. It wasn't a hostile takeover. It was a white-flag surrender. Stanley Tam, the founder of the United States Plastic Corporation, voluntarily divested himself of 51 percent of his shares. Who became the majority shareholder? Stanley transferred his shares to the person he referred to as his Senior Partner: God. The first lawyer that Stanley asked to broker the deal actually laughed at him, but I think it's fair to say that God has gotten the last laugh.

At the time of the takeover, the United States Plastic Corporation had annual revenues of less than $200,000. But Stanley believed that God would bless his business if he honored God from the get-go. Stanley was seeding the clouds. I'm guessing that most of us would have been patting ourselves on the back for divesting ourselves of 51 percent, but not Stanley. While reading Jesus's parable about the merchant who sold everything to obtain the pearl of great price,[3]

Stanley decided to divest himself of *all* shares and become a salaried employee of the company he started. Who does that? Someone who has carefully calculated the opportunity cost! Over the next sixty years, Stanley gave away more than $120 million. He also led thousands of people to go all in with his Senior Partner, just like he did.[4]

When Stanley Tam spoke at National Community Church, he was the oldest guest speaker we'd ever had by a long shot. He more than tripled our median age of twenty-eight. His message was inspiring, but it was the meal we shared afterward that was unforgettable. I've shared meals with some pretty impressive people, ranging from former presidents to NFL MVPs. I've even broken bread with a few billionaires, and I enjoyed them all very much. But that meal with Stanley Tam is in a category by itself. The net worth of his wisdom is impossible to calculate. If there had been a mic in the room, Stanley would have been dropping it all night long! In between bites, Stanley offered up sound bites like "God can't reward Abraham yet because his seed is still multiplying!" I've been chewing on that one ever since! Then he added this: "God's shovel is bigger than ours!" Yes, it is!

One topic of conversation revolved around the idea of income ceilings, and it was quite convicting. For most people, spending increases in direct proportion to their income. Stanley, on the other hand, hadn't taken a raise in three decades. Why? In his words, "A man can eat only one meal at a time, wear only one suit of clothes at a time, drive only one car at a time. All this I have. Isn't that enough?"

How much is enough?

If you read this book without answering that question for yourself, you've done yourself a disservice. And you won't tap your full potential to be a double blessing. The industrialist and philanthropist John D. Rockefeller answered that question this way: "One more dollar." Many of us, if we're honest, can identify with that sentiment. Our insatiable appetite for more means that enough is never enough, unless you predetermine an amount in your heart. Considering the fact that half of the world's population lives on less than two dollars a day, "How much is enough?" is a difficult question. Do you remember how the earliest Christians answered that question in the face of great need?

They sold property and possessions to give to anyone who had need.[5]

There is nothing wrong with making more money, but there is something wrong with spending it all on yourself. I'm not suggesting that everyone take a vow of poverty, but what would happen if every person who claimed to follow Christ simply set an income ceiling? It's a counterintuitive way to live, but what would the world look like if we practiced radical generosity with everything we made above and beyond that threshold? Our generosity would turn the world upside down, just like the first-century church. We'd be a double blessing to a hurting world, and I bet our impact would more than double!

Keeping Up with the Joneses

In the Declaration of Independence, Thomas Jefferson outlined three unalienable rights endowed on us by our Creator. The first two are pretty self-explanatory: life and liberty. But the third is a mystery to most—the pursuit of happiness. Fewer people have defined *happiness* than *success,* and even fewer have found happiness.

If we don't define success for ourselves, we generally adopt a cultural definition by default. The same is true of happiness. In American culture, we've turned happiness into a sport and called it "Keeping Up with the Joneses." We count our *neighbors'* blessings rather than our own, and we wonder why we can't get no satisfaction! That idiom originated with a 1913 comic strip by the same name,[6] but the struggle it represents is as old as Cain and Abel. If you benchmark success by comparing yourself with other people, it's a no-win scenario. The comparison game ends with either surplus pride or inflated jealousy, and both are dead ends. The reality is this: you cannot keep up or catch up with the Joneses! And the Bible has a word for it, *covetousness.*

Trying to obtain happiness by mimicking the materialistic tendencies of the average American is a poor prescription for happiness. Yet that's what so many of us do by default. We buy things we don't even want to impress people we don't even like! That is not #blessed; it's the exact opposite. Blessing is defined not by what we get but by what we give. Therein lies the mystery of the double blessing. And while that may seem counterintuitive, it's as irrefutable as the words of Jesus:

It is more blessed to give than to receive.[7]

I like being on the receiving end of other people's generosity as much as the next person. If you give me a gift, I will not rob you of your blessing! I will receive it with genuine gratitude, and I will say a sincere thank-you. But the blessing isn't stewarded until I do one more thing—take inventory! I take note of the ways I've been blessed; then I restock the blessing by giving to others what has been given to me! And when we flip the blessing, we experience what Jesus promised. The most profound form of joy is found on the giving side of life.

Flip the Blessing

The three-word phrase *flip the blessing* is more than a memorable mantra. It started out as a game of sorts. But it was so much fun that it turned into a way of life. If you give me something—anything—I attempt to return the favor by blessing someone else in the same way. If it helps, think of it as a gift-in-kind.

When we hear the word *generosity,* we tend to think in terms of dollars and cents. But it's so much more than that. There are ways to be generous that have nothing to do with money! Generosity involves time and talent as much as treasure. If I'm being honest, I find it far more difficult to be generous with my time and talent than my treasure. Sometimes, writing a check is a cop-out, the easy way out. It's a false substitute for personal involvement. We hand a person experiencing homelessness a few dollars and think we've done our duty. Not if we don't match those dollars with dignity! Over the years we've had hundreds of friends experiencing homelessness find a church home at NCC. And I know that what they really want—what they really need—is for someone to look them in the eye and see into their soul. Of course, that takes more time than many people are willing to give.

Remember the frustration I felt as an unpublished author for thirteen years? Yes, setting a self-imposed deadline was a key benchmark, but so was a two-hour conversation with a pastor-author who I know for a fact was far too busy to meet with me. But he met with me anyway!

I've never forgotten that investment of time, and it's a blessing I've tried to flip for those who know they have a book in them but don't know how to get it out. That pastor-author also helped me find my first agent, leveraging his influence on my behalf. That's a difficult blessing to flip, but I've helped dozens of authors find their first agent as a gift-in-kind. I've also seeded a few self-published books for good measure. That's how I turn the original blessing I received into a double blessing for someone else. It also reminds me of where I've come from, which helps me resist the urge to jump on the "more is better" bandwagon or settle down in "Jonesville."

Now let me add a little caveat.

I don't just flip the blessing when I'm on the receiving end of someone else's generosity; I also try to flip the blessing when I feel like flipping the bird. Can I say that? Not only does flipping the blessing on someone who ticks you off defuse your negative emotions, but it can also interrupt the pattern and have a profound impact on the other person. If you don't believe it, try it. When you return rudeness with respect or meanness with kindness, it leaves people dumbfounded. Like Spock's stun gun, they don't even know what to do with it. It's not foolproof, especially if your situation involves a fool. But it's more effective than fighting fire with fire—and far more fun.

#Blessed

Did you know that the word *clue* originally referred to a ball of yarn, not unlike Ariadne's thread? *To flirt* meant "to flick away." The word *awful* meant "worthy of awe." The word *naughty* meant "having nothing." And *fizzle* referred to a silent fart. Sorry—couldn't resist including that last one. Many words aren't what they used to be! Words have a way of leaking their original meaning or they take on new connotations. Either way, words morph in meaning. And the word *blessed* is a classic example. In many ways, our culture has reduced it to a hashtag that comes across as a humblebrag. We use it to tag Instagram photos in exotic places or put on the license plates of very expensive cars. But the more exotic the place or expensive the thing, the more we devalue the original idea.

The blessing of God cannot be equated to external circumstances or material things. It's an internal reality—a state of mind, a state of soul. It's joy unspeakable. It's peace that surpasses understanding. It's things you can't possibly put a price tag on. Are you good with God? Then you are blessed beyond measure, even if you drive a car that spends most of its time with a mechanic or if the most exotic place you've ever been is your grandma's house.

The Greek word for "blessed" is *makarios,* and it's the word Jesus employed to delineate the difference between giving and receiving. It's a multidimensional word that means "make large."[8] In that sense, it aligns with the prayer of Jabez: "Oh, that you would bless me and enlarge my territory!"[9] It also allies itself with Isaiah's exhortation: "Enlarge the place of your tent, stretch your tent curtains wide, do not hold back; lengthen your cords, strengthen your stakes."[10] It doesn't mean "to make large" as in "large and in charge." It's a humble heart that grows bigger and bigger the more and more it gives. It may even grow three sizes in one day, giving you the strength of ten Grinches, plus two![11]

Sorry—I couldn't resist. Seussisms aside, nothing expands the borders of life like generosity! It will take you places you couldn't get to on your own merit and introduce you to people you have no business being in the same room with. In the words of King Solomon, "A man's gift maketh room for him, and bringeth him before great men."[12]

Blessed Beyond

God wants to bless you beyond your ability to contain it. Of that I'm sure. But don't reduce that blessing to a balance sheet. Your net worth is not a profit-and-loss statement. If you've been blessed with more money than you know what to do with, that's great. But please recognize the reason!

> You will be enriched in every way so that you can be generous on every occasion.[13]

It says "enriched in every way," so let me take an emotional angle. If you have joy unspeakable, it can shift the atmosphere of an organization. If you have peace that surpasses understanding, it can help everyone stay calm and carry on.

And if you have more love than you can contain, it can start a revolution. Of course, what's true of love, joy, and peace is true of money too. God enriches us so that we "can be generous on every occasion!"

The word *makarios* means "joy without measure." It's also translated "as good as it gets,"[14] which I interpret to mean "beyond blessed" or "blessed beyond." But perhaps the simplest definition—and the least common denominator—is good old-fashioned happiness!

Happiness isn't something we *get*.

Happiness is something we *give*.

Let me say this as succinctly as I can: *happiness is giving more than you receive!* The more you give, the more you have. You may be tempted to read right over that, but most of us pursue happiness the wrong way. It's not the result of what we receive. It's the by-product of what we give. The secret to happiness is the mystery of the double blessing—*you get it by giving it.*

Accumulate Experiences

The story of the Rich Young Ruler is a cautionary tale that provides a compelling clue in our pursuit of happiness. From the outside looking in, he had everything we think we want. He was rich, he was young, and he was a ruler. On paper, his life was perfect. He had everything money could buy, but the question he asked revealed how unhappy he was: "What do I still lack?"[15]

The answer to that question? He was missing the rush of holy adrenaline that courses through your veins when you go all in with God. The Rich Young Ruler was living for himself, and when you live for yourself, you eventually lose yourself. Jesus prescribed a counterintuitive cure, a giving challenge:

If you want to be perfect, go, sell your possessions.[16]

I haven't met many people possessed by a demon, but I've met lots of people possessed by their possessions. The Rich Young Ruler could have leveraged his wealth and his power to do so much good for so many people. The opportunity cost was off the chart. But his self-worth was too tied to his net worth. The very thing that he thought would give meaning to his life made him miserable.

Wealth should come with this warning: *your greatest asset will become your greatest liability if you don't use it for God's purposes.*

Be honest: Have you ever felt just a tad bit sorry for the Rich Young Ruler? I probably would have pulled Jesus aside and told Him to dial it down a little: "Why not start with the tithe?" But Jesus loved him too much to ask for anything less than everything! We focus on what Jesus asked him to give up, the actual cost. But we fail to consider what He offered in exchange—a three-year internship with the Son of God. That's the opportunity of a lifetime, and it's gotta look good on LinkedIn.

The disciples who chose to follow Jesus didn't take a vow of poverty, but they did drop their nets. They sacrificed upward mobility for a wealth of experience unrivaled in human history. They spent three years hiking, camping, and fishing with the Son of God. They drank the water that Jesus turned into wine! They filleted the miraculous catch of fish! You can't put a price tag on those kinds of experiences, but wait—that's not all.

> Everyone who has left houses or brothers or sisters or father or mother
> or wife or children or fields for my sake will receive a hundred times
> as much and will inherit eternal life.[17]

Jesus seems to be saying that we get to have our cake and eat it too. My advice? Don't accumulate possessions; *accumulate experiences!* More specifically, accumulate the kind of experiences that can come only from following in the footsteps of Jesus.

Let me share two more convictions.

First, *you cannot give God anything that doesn't belong to Him already.*

You can only *give back* what God has given you in the first place! That doesn't make your giving less meaningful. It makes it more worshipful.

Second, *no one has ever sacrificed anything for God.*

I'm not making light of those who have made tremendous temporal sacrifices, especially those who have been martyred for their faith like eleven of the twelve disciples. Sacrifice can involve tremendous pain, but if it's God-ordained, it nets eternal gain. Please hear me out. If you always get back more than you gave up, have you sacrificed anything at all? That doesn't make the sting of sacrifice hurt any less, but that's the risk-reward ratio every time we flip the blessing! The return on investment? Compound interest for eternity!

At the end of our lives, our greatest regret won't be the mistakes we've made. It'll be the opportunities we left on the table. It'll be the blessings we failed to flip!

Count the cost.

Flip the blessing.

Repeat.

THE GIVING GAME

Whatever you did for one of the least of these
brothers and sisters of mine, you did for me.

MATTHEW 25:40

Invented by Simon Prebble in 1967, Newton's Cradle is a rather ingenious device that demonstrates the conservation of momentum by a series of swinging spheres. When a ball on one end of the cradle is lifted and released, it strikes the stationary spheres, thereby transmitting a force that causes the ball on the opposite end of the cradle to swing in the opposite direction.

Named in honor of Sir Isaac Newton, the cradle illustrates his three laws of motion. According to the first law, an object will remain at rest unless acted on by an external force. The second law states that force equals mass times acceleration. And Newton's third law may be his most famous: for every action there is an equal and opposite reaction.[1]

Like the laws of nature that govern the physical universe, there are supernatural laws that govern the spiritual realm. The law of measures is exhibit A: "With the measure you use, it will be measured to you."[2] You cannot break the law of measures; it will make or break you. It's the spiritual equivalent of Newton's third law of motion, and it's the key to double blessing.

When God blessed Adam and Eve, they were acted on by an external force. He transmitted a blessing, but entropy ensued. Nothing will stop the momentum of blessing like sin, but original sin met its match in Jesus. The cross is where the curse of sin is broken and the blessing of God is bestowed.

So how do we conserve the momentum of God's blessing?

At the risk of sounding like a memorandum issued by the department of redundancy department, the only way to maintain momentum is to *flip the blessing*. If we fail to flip the blessing, we hit the point of diminishing return. Eventually, we lose all spiritual momentum and wonder why. I'll tell you exactly why: God doesn't bless selfishness. If the blessing stops with you, it'll eventually stop altogether! Instead of being a conduit for blessing and maintaining forward momentum, we settle for sideways energy.

The Grace of Giving

If you were truly selfish, you would be more generous. That seems illogical on many levels, including the theological level. But study after study corroborates what Jesus conjectured: it is *happier* to give than it is to receive.[3]

In a study published in *Science*, researchers Elizabeth Dunn, Lara Aknin, and Michael Norton gave people five dollars or twenty dollars and divided them into two groups. The first group was told to spend the money on themselves. The second group was told to spend the money on someone else. Those who spent the money on someone else experienced an uptick in happiness. Those who spent the money on themselves did not. The question, of course, is, why not? The same researchers tracked a group of employees who received a year-end bonus. Measuring their baseline happiness before and after receiving the bonus, the only significant predictor of increased happiness was charitable giving. It was only those who flipped the blessing that found the blessing![4]

Can I be blunt? If a televangelist tells you that God told him he needs an airplane, please call that bluff. I promise you, someone needs a meal more than he needs a plane! That said, we should make no apologies for any investment that advances God's kingdom in the way Jesus commanded: feeding the hungry, clothing the naked, and caring for the sick.[5]

I recently led our church through a journey of generosity. The goal was building out a city block so that we can be a bigger blessing, a longer blessing to our city. I was a little reticent at first because asking for money, even with good intentions, is easily misinterpreted. But I was moved to tears by some of the sacrifices people made. Again, I'm not sure that our twenty-first-century sacrifices are on par with the first-century church, but they are pleasing to God nonetheless.

We had people give year-end bonuses and tax refunds. A few people unemployed by a government shutdown made a pledge by faith during that furlough. And one couple even gave the down payment they had saved for their first home! I would never ask anyone to do that, but I would never tell them to *not* obey the prompting of the Holy Spirit. A little part of me wanted to refuse some of those gifts or at least ask, "Are you sure?" But there is only one way to grow in the grace of giving, and that is by giving more! The biggest blessings involve the greatest sacrifices, and Jesus set the standard. That's the way we maintain our spiritual momentum and keep Newton's Cradle swinging.

Four Levels of Generosity

I've already referenced *excellence* as a habit of highly blessed people, but let me come at it from a little different angle:

> Since you excel in everything—in faith, in speech, in knowledge, in
> complete earnestness and in the love we have kindled in you—see that
> you also excel in this grace of giving.[6]

The English word *excel* comes from the Greek root *perisseuó*, which means "above and beyond" or "to go beyond all measure."[7] This is Ephesians 3:20: "To him who is able to do *immeasurably more* than all we ask or imagine." This is Jesus feeding five thousand with five loaves and two fish, then having twelve baskets of leftovers: 5 + 2 = 5,000 R12.[8]

This Greek word is similar to the Japanese concept called *kaizen*, which advocates continuous improvement. In psychology, it's a growth mindset. In business, it's benchmarking. And you never really arrive, because there is always room for improvement. Can I let you in on a little secret? When you have a God-sized vision, you never get there! You grow with the vision, and the vision grows with you. But if you continue to excel, you will eventually reach excellence and beyond.

Generosity cannot be reduced to a formula, per se. And the process is as unique as you are. But if you want to grow in the grace of giving, here are some next steps to take.

The first level of generosity is giving *spontaneously*.

Giving spontaneously is Spirit-led generosity. But please note, *Spirit-led* does not mean "poorly planned." This involves budgeting. You have to create financial margin so you can meet needs and seize opportunities when the Holy Spirit prompts you to do so. If you want to put some fun back into your finances, this is a game changer! But remember, there are ways to be generous that have nothing to do with money! If you are going to give of your time spontaneously, you have to create margin in your calendar too! The apostle Paul applauded the spontaneity and generosity of the Macedonian Christians this way: "This was totally spontaneous, entirely their own idea, and caught us completely off guard."[9] That is pure generosity, and few things are more fun than being on either side of it.

The second level of generosity is giving *consistently*.

The key to growth in any area of our lives is establishing consistent habits, daily disciplines, and regular routines. Consistency beats intensity seven days a week and twice on Sunday. After all, "we are what we repeatedly do!"[10] Perhaps that is why Paul set a precedent: "On the first day of every week, each one of you should set aside a sum of money in keeping with your income."[11] One of the ways Lora and I put this principle into practice is by setting up recurring giving with the kingdom causes we care about. Does that mean we stop giving spontaneously? Of course not. But consistent giving points us in the direction of our giving goals. It establishes a baseline, a trend line of generosity.

The third level of generosity is giving *proportionately*.

The idea of proportionate giving traces back to the Old Testament tithe, which literally means "10 percent." And we'll unpack this idea in the next chapter. Suffice it to say, if you are going to grow in the grace of giving, you can't think in terms of dollar amounts. You have to think in percentages. This idea carries over in Paul's exhortation: "Give in proportion to what you have."[12] The tithe is a key benchmark in the journey of generosity, but it's not the end goal.

The fourth level of generosity is giving *radically*.

This is giving that is over and above the 10 percent tithe. In Old Testament terms, it would be called a *freewill offering*. As the name suggests, it was not obligatory. A radical giver is someone with an abundance mindset. It's someone who counts the opportunity cost. It's someone who doesn't just love to give; this person *lives to give!* The Macedonian Christians were being harassed and oppressed by trials and tribulations, yet Paul pointed out that "their extreme poverty welled up in rich generosity."[13] Seems like an oxymoron, doesn't it? He then footnoted their radical generosity this way: "They gave as much as they were able, and even beyond their ability."[14] Radical generosity is giving above and beyond your ability. That kind of generosity doesn't happen overnight, but that is where generosity sets its sights. Maybe it's a double tithe. For some, it could even be a reverse tithe—living off 10 percent and giving 90 percent back to God.

Now let me broaden the idea of double blessing. Yes, the giving game has a lot to do with dollar signs. But there are many ways to win! These four levels of generosity must be applied to time and talent as well as treasure.

Regifting

In our early years of marriage, Lora and I could not afford to take a vacation. I know—first-world problem! That's hardly a complaint given the fact that there are those who don't know where their next meal is coming from! But during those days when we couldn't afford to get away, we were blessed by the generosity of people who let us stay at their vacation home or even paid for us to take a trip. That's what inspired us to start flipping the blessing in the first place. We were blessed by the generosity of others, and we wanted to get on the giving side of that equation!

I remember well the first time I felt prompted to flip this particular blessing. I was speaking at a conference in California, and a local pastor was kind enough to pick me up at the airport. During the ride back to the church, he shared a bit of his story. I could tell his stress level was running a little high and understandably so, because one of his children was going through a physical challenge with medical and financial repercussions. I knew in my spirit that Lora and I needed to do something about it, and we did. I'll never forget the feeling of flipping that blessing. I was a little nervous about our gift being received in the spirit that it was intended, but when it was, we discovered that financing their much-needed vacation was as much fun as taking one! In fact, it was almost like we vicariously went on vacation with them!

I've already explained the giving game, but let me share some rules of engagement. First, it's *giving-in-kind*. If someone gives me a gift card, I can almost guarantee that I'm going to regift it. I know that sounds wrong, right? Isn't that insulting to the person who gave it to me in the first place? If it is, so be it. I find far more joy in regifting those cards than I do in using them on myself! Plus, there are situations when a cash gift would be misperceived or even insulting. But a gift card gives you a built-in excuse. Very few people argue with "I have a gift card; let me pay!"

I realize that giving gifts of equal value to those we have received seems like a zero-sum game. Doesn't that net zero? My honest answer is *No!* For starters, it nets joy incalculable. And while I cannot quantify this, it seems like the more gift cards I give away, the bigger my pile of gift cards gets! And that's true of every blessing. I'm certainly not suggesting that everyone give away every gift card they get. You need to figure out how to play the giving game in your own unique way.

The second rule of engagement is this: *give in keeping with who you are.* In other words, you be you! Do you know someone whose ability to bake qualifies as a spiritual gift? Or what about the person who is able to fix anything and everything? I'm neither of those people! I can barely bake the refrigerated store-bought cookies, and I cannot fix a blame thing! Any attempt on my part to bless you in that way will come across as a curse! Why? Because that's not who I am! Flipping the blessing is leveraging *your* time, *your* talent, and *your* treasure for others. Your generosity is as unique as you are, but you have to figure out how to put your fingerprint on it.

Smile Quota

Once you get the hang of it, flipping the blessing is a ton of fun. But it's not always easy. One of the hardest things to flip is our flipping attitude! Attitude is a big piece of the blessing puzzle, and it doesn't cost a dime!

One of the simplest ways to bless someone is with a smile. Make no mistake—your smile is a superpower! Scientifically speaking, a smile reduces stress by suppressing cortisol and increases happiness by releasing endorphins. Of course, it doesn't take a scientific study to convince us of the benefits of smiling. It's intuitive. What's counterintuitive is this: We don't just smile *because* we're happy. We're happy *because* we smile. A smile has the power to hack your emotions and trick your brain.[15]

Did you know that children smile approximately four hundred times per day, while adults smile an average of twenty times per day? Somewhere between childhood and adulthood, we lose 380 smiles![16] We've got to get some of those smiles back! Smiling is the way we steward our forty-three facial muscles as well as the seventh cranial nerve that controls them.

When I was in high school, I remember doing "yawn experiments" during study hall to pass the time. If I remember right, our record was a chain reaction of seventeen people yawning. It's amazing how subconsciously contagious a yawn is. So is a smile! If you want to have some fun during a meeting or party or dinner gone dull, try a smile experiment. Target the person who seems like the least likely person to crack a smile; then start sending some smiles their way. If a regular smile doesn't work, you have permission to silly smile!

In all seriousness, what if we leveraged our smiles as a subtle way of blessing others? Your smile has the power to turn someone's frown upside down! Of course, I better add one warning: smiling is scientifically proven to make you more attractive!

The Gift of Undivided Attention

Along with stewarding your smile, try giving people your undivided attention. Yes, that means putting your phone away! In a digitally distracted day and age, undivided attention is one of the greatest gifts you can give another person. Have you ever been with someone who made you feel like the most important person on the planet? Like the only person on the planet? It's a gift, isn't it? More than that, it's a blessing!

Winston Churchill's mother, Jennie Jerome, once dined with two of England's prime ministers on back-to-back evenings. When asked her impression of each, she said of William Gladstone, "When I left the dining room after sitting next to Gladstone, I thought he was the cleverest man in England." After dining with Benjamin Disraeli? "I left feeling that I was the cleverest woman in England."[17]

Can I let you in on a little secret that isn't so secret? The most interesting people on the planet are those who take the greatest interest in others. That is the blessing of undivided attention, and no one was better at it than Jesus.

Remember the woman with a twelve-year history of hemorrhaging who touched the hem of Jesus's garment? When Jesus asked, "Who touched my clothes?"[18] the disciples were stupefied, saying, "You see the people crowding against you . . . and yet you can ask, 'Who touched me?'"[19] Jesus didn't stop looking until He found the woman. Then he looked into her soul. He didn't just heal the hemorrhaging; He gave her the gift of His undivided attention! What if we made that our mission, just like Jesus?

This past football season, I did a little pep talk on the opening day of training camp for the Baltimore Ravens. I'd never met their head coach, John Harbaugh. But John had read my book *Chase the Lion* and wanted it to be their team theme. For the record, they won the AFC North in the last minute of the last game of the season. When they did, John ran off the field with the lion spike I had given him held high over his head. I wasn't born or bred a Ravens fan, but it's hard not to root for them now!

Here's what I remember from that opening day of training camp, besides feeling relatively small in a room full of very large men. John spent more than an hour with me and the staff members I brought with me. We ate breakfast together. He showed us the weight room and practice facility. We even got on the biometric scale in the locker room and measured body fat.

Did I mention it was the first day of training camp? I expected a quick hi and bye. John Harbaugh gave us the gift of undivided attention—and lots of Ravens gear to go with it. That's a gift I won't forget, and it challenged me to be more present with the people I cross paths with.

The Bible takes it one step further:

Do not neglect to show hospitality to strangers, for thereby some have entertained angels unawares.[20]

What would happen if we treated everyone like angels? I think God's kingdom would come! I think God's will would be done! And there would be far more double blessings to go around. The church ought to be the most hospitable place on the planet. No one should beat us at the hospitality game!

There You Are

Can I share one of my frustrations as a pastor?

Too many people measure a church by what they get out of it—the message, the worship, the kids' programming. Listen, those things should be done with an excellence that honors God. And you need to find a church that fits—that's for sure. But that can't be the only measuring stick. You can't go to church just because of what you'll get out of it. You need to go to church because of the time, talent, and treasure you bring to the table! You have something to offer that no one else does.

Sure, the church you attend should stretch you spiritually! But the true measure of spiritual maturity isn't *what you get out of it* but *what you give to it*. We live in a consumeristic culture, and it's hard to check that consumer mindset at the door. But if you don't, it will always leave you feeling shortchanged. If your objective is to bring a blessing, opportunity abounds!

My spiritual father, Dick Foth, says there are two kinds of people in the world. There are those who walk into a room internally announcing, *Here I am!* They think the world revolves around them, and their ego barely fits through the door! Then there are those who walk into a room outwardly focused, internally saying, *There you are!* They check their ego at the door, and it's all about everyone else!

That's the difference between William Gladstone and Benjamin Disraeli. Gladstone was incredibly clever, but he was a "here I am" person. In fact, Queen Victoria famously said of Gladstone, "He always addresses me as if I were a public meeting."[21]

I certainly hope that every person who walks into National Community Church walks out feeling blessed, and we often give the benediction by pronouncing the priestly blessing. But church isn't a "bless me" club. The goal isn't just to get a blessing. The goal is to bring a blessing, to be the blessing. When a church is composed of people with that mindset, you better buckle your seat belt. That's a church that will change a city!

One last observation, since I'm already on my soapbox.

Do you know why C. S. Lewis went to church? It's not because he loved the songs. He thought they were "fifth-rate poems set to sixth-rate music."[22] It's not because he loved the sermons or liked the people. He did not. C. S. Lewis went to church because he believed that if he did not, he would fall into something he called "solitary conceit."[23]

When we isolate ourselves from others, we become an island unto ourselves. Simply put, I need you, and you need me. Together, we become a double blessing to the second power. Like the extraterrestrial twins in the *Super Friends* comic, Zan and Jayna, our powers cannot activate if we're out of reach, out of touch. My point? The giving game is a tag-team sport. "Wonder Twin powers, activate!"[24]

Elfing

At this point, you might feel a little overwhelmed by the giving game. How do I start the game? How do I keep score? How do I know whether I'm winning? First of all, the giving game is a *game*. Yes, the stakes are stewardship. But a game is meant to be fun, and that's how you know whether you're winning at double blessing!

I was recently going through a stack of letters that had accumulated in my inbox, and I found one that was many years old. I had no recollection of the incident cited in the letter, but it reminded me of what a big deal little blessings can be!

Dear Mark, I wanted to send you a note of thanks for a simple kindness extended to my son yesterday. I'm not exactly sure what time of the day it happened. It appears from my son's text that it was around 5 PM, but you were in the school café at the same time he was and you purchased his soda for him.

A soda? Does that really warrant a thank-you letter? The soda probably cost less than the postage to mail that letter! As it turns out, the student whom I purchased the soda for was struggling to make ends meet. He was working thirty-five hours a week while taking a full class load so he could graduate early. It didn't involve much effort on my part, but sometimes the smallest acts of kindness are the most meaningful. And few things are more fun!

Speaking of fun, we have friends who go *elfing* every Christmas. It's ding-dong ditch with a twist. Each year, this couple, whose identity I will protect, choose a family to bless. Then for twelve consecutive days, they stealthily deliver gifts, ring the doorbell, and disappear like elf ninjas. On day twelve, they reveal their identity and throw a little party!

Where did the idea come from? The husband, whom we'll call Buddy, got elfed as a kid. His family flipped the blessing, and then Buddy flipped it again when he got married. A few important footnotes if you decide to go elfing.

First, the police have been called because of suspect packages!

Second, at least one child was devastated that they weren't real elves!

And third, make sure you have the right address!

The world could use a few more elves, could it not? Yes, the best way to spread Christmas cheer is by singing loud for all to hear.[25] But flip some blessings while you're at it.

Three-Minute Parties

Few people are better at the art of blessing than Bob Goff. If you haven't read *Love Does* or *Everybody, Always,* add them to your reading list! Anyone who hosts an annual parade on New Year's Day for his neighbors is someone we can learn from. And I've been on the receiving end of Bob's over-the-top blessings.

A few years ago, Bob invited some friends to his lodge in Canada. It's not the easiest place to get to. It involved a six-hour flight and an eight-hour boat ride, but it was worth the roundtrip! As we approached Bob's lodge in the middle of nowhere, Canada, a flat-bottom boat came speeding toward us. It was towing water-skiers, and there was a fully uniformed marching band on board. There was even a kilt-wearing bagpipe player on board! That's what I call a welcoming party! Honestly, it gave me a glimpse of the welcome-home party that awaits us in heaven.

At the end of our time together, we took a group photo. It happened to be summertime, but right before snapping the picture, it started to snow! Bob had set up a snow machine because he thought it would be more fun. I don't know how else to say this, but Bob Goff parties like Jesus! There is one more story about Bob that brings this idea of blessing down to earth.

If you follow Bob on Instagram, it seems like he's everyplace all the time. Bob logs half a million miles a year, which means he spends a lot of time with TSA. Most of us proceed through the security checkpoint like automatons, but not Bob. He noticed a TSA agent who seemed to treat every traveler with a little extra courtesy. So one day, Bob called him out. Instead of handing him his ID, Bob extended his hand to shake his. He said, "I've passed by you a dozen times and I just wanted to thank you for the way you treat each person in line. It's really amazing. The way you treat people reminds me a lot of the way Jesus loved."

This TSA agent looked up, and then he got up, stepped out from behind his desk, and went in for a hug! Here's the thing: Bob is very tall, and this agent is very short. As the agent wrapped his arms around him, Bob heard a muffled "I'm Adrian." Hundreds of travelers witnessed their man hug, which looked more like an awkward slow dance.

"This was the beginning of my friendship with Adrian," said Bob, "three minutes at a time."[26] I love that approach to life—*three minutes at a time!* That's all it takes to bless someone, maybe less. One of the best ways to obey the Great Commandment is by throwing three-minute parties. Where? Wherever! When? Whenever! Who? Whoever! But you might as well start with the person right next to you.

Some of the best blessings in life are bestowed on us for no reason at all. Like surprise parties, spontaneous blessings seem to come out of nowhere. And it's their unpredictability that makes them so unforgettable. An ex nihilo blessing can turn an ordinary moment into a memory that lasts a lifetime.

When I survey those who have blessed my life in profound ways, I see a few common threads. Bob Schmidgall came to the hospital to pray for me in the middle of the night. Dick Foth took an unselfish interest in me at a vulnerable time in my life. Bob Rhoden believed in me more than I believed in myself. Then there are people like Dick Eastman and Pat Morley and Michael Hall who intercede for me and my family by name. And, of course, Bob Goff, who loves everybody, always!

One way or the other, all of them have blessed me with their smiles, their words, and their undivided attention. And they have done so at critical junctures in my life. The only way for me to steward those blessings is to flip the blessing, and that's precisely how the kingdom advances. You start playing the giving game, and everybody wins.

Go throw a three-minute party!

PAY IT FORWARD

With the measure you use, it will be measured to you.

Luke 6:38

On July 30, 1945, *Time* magazine published an article about a rather fascinating experiment.[1] It wasn't a science experiment like the Manhattan Project, which had tested the first atomic bomb two weeks before. It was an experiment of a very different nature. The hypothesis to be tested was a verse of Scripture, Malachi 3:10:

> "Bring the whole tithe into the storehouse, that there may be food in my house. Test me in this," says the Lord Almighty, "and see if I will not throw open the floodgates of heaven and pour out so much blessing that there will not be room enough to store it."[2]

The mad scientist was a businessman named Perry Hayden, the president of Hayden Flour Mills. He wanted to test the tithe in a unique way, but first, a little backstory. When he was twenty-nine years old, Perry Hayden felt conflicted. He wanted to go into business, but he also wanted to be a missionary to China. Perry had no idea which path to pursue when he attended a conference in Columbus, Ohio. A conversation with one of the speakers after one of the sessions changed the trajectory of his life. After explaining his conundrum, the speaker said, "Perry, go home and make all the money you can. Then give all the money you can." Perry's decision was made right then and there!

In the months following that conference, someone sent Perry a pamphlet on tithing. He had grown up in church, but somehow he had never heard of the concept. He decided to take the tithe challenge and began giving God the first 10 percent of his income. It wasn't an easy decision, given the fact that his business was losing money at the time. But his business experienced such a significant turnaround in the wake of that decision that he felt like the turnaround could be attributed only to God.[3]

Many years later, Perry Hayden got a crazy idea while listening to a sermon on John 12:24. Jesus said, "I tell you the truth, unless a kernel of wheat is planted in the soil and dies, it remains alone. But its death will produce many new kernels—a plentiful harvest of new lives."[4] Perry Hayden wanted to prove the veracity of this verse in a unique way and test the hypothesis in Malachi 3:10. That's where we double back to the experiment featured in *Time* magazine.

On September 26, 1940, Perry Hayden planted 360 kernels of "sturdy Bald Rock wheat seeds" on a plot of ground measuring four-by-four feet. It may have been the world's smallest wheat field. He then vowed to tithe on the harvest one year later and do so for six years according to the ancient Jewish agricultural laws found in Leviticus 25. Perry would sow the field for six years, then let it sabbath the seventh year.

In 1941, one square inch of kernels turned into forty-five cubic inches after the tithe. In 1942, they experienced a fifty-five-fold yield, or seventy pounds. They tithed the wheat and replanted the remaining sixty-three pounds on a farm owned by Perry's friend, Henry Ford. In 1943, one acre of land yielded 16 bushels from one bushel of seed. Henry Ford provided the reaper and thresher. Then he provided his farm for the fourth planting. In 1944, 14 acres yielded 380 bushels. A tenth of the crop was tithed, and the rest was replanted. It took 230 acres and a fleet of forty combines to harvest it in 1945. It yielded 5,555 bushels. At that point, after tithing on the fifth year's harvest, the 5,000 bushels of wheat were turned over to 276 farmers who planted them on 2,666 acres. Every one of those farmers agreed to tithe on the harvest to the church they belonged to.

In 1946, Michigan's governor, Harry Kelly, declared August 1 "Biblical Wheat Day." That's the day Perry Hayden celebrated the sixth and final harvest. What started as 360 kernels planted on a four- by-four-foot plot resulted in a harvest of 72,150 bushels of wheat valued at approximately $150,000. Adjusted for inflation, it'd be worth $1,449,577 in today's dollars! Thus ended one of the most amazing tithing experiments in history.[5]

I've already issued a gratitude challenge, so why not a tithe challenge too? A book on blessing would be incomplete without it. Remember the four levels of generosity? The tithe is one small step but one giant leap toward level-three generosity—giving *proportionately*. Like any goal, it might take a minute to get to 10 percent. It will involve a measure of faith and a measure of sacrifice, no doubt. But if you set your sights on that giving goal, you'll get there in God's timing. And the God who celebrates two small coins will celebrate every risk you take and every sacrifice you make.

Let's go back to the basics.

Firstfruits

The tithe is as old as Abraham. It is pre-Sinai, which is not insignificant. There are those who would argue that the tithe is an old covenant practice, but it actually predates the giving of the law. It traces back to a rather cryptic encounter between Abraham and the priest of Salem, Melchizedek. This is what some theologians would call a preincarnate appearance of Christ. *Melchizedek* means "king of righteousness,"[6] and the King did two very curious things. First, He blessed Abraham. Second, He served him bread and wine. This foreshadows something we call communion and the cup of blessing. What was Abraham's response to this blessing, to this communion? He gave Melchizedek a tenth of all he owns.

Fast-forward fifteen hundred years, and the prophet Malachi challenged the people of Israel to give proportionately. That challenge is coupled with the promise of more blessing than they can contain. And it happens to be the only place in Scripture where God explicitly tells us to test Him. How? By giving Him the tithe.

Again, *tithe* literally means "a tenth part of one's annual income."[7] But let's go to the graduate school of generosity. It's not any 10 percent; it's the first 10 percent. The technical term is *firstfruits*. As such, the tithe wasn't just an act of obedience under the old covenant. It was a statement of faith.

Jewish farmers wouldn't harvest their fields all at once. They would harvest the firstfruits, take that first 10 percent to the temple, and give that offering to the priests. Then, and only then, would they return to their farms and harvest the rest of their fields. According to Levitical law, if they honored God with the tithe, God would bless what was known as the *second harvest*.

Second Harvest

Can I push the generosity envelope a little further? If you've made it this far, hopefully I've earned a level of trust. This is not an accusation; it's an observation. If you aren't experiencing a second harvest, maybe it's because you aren't honoring God with your firstfruits. And I would be remiss if I didn't mention that the Israelites were under a curse because they weren't giving God the whole tithe. Remember what the Talmud says about failing to thank God for His blessings? It's as if we've stolen them from Him.[8] The same is true of the tithe. You can't hold out on God and expect His full blessing.

This is where I tread very carefully, and I hope you hear the heart of God. The tithe is *not* a threat; it's a promise! If you grew up in a church that was legalistic, I would be willing to bet that the tithe has some negative connotations. It may even create some internal tension, and I'll tell you why. Because legalism focuses on the law rather than grace! But we're not under the law; we are under the umbrella of grace! Again, the goal is to grow in the *grace* of giving. *Grace is the genesis of generosity!* Or you can flip that coin: *generosity is the revelation of grace.* Either way, grace is the game changer! If the tithe causes your blood pressure to go up, you're thinking about it the wrong way!

Can I share some lessons learned, having put this promise into practice for more than a quarter of a century?

First, *tithing is trusting.*

It's as simple and as difficult as that. Again, God doesn't need your money! But He wants your heart, and those two tango!

Second, *the tithe keeps greed in check.*

Don't get me wrong—greed never goes away! It rears its ugly head every time I walk through the mall and see all the things I don't have! On that note, there are those who would argue that the tithe *belongs* to God. I disagree! It *all* belongs to God, but God generously lets us keep 90 percent. Our tithe is really God's reverse tithe!

Third, *God-honoring goals are never easy.*

If the tithe is new to you, 10 percent can seem like an awfully big chunk of change. That's especially true if you're trying to get out of debt or make ends meet. Can we take a step back? When I decided to run a marathon, I didn't go out and run 26.2 miles. I would have pulled a hamstring! I ran three miles—very slowly! And I was very sore the next day! It took seventy-two training runs over six months to work my way up to that goal. If the tithe seems like a giant leap, it might take more than one step. And that's okay. God will applaud every step along the way!

Fourth, *you cannot outgive God.*

I better issue a warning right here: please, don't try to play God like a slot machine. If you give for the wrong reasons, it doesn't even count. But if you give for the right reasons, it's game on. I promise you this: *God can do more with 90 percent than you can do with 100 percent.*

Let me close one last loophole.

Even if you consider the tithe an old covenant concept, I doubt the percentage went down under the new covenant! Grace doesn't discount the law; it supersedes it. Besides, the tithe isn't the ultimate goal. It's the starting line. When God gets ahold of our hearts, we stop asking, "How much do I have to give?" and we start asking, "How much can I possibly give away?"

The Tithe Challenge

Remember the umbrella of blessing? The tithe is exhibit A—your bottom line becomes God's responsibility. Of course, Malachi mixes my metaphor. God promises to pour out more blessing than we can contain, in categories we cannot conceive of.

Paul and Lynne Farrell are some of the most generous people I know. Paul's professional endeavors in the field of technology have been blessed beyond measure, and they are level-four givers. I first encountered their radical generosity when they offered scholarship money for church staff who wanted to pursue a graduate education. Many of our staff have benefited from their generosity! They also took it upon themselves to help their nieces and nephews pursue a college education.

After many years of blessing others in this way, their son applied to

Vanderbilt University. Not only was he accepted, but he was also awarded a scholarship that added up to $176,000 over four years. Paul and Lynne didn't connect the dots until they decided to inventory how much they had invested in the education of others. Want to take a wild guess? Their gifts totaled their son's scholarship, $176,000. Coincidence? I think not. Is that why Paul and Lynne made the investment? Of course not! But let me say it again: you cannot break the law of measures. Said another way, you cannot outgive God. Those who sow greed reap scarcity. Those who sow generosity reap God's abundance—with a double measure of joy!

Now let me double back to the tithe challenge.

How do you take it? It's pretty simple: *take your annual income and divide it by ten.* That tenth is your tithe! And I'll go ahead and get this question out of the way: Is it *gross* income or *net* income after taxes? That depends. Do you want a gross blessing or a net blessing? Are we having fun yet? And just to make sure everyone feels included, if you are already tithing, you can have twice the fun by double tithing! Consider this your challenge! If you double down on your giving, I bet it'll become a double blessing!

Begat That

Remember the film *Pay It Forward*? It may not have received the highest critical acclaim, but I love the storyline. A social studies teacher named Mr. Simonet gave an extra-credit assignment to a class of seventh graders: "Think of an idea to change the world and put it into action." Trevor McKinney, played by Haley Joel Osment, challenged his classmates: "Do something nice for someone who really needs help—it has to be something hard, something they can't do for themselves—and in return, that person passes on the gesture to three other people; they pay the kindness forward."[9]

Pay It Forward isn't just a Hollywood script; it's a subplot of Scripture.

Remember the battle of Jericho? The key to victory wasn't just circling the city for seven days; it was a single act of kindness. Before the walls came tumbling down, Israel sent two spies into Jericho on a reconnaissance mission. The spies were nearly captured, but a prostitute named Rahab saved the day. Harboring Jewish spies was akin to treason, so Rahab cut a deal with them before help-ing them escape. She asked them to, well, pay it forward:

> Please swear to me by the LORD that you will show kindness to my
> family, because I have shown kindness to you.[10]

I'm sure Rahab was thinking of her immediate family. It was a present-tense request, but it had future-tense ramifications. According to rabbinic tradition, Rahab converted to Judaism at the age of fifty and fell in love with Salmon, a Jewish man from the tribe of Judah.[11] They had a son named Boaz, who had a son named Obed, who had a son named Jesse, who had a son named David. Oh, and Rahab is one of only five women listed in the genealogy of Jesus![12] Begat that!

You never know to whom you are showing kindness! It could be the great-great-grandmother of a king. Or it could be your future son-in-law.

When I was thirteen years old, I was in the intensive care unit at Edward Hospital in Naperville, Illinois. Around two o'clock in the morning, the doctors issued code blue because I was on the verge of respiratory arrest. That's when my parents called our pastor, Bob Schmidgall. We had just started attending the church, and it was a church of thousands, so he didn't know us from Adam. But that didn't keep him from coming to the hospital in the middle of the night to pray for me. He didn't know it at the time, but he was praying for his future son-in-law. I married his daughter nine years later, and we gave him his first grandchild.

Sometimes the seeds of blessings germinate in a matter of minutes. More often than not, it takes generations for those seeds to affect nations. Either way, your blessing is someone else's begat. So go ahead and flip the blessing. It's the way we pay back the blessings God has given us on loan. It's also the way we pay it forward.

Lead with Blessing

When Jesus sent out His disciples on their inaugural mission, He gave them some counterintuitive commands. Flying in the face of the proverbial "Pack an extra pair of underpants," Jesus said to His disciples, "Don't carry a traveler's bag with a change of clothes."[13] Things that make you go *hmmm!* He also red-flagged them: "I am sending you out as sheep among wolves."[14] That doesn't sound safe, does it? But the most counterintuitive piece of advice may have been the approach He told them to take when meeting someone for the first time:

> When you enter the home, give it your blessing. If it turns out to be a worthy home, let your blessing stand; if it is not, take back the blessing.[15]

A default, in computer science, refers to a setting automatically assigned to a software application. Those default settings, called presets, are the operating instructions we return to when all else fails. Much like the default settings in software applications, we download default settings during the course of our lives that dictate the way we interact with the world. Those default settings are as different as introversion and extroversion and as subtle as subconscious motivations.

If we're being honest, the operating instructions that Jesus gave His disciples seem like the wrong default settings, don't they? Most of us do a quick moral calculation before offering someone our blessing. Why? Because we want to know whether they are worthy of the blessing *before* we give it! But Jesus takes a totally different tack. He taught His disciples to do what He did—lead with blessing. If it turns out that the person wasn't worthy of the blessing, so be it. You can take the blessing back. How? By shaking the dust off your feet. Not every attempt at blessing pans out. In fact, some blessings seem to backfire. So be it. You pick up the pieces and continue leading with blessing!

I'm not suggesting that you don't exercise a measure of discernment in dispensing blessing. After all, Jesus also said, "Do not throw your pearls to pigs."[16] In other words, don't entrust what is valuable to those who will waste it. To put it in economic terms, don't throw good money after a bad investment. The sunk-cost fallacy is as applicable to our spiritual lives as it is to our financial lives. For clarity, no one is a lost cause! But until that person is ready to receive your blessing, it might return-to-sender. That's okay. Give your blessing anyway!

There is an old axiom that might help us decipher the difference: "Fool me once, shame on you; fool me twice, shame on me." I'm not saying we don't give people second chances. But if you're giving a pig his hundredth chance, that's not forgiveness. That's called codependency! And this is where we need Spirit-inspired discernment.

If you look at the teachings of Jesus through a wide-angle lens, it could be argued that much of what Jesus was attempting to do was change default settings. There is a common refrain in the Sermon on the Mount. It starts with "You have heard that it was said" and ends with "But I tell you."[17] What was Jesus doing? He was uninstalling Old Testament presets and uploading New Testament mindsets. Instead of "an eye for an eye,"[18] He taught His disciples to "turn to them the other cheek."[19] That is a very different default setting!

Simply put, our preset as Christ followers is *lead with blessing*.

Ex Nihilo Blessings

A few years ago, I was at a conference at Covenant Church in Dallas, Texas. After I spoke, Pastor Mike Hayes got up and said he felt prompted by the Spirit to take up an offering. What he said next shocked me: "We're going to raise $100,000 in five minutes to bless National Community Church." What? I was not expecting an offering! And quite frankly, I'd never experienced anything like this before and never have since. I call those kind of blessings ex nihilo blessings. The Latin phrase *ex nihilo* means "out of nothing."[20] An ex nihilo blessing is a surprise blessing or spontaneous blessing. It's a blessing that comes out of nowhere, a blessing that seems to materialize out of thin air.

Pastor Mike and Kathy Hayes pledged $5,000 and asked five people to follow suit. Five hands shot up in five seconds. Then he asked twenty-five people to give $1,000. Finally, he asked one hundred people to give $500. It was like a kindergarten classroom, with hands flying up right and left. I'd known Mike and Kathy all of fifteen minutes. We met for the first time right before the service, yet they raised $100,000 in five minutes flat. Who does that? People who understand that you get the blessing by giving the blessing. That's who!

Now here's the rest of the story.

Mike and Kathy Hayes would have had no way of knowing this, but that very day we had purchased an old apartment building in Ward 7 of Washington, DC, that would become our DC Dream Center. We purchased it for the back taxes that were owed on it, which were significantly less than $100,000. So that gift from Covenant Church not only paid for the old apartment building but also provided the down payment on our Dream Center.

A few months later, we cast the vision for the DC Dream Center to our congregation. As you might imagine, I shared the story of that ex nihilo blessing. I think it's a huge part of what inspired our congregation to give $5.5 million to build our Dream Center debt-free.

That Dream Center now ministers to hundreds of kids in an underserved part of our city. We're changing our city one child at a time! It's a place where hope becomes habit. It's a place where reconciliation is real. My favorite part of the Dream Center? We have a "dream wall," where kids can chalk their God-sized dreams. Mike and Kathy didn't know it at the time, but they were paying it forward through each one of those children. Like the drop of water that causes a ripple effect, their gift will be felt far and wide for years to come!

But there is one more ripple effect. That experience affected me in a profound way, not unlike J. C. Penney's biography. It planted a seed in my spirit, and I marked that moment with a prayer: *Lord, give us the privilege of doing for someone else what's just been done for us.* In other words, give us the joy and privilege of flipping that blessing!

I Like Churches

A few months after that ex nihilo blessing, we did a series of sermons titled I Like Giving. The title of that series is also the title of a wonderful book written by my friend Brad Formsma. He's also the executive producer of short films you can watch at www.ilikegiving.com. A few of my favorites include *I Like Car, I Like Adoption,* and *I Like Being 98.* But I better warn you—have some Kleenex handy!

Brad and his wife, Laura, are some of the most creatively compassionate and radically generous people whom Lora and I know. Few people are better at identifying needs and meeting them. And it was Brad's example that inspired something we called I Like Churches.

We have a mantra we repeat with regularity at NCC: "It's not about the name over the church door; it's about the Name above all names." Too many churches are too territorial. News flash: we're on the same team! One of the ways we've tried to put this #sameteam mentality into practice is by investing in any church plant in the DC area that is preaching and practicing the gospel. We've invested in dozens of church plants, some just blocks away from our seven campuses. We genuinely believe that we need one another. Simply put, we need lots of different kinds of churches because there are lots of different kinds of people! And investing in those churches keeps our hearts in the right place!

During our I Like Giving series, we decided to put our money where our mouth was by taking a special offering for a dozen area churches. We empowered our campus pastors to identity the pastors and churches we would bless out of the blue. To say that those pastors were surprised would be an understatement.

I look back on that ex nihilo offering as a defining moment. Did we hit $100,000? No, but we got more than halfway there! And we were finally able to pay forward that Covenant Church blessing this past year by investing $100,000 in our first network church, Bridges Church in Nashville, Tennessee.

Every time I see Mike and Kathy Hayes, I thank them all over again. We are eternally indebted to Covenant Church, and I mean that literally. We're having an impact on hundreds of kids through the DC Dream Center, and Covenant Church is a shareholder in each and every one of them. And someday, those kids will pay it back by paying it forward.

Back to the Future

Before taking the next step in our journey of generosity, let's take a step back. Are you playing the giving game? If so, at what level? More importantly, what's the next step for you?

Please don't play the game for the wrong reasons! What are the wrong reasons? Anything not commanded by Christ or prompted by the Holy Spirit. Can I remind you of a simple yet all-important truth? "God loves a cheerful giver."[21] Who qualifies? Well, it's certainly not someone who gives because of external pressure! Generosity is always inside out, and the conviction of the Holy Spirit is often the catalyst.

After you check your motives, let's continue to checklist our generosity.

Are you leading with blessing? Or are you leading with something else?

Have you taken inventory of your blessings? And are you flipping them?

What about the tithe challenge? Have you taken it? If not, why not? If not now, when?

This might also be a good place to hit pause. You cannot flip the blessings you have not inventoried. You have to look back. Then, and only then, are you ready to pay it forward.

KINGDOM CALCULUS

Whoever finds their life will lose it, and whoever
loses their life for my sake will find it.

MATTHEW 10:39

On November 12, 1859, a French acrobat named Jules Léotard performed the
very first flying trapeze act at the Cirque Napoléon in Paris. As a teen, Jules tied
ventilator cords over his father's pool, where he practiced his midair maneuvers.
His new art form wowed circus audiences, in part because it was done with no
safety net. His close-fitting outfit caught their attention too! Jules Léotard is re-
sponsible for—you guessed it—the leotard.[1]

The trapeze quickly became the featured act of the big-tent circus because
of its inherent intrigue, the faultless timing necessary to pull it off, and the
beauty of aerial ballet. In traditional trapeze, the flyer and the catcher climb tall
ladders to small platforms, approximately forty feet in the air. The flyer has a fly
bar. The catcher has a catch bar. And when it's time for the flyer to let go, the
catcher gives the signal.

Miguel Vargas is a fifth-generation circus performer who does training for
Cirque du Soleil. According to Vargas, who's been a trapeze artist since age
seven, the greatest challenge when trying a new trick is the mental block—it's
hard to let go of the fly bar, because you're about to do something you've never
done before, forty feet in the air.[2]

Letting go of the fly bar goes against every natural instinct, and the same is
true of living generously. Our natural inclination is to hold on to what we have
with tightly clenched fists. The mental block? Again, enough is never enough!

You've got to overcome that mental block if you're going to let go of the fly bar and flip the blessing.

John D. Rockefeller, widely considered the wealthiest American of all time, somehow managed to overcome that natural inclination to hold on and became one of history's great philanthropists. It's tempting to discount Rockefeller's generosity because of how much money he made, but his generosity didn't start when he had millions of dollars. It started with a God-fearing mother who urged a little boy to trust God with his pennies! Rockefeller let go of the fly bar at an early age, and he never stopped trusting the catcher! He lived by John Wesley's maxim: "Gain all you can, save all you can, and give all you can."[3]

Faith is a two-sided coin. Heads, faith is *hanging on*. It's white knuckling the promises of God and refusing to let go. Tails, faith is *letting go*. That may seem like a contradiction, but if we had not let go of a fifty-dollar fly bar in 1996, I don't think National Community Church would have backflipped into nearly $20 million in missions giving over the last seventeen years. I bet you can think of a few examples of things you had to let go of to gain what you now have. And that's not just true financially; it's true spiritually, emotionally, and relationally.

Is there something you need to let go of? Is there something you're holding on to out of fear, not faith? Like the Rich Young Ruler, you may think your savings account is your safety net. But it may be the very thing keeping you from flying. Or maybe you're safeguarding your time instead of volunteering it. Perhaps it's time to let go of your time, talent, and treasure in greater measure and see what God can do!

"I have held many things in my hands, and I have lost them all," said Martin Luther. "But whatever I have placed in God's hands, that I still possess."[4]

The Mental Block

I love food, and I love miracles, so as you can imagine, I really love food miracles! My personal favorite may be the feeding of the five thousand.

Jesus and His disciples were surrounded by a sea of people—hangry people. Jesus turned to Philip and asked the obvious question: "Where shall we buy bread for these people to eat?"[5] Philip was from Bethsaida, a few miles away. If anyone knew where to find food, it was him. But there was no Panera Bread around the corner! And even if there were, Philip knew they couldn't afford to feed even a fraction of that crowd. Philip's response borders on rebuke: "It would take more than half a year's wages to buy enough bread for each one to have a bite!"[6]

Galilee, we have a problem!

Can I make an observation? *Everyone wants a miracle, but no one wants to be in a situation that necessitates one.* Of course, you cannot have one without the other. By definition, a miracle requires an impossible situation! So if you find yourself where enough isn't enough, maybe God is setting you up!

Jesus was not asking Philip where they could find bread because He didn't know what to do next. This was a prank, not panic. Jesus was setting him up for the miracle with a pop quiz.

He was testing Philip, for he already knew what he was going to do.[7]

This is awfully reassuring, isn't it? Even when we feel like we're up a creek without a paddle, God still has a game plan. And remember, you cannot have a comeback without a setback. Just when it seems like there was no way out of this predicament, a little boy carrying a sack lunch entered the scene, stage right. Andrew played Captain Obvious: "There's a young boy here with five barley loaves and two fish. But what good is that with this huge crowd?"[8] Andrew is doing some quick calculations, and it doesn't add up. Not even close! What do you do when you don't have enough? For starters, pray like it depends on God. Then keep your eyes open because you never know how or when or through whom God may make provision.

Let me add a little caution right here: budgeting is not bingo. For what it's worth, National Community Church budgets on 95 percent of our previous year's income. That's not a lack of vision or a lack of faith; it's living within our means. And it gives us financial margin to go after God-sized visions when those opportunities present themselves. That said, *don't let your budget determine your vision.* A God-sized vision will always be beyond your resources, but it's not beyond God's ability! Faith is vision beyond your means, and it often spells *miracle*.

Only God

Scripture doesn't tell how old the little boy with five loaves and two fish was, but I bet he was old enough to know that 5 + 2 = 7. Or does it? If you add God to the equation, the math morphs. I call it kingdom calculus. If you put what you have in your hands into the hands of God, it doesn't just add up. It multiplies! That's the original blessing—"Be fruitful and multiply."[9] By my count, 5 + 2 = 5,000 R12. Not only did Jesus feed all the people until they were full, there was more left over than they started with. Only God!

The moral of the miracle is this: *your generosity is someone else's miracle!*

You may not be able to meet the needs of five thousand people out of pocket. But if you're faithful with your 5 + 2, there is no telling what God can do!

This little boy's generosity turned into a miracle for five thousand people, but miracles are not one and done. Miracles have a ripple effect, like the drop of water on the cover of this book. This miracle didn't just fill their stomachs; it fuels their faith. And I bet their testimony of what happened on that hillside that day eventually fueled someone else's faith. How do you steward a miracle? By boldly believing God for even bigger and better miracles. By humbly telling others about His goodness and His greatness!

I can't quantify this with a study, but miracles seem to multiply in pockets. Since we're focused on food miracles, we'll call them Hot Pockets. My theory is pretty simple: when God does a miracle of a certain nature, it enables people to believe God for the same miracle. If God did it for them, maybe He'll do it for me. If God did it before, maybe He'll do it again. Again, every testimony is a prophecy! You can pay it forward with your story! In fact, your testimony is one way of flipping the blessing! You share the story of God's work in your life, and it becomes a seed of prophecy sown in someone else's life.

There is no way to know how many miracles this one miracle seeded, but there were undoubtedly second, third, and fourth-generation miracles that trace their genealogy back to a little boy who let go of the fly bar!

Givers, Takers, and Matchers

Let's assume the disciples didn't strong-arm this little boy into volunteering his sack lunch. The fact that he willingly gave his lunch to Jesus is no small thing. If you have young children, you know that getting your kids to share anything takes a minor miracle! That's the miracle before the miracle, the premiracle.

When our children were young, I came across a snippet titled "Introduction to Property Law from a Toddler's Perspective." It's a pretty accurate description of a toddler's mindset:

> If I like it, it's mine.
> If I can take it away from you, it's mine.
> If it looks like mine, it's mine.
> If I saw it first, it's mine.
> If you're having fun with it, it's mine.
> If you lay it down, it's mine.
> If it's broken, it's yours.

I wish it was only toddlers who operated with this mindset, but some people never outgrow their selfish streak or sandbox mentality. According to the Talmud, the Jewish commentary on the Old Testament, there are four types of people:

> What's yours is mine
> What's yours is yours
> What's mine is mine
> What's mine is yours[10]

The first person is a *taker*—what's yours is mine. Actually, the Talmud calls that person a *boor*.[11] The second and third persons are *matchers*—what's yours is yours and what's mine is mine. The fourth person is a *giver*—what's mine is yours. This person qualifies, by Talmudic measure, as a *saint*.[12]

Which one are you?

Let me break this down a little bit more. Takers are the heroes of their own stories. Adam Grant described them this way: "*Takers* have a distinctive signature: they like to get more than they give. They tilt reciprocity in their own favor, putting their own interests ahead of others' needs."[13] For takers, life is a zero-sum game played with a scarcity mentality. The person with the most toys at the end of the game wins!

Givers, on the other hand, love to add value. They lead with blessing, and their goal is always to outgive others. Why? Because they know it's all from God and it's all for God. For givers, life is a win-win proposition. They know that at the end of the game, all the toys go back in the box![14] So they operate with an abundance mentality. That is what underpins their double-blessing mindset.

How do you know whether someone is a giver or a taker? It doesn't take long to discern, does it?

There are certainly takers in givers' clothing, but they usually show their true colors when there is one piece of pie left. Just in case you can't guess a person's tendency based on behavior, the use of pronouns is a linguistic tip-off.

Takers are more likely to use first-person singular pronouns—*me, myself,* and *I.* Givers are more likely to use first-person plural pronouns—*we, us,* and *our.*[15] Why? Because takers take credit, while givers give credit. They are *we* people, not *me* people! Nitpicking about pronouns may seem overly analytical, but pronouns reveal what's in our hearts. Jesus said, "The mouth speaks what the heart is full of."[16] And that includes our use of singular or plural pronouns!

Net Worth

Moses Montefiore was the first Jewish man to hold high office in the city of London. A friend of the royal family, he was knighted Sir Moses by Queen Victoria in 1837. That same year he was elected sheriff of London. In later life, Sir Moses became famous for his philanthropy. He made seven trips to the Holy Land, the last one at the age of ninety-one. His love for the Holy Land was demonstrated by his funding of a textile factory, a printing press, a windmill, and several agricultural colonies in Palestine.[17]

On his one hundredth birthday, the *London Times* devoted its editorial page to his praise. One of those editorials recorded a remarkable exchange. Queen Victoria once asked Sir Moses, "What is the extent of your wealth? How much do you own?"[18] Sir Moses, who had amassed a fortune through business ventures and real-estate acquisitions, told the queen it would take a few days to appraise his wealth. When he came back to the queen with a number far less than she surmised, she found it unbelievable. With a smile, Sir Moses explained, "Your majesty, my only true wealth is money that I have given to charity. Anything else I possess is merely temporary and may someday be lost or confiscated."[19] What you *own* and what you are *worth* are two very different things!

What's your net worth?

One of my mentors, Dr. Robert Rhoden, defines success by making a wonderful distinction. The world measures success by *how much money you make* and *how many people serve you*. In God's kingdom, it's the exact opposite. Success is measured by *how much you give* and *how many people you serve*.

Net worth isn't calculated by a stock portfolio, equity in property, or the balance in your savings account. Your net worth is the sum total of all you've given away, not a penny more or a penny less. I love the way author Gary Thomas frames this fundamental shift in perspective:

> Thinking about eternity helps us retrieve [perspective]. I'm reminded of this every year when I figure my taxes. During the year, I rejoice at the paychecks and extra income, and sometimes I flinch when I write out the tithe and offering. I do my best to be a joyful giver, but I confess it is not always easy, especially when there are other perceived needs and wants.
>
> At the end of the year, however, all of that changes. As I'm figuring my tax liability, I wince at every source of income and rejoice with every tithe and offering check—more income means more tax, but every offering and tithe means less tax. Everything is turned upside down, or perhaps, more appropriately, right-side up.
>
> I suspect judgment day will be like that.[20]

I suspect he's right. Balance sheets will look different in eternity. The math will morph as blessings carry over! Everything else is a sunk cost.

Set Giving Goals

What is the root of all evil?

If you asked the average Bible-believing person to fill in the blank, many, if not most, would answer "Money." And they would be wrong! Money is *not* the root of all evil. The *love* of money is the root of evil.[21] What is the love of money? It's good old-fashioned greed, and the problem with greed is that it's never satisfied.

When I was in my twenties, I made some poor investment decisions. I fell for a few get-rich-quick schemes, learning some costly lessons the hard way! I discovered that if an investment seems too good to be true, it probably is! I have quite a few shares of quite a few stocks that went belly up in my brokerage account serving as a tangible reminder of that truth.

I also traded options on a daily basis. An option is a leveraged investment that gives you the right to buy or sell a stock on or before a certain date. It's high risk, high reward. Unfortunately, I tripled my initial investment my first month of trading. Why was that unfortunate? Because a 300 percent return in thirty days is intoxicating. At the time, I would have called it "investing." In retrospect, I was trading way past my pay grade! For me, it was gambling. I eventually got out of the options game because my emotions were beginning to rise and fall with calls and puts.

Well into our thirties, Lora and I were barely making ends meet. As church planters, we didn't make a full salary for quite a few years. I worked a couple of jobs to make ends meet. And when they finally did, it wasn't much. Plus, the cost of living in the nation's capital is the reason so many people play the lottery here! That was my justification for trading options, but the net gains weren't worth the price I was paying! That's when I decided to stop playing the get-rich-quick game and start playing the long game.

When I created my first life-goals list, the financial goals were earning goals and savings goals. On one level, there is nothing wrong with setting those kinds of goals. It's called financial planning, and if you don't have a budget, now might be a good time to start thinking about making one. Budgeting is one way to create the financial margin to be a bigger blessing to others! But for me, those macro goals of saving and earning revealed a faulty focus—I was focused on *getting* rather than *giving*. And that's backward. When I started setting giving goals, the game changed. It flipped a switch in my spirit.

A few years after that flip, I wrote *The Circle Maker*. Publishing my life-goals list in that book is one of the scariest things I've put in print. Why? Because it was "going public" with very private goals. I knew that some people would take potshots at some of my goals and second-guess the motivation behind others. I also knew that some of those life goals are long shots that might make me look a little foolish. So be it. I included five financial goals in that list of 115 life goals:

1. Be debt-free by fifty-five.
2. Give back every penny we've earned from National Community Church.
3. Live off 10 percent and give 90 percent by the time we retire.
4. Give away $10-plus million.
5. Lead National Community Church to give $25,000,000 to missions.[22]

It's still hard to put those numbers in print, but let me reveal a little secret. Sometimes I write things in books and preach things from the pulpit to hold myself accountable! Once they're out there, they're out there. It's hard to back off publicly stated goals.

Do you have a list of life goals? Financial goals? Remember, you won't achieve 100 percent of the goals you don't set. Please pray about them first, but don't be afraid to set some God-sized goals. Just make sure your motivation is God-honoring. And when you're ready to be held accountable, find your own unique way of going public.

Die Broke

Remember the old axiom "Finders keepers, losers weepers"? In God's kingdom, it's the exact opposite. Jesus said, "What will it profit a man if he gains the whole world, and loses his own soul?"[23] The answer is "Absolutely nothing!" Jesus also said this: "Whoever finds his life will lose it, and whoever loses his life for my sake will find it."[24]

Simply put, finders weepers, losers keepers!

Do you know the name Chuck Feeney? Most people do not, yet he's the man whom Bill Gates and Warren Buffett call their hero. Buffett went so far as to say, "He should be everyone's hero."[25] Dubbed the James Bond of philanthropy by *Forbes* magazine,[26] Feeney made his fortune as the founder of Duty Free Shoppers. Instead of using that money to live a lavish lifestyle, Feeney was determined to do his giving while he was living. To date, he has given away more than $8 billion.[27]

It was Feeney's example that inspired Warren Buffett and Bill and Melinda Gates to launch their Giving Pledge, a campaign aimed at recruiting the wealthiest people in the world to commit at least half their fortunes to charity before they die. Honestly, I think that's a pretty good goal no matter how much you make!

Chuck Feeney's goal? *Die broke!*

What if we followed suit? Why wait until you're dead? What's the fun in that? Why not do your giving while you're living? Truth be told, we can't take it with us. I've never seen a U-Haul hitched to a hearse or an armored truck doing a drop-off graveside.

I realize that this idea is a stretch for some. You'd love to grow in generosity and *die broke,* but you're already broke! In fact, you can barely make your car payments, child-care payments, or credit-card payments. If you're in a season where it's difficult to make financial ends meet, double down on giving your time and talent. And when you get back on your financial feet, add money to the mix. But whatever you do, don't let what you *cannot* do keep you from doing what you *can.*

Practically speaking, should we save for retirement? I think we should. Leverage the tax code and max out your Roth IRA while you're at it. That's good stewardship. How about leaving an inheritance? I think it's biblical, and your children would probably appreciate it. But what you leave *for them* isn't nearly as important as what you leave *in them*—a legacy of generosity! Set an example for them to follow; that's the gift that keeps on giving.

There is nothing wrong with targeting financial independence, but let's aim higher than that. There is nothing wrong with saving for retirement or leaving an inheritance, but let's think longer than that. If you die rich, you die broke. If you die broke, you die rich.

Die broke!

THE EIGHTH WONDER
OF THE WORLD

To whom much was given, of him much will be required.

LUKE 12:48, ESV

A shoemaker named George Robert Twelves Hewes, a homemaker named Lydia Darragh, an army physician named William Gorgas, and a slave named Anna Williams. These are not household names you know from history class, but without their collective courage, history books would read very differently.

George Robert Twelves Hewes led one of the boarding parties during the Boston Tea Party because of his "whistling talent."[1] Lydia Darragh uncovered a British plot to attack American troops at Whitemarsh and risked her life to warn General George Washington and his troops.[2] And it could be argued that William Gorgas was the key to constructing the Panama Canal. It ranks as one of history's most ambitious engineering endeavors, but it cost 30,609 human lives, most of us which were lost to yellow fever and malaria.[3] It was Gorgas, the chief sanitary officer, who ordered the draining of swamps and the use of mosquito netting because of his contrarian belief that these were mosquito-borne diseases.[4] That leaves a slave named Anna Williams, but her story takes a little longer to tell.[5]

There is statue that sits outside the National Archives in Washington, DC, with an inscription that reads, "What is past is prologue." It's taken from act 2 of *The Tempest* by William Shakespeare. The sad irony is that very few people know the history of the city block where the National Archives now sits. In Pierre Charles L'Enfant's original plan of the capital city, that block was designated for a national church halfway between the White House and the Capitol. That idea was vetoed by Founding Fathers who believed that it might hamper freedom of religion by establishing a "state" church. So in 1797, President George Washington designated that two-acre plot to serve as a public marketplace.

Center Market opened its doors in 1802, with farmers and fishers and bakers selling their wares. At its peak, there were as many as seven hundred vendors. But Center Market didn't just sell groceries and other goods. It sold slaves, slaves who were held captive in slave pens on what is now the National Mall. After being auctioned to the highest bidder, those slaves were coffled in chains, and marched on foot as far south as Georgia. That brings us to a woman who at the time was known only by her first name.

In November of 1815, Anna was sold to Georgia slave traders for $5.[6] The night before her march south, she was held hostage at George Miller's tavern at 13th and F Streets, NW. She could not bear the thought of being separated from her family, so Anna attempted to escape by jumping from the third-story window. The fall broke both of Anna's arms and shattered her lower spine, but she survived. A young Pennsylvania doctor named Jesse Torrey, who happened to be visiting the capital city, heard about Anna's jump, as did most of the city! Torrey's conscience couldn't believe that slaves were being sold in the shadow of the Capitol, so he canceled his congressional visit and took up the abolitionist cause.[7]

In 1817, Jesse Torrey published an eighty-four-page volume titled *A Portraiture of Domestic Slavery* with an artist's rendering of Anna's jump on the front cover. That painting pricked the conscience of some and inspired the courage of others to ban slave trade in the capital city. Until 2015, Anna's last name was a mystery. Then researchers at the National Archives, the very place where so many slaves had been sold when it was Center Market, discovered her full name. Anna's full name was Ann Williams. Researchers also discovered her case file, evidence that she had filed a petition for and had won freedom for her and her children.

What makes a hero a hero? There is no single answer, no easy answer. But heroes are givers, not takers! Heroes do not announce, "Here I am." They are all about everyone else, "There you are." A true hero is someone who selflessly sacrifices for someone else's benefit. It's someone who goes the extra mile. It's someone who takes personal responsibility when things go wrong and gives credit to others when things go right. A hero is someone who invests time, talent, and treasure for God's glory and others' good, a double blessing. Heroes are not always recognized as such during their lifetimes, but their courage echoes on across the ages!

Patron Saints

The Old Testament is headlined by heroes such as Moses and David, but it's the supporting actors who inspire me the most. Without Aaron and Hur, Moses wouldn't have had the perseverance to prevail in prayer.[8] Without Jonathan, David wouldn't have survived Saul. And he wouldn't have assumed the throne without his thirty-seven mighty men either. Then there's Barzillai. If you haven't heard his name before, you aren't alone.

When Absalom rebelled against his father, David fled the capital city. Who risked his life and livelihood to help David when his world was falling apart? A man from Gilead named Barzillai. We know two things about him: he was "very old" and "very wealthy."[9] Barzillai supplied David with sleeping mats, cooking pots, and serving bowls. He then served David and his escape party a smorgasbord—wheat, barley, grain, lentils, honey, sheep, and cheese.[10] Barzillai's generosity saved David's life, and David did not forget.

When David returned to Jerusalem to take back his throne, it's Barzillai who escorted the king across the Jordan River. David actually invited Barzillai to come and live with him! Barzillai refused the offer, saying, "Just to go across the Jordan River with the king is all the honor I need!"[11] What did David do next? "The king kissed Barzillai and blessed him."[12]

What if the joy of blessing others was the only honor we sought?

What if all we wanted was to add value to others?

What if our chief goal in life was to help others cross the Jordan River?

In the New Testament, there are headliners like Peter, Paul, and Mary. But again, it's the unsung heroes who save the day. The last chapter of Romans reads like the rolling credits at the end of a film. We don't pay much attention to the cast and crew. To us, Romans 16 is a long list of difficult-to-pronounce names. To Paul, it's his who's who list. And each one gets an honorable mention! The first person Paul singled out was a woman named Phoebe, a deacon in the church in Cenchreae. What did she do that put her on Paul's list?

> She has been a patron of many and of myself as well.[13]

In the ancient Roman context, a patron was the protector of a freed slave. From its etymological origins, the word evolved to mean "someone who financially funds a person, organization, or cause." In his book, *Gospel Patrons*, John Rinehart shares the story of those whose generosity has changed the world. He combines the words *gospel* and *patron* to form *gospel patrons* and defines it as "people who resource and come alongside others to help them proclaim the gospel."[14]

Isn't that precisely what Phoebe was? She was the patron saint of Paul's ministry. It was Phoebe's generosity that helped fund Paul's missionary journeys, making her a shareholder in every church Paul planted. Talk about return on investment—that's compound interest for eternity! Of course, Phoebe wasn't the only angel investor. Paul also mentioned Lydia of Thyatira. Not only was Lydia the first documented convert to Christianity in Europe; she was an entrepreneur whose profit margin probably helped fund Paul's ministry as well.

Phoebe and Lydia were venture capitalists, helping the kingdom of God advance across the ancient Middle East. But they weren't the first angel investors. In fact, they may have been inspired by a group of women who formed a rather unique hedge fund.

Angel Investors

Have you ever stopped to think about how Jesus and His disciples made ends meet? I'm pretty sure Jesus didn't continue a side hustle as a carpenter! And His disciples quit their day jobs. So how did they eat? Or travel? Or do anything that cost money for that matter? The answer is found in a group of women with a vision for the kingdom.

> Soon afterward Jesus began a tour of the nearby towns and villages,
> preaching and announcing the Good News about the Kingdom of

God. He took his twelve disciples with him, along with some women who had been cured of evil spirits and diseases. Among them were Mary Magdalene, from whom he had cast out seven demons; Joanna, the wife of Chuza, Herod's business manager; Susanna; and many others who were contributing from their own resources to support Jesus and his disciples.[15]

Call it an investment club. Christen them venture capitalists. Or dub them gospel patrons. Call it what you will, these women got in on the greatest IPO in history. They were the first to purchase stock options in the good news of the gospel.

In the entrepreneurial world, an angel investor is someone who resources a start-up with seed money in exchange for some form of equity. The application of the term *angel* to *investor* traces back to Broadway in New York City and referred to wealthy individuals who funded theatrical performances that would have been shut down otherwise.[16]

The first angel investor profiled by Luke is Mary Magdalene, who had seven demons cast out of her. She had issues—at least seven of them! But Jesus did something for Mary that money can't buy. So is it any wonder that Mary would invest her life savings in the kingdom? And not just her life savings but her life! Remember the way the disciples scattered when Jesus was arrested? Mary was present and accounted for at both the Crucifixion and the Resurrection. In fact, Augustine dubbed her the apostle to the apostles because she announced Jesus's resurrection to the apostles![17]

The second angel investor is a woman named Joanna, whose husband happened to be Herod's business manager. Stop and think about that. Chuza got his paycheck from Rome; then Joanna took what was Caesar's and gave it to God. She reinvested her Roman currency in kingdom stock.

The third angel investor is Susanna, whom we know next to nothing about except her first name. And Luke notes that there were "many others" who invested in this hedge fund that go unnamed altogether! My point? Jesus and His disciples could not have done what they did without these women! And the net gain is eternal dividends for every investor! These are the unsung heroes of the kingdom.

I recognize that some may be a little uncomfortable using investment termi-
nology to describe what these women did, but risk-reward ratios and returns on
investment are as old as the Parable of the Talents. It's not just biblical; it's part
and parcel of the double blessing. And I think we'd be better stewards if we
thought in those terms.

Compound Interest

On January 26, 2014, Josh and Monica Mayo launched Cross Church in Atlanta. We had the privilege of being shareholders in that vision, investing $5,000
in their initial public offering. A few years later, Josh called me to tell me that
we'd had a hundredfold return on the investment. What did he mean? Cross
Church had just passed the $500,000 threshold in their missions giving! That's
compound interest on a kingdom cause.

By definition, compound interest is *interest on interest*. Albert Einstein
called it the eighth wonder of the world, a force more powerful than $E = mc^2$.[18]
We understand how compound interest works with stocks and bonds, but how
about the kingdom of God? In a sense, we all owe our faith to this group of
women. If the kingdom of God were a multilevel-marketing company, these
women got in on the ground floor. They would be our uplines and we would be
their downlines!

Let me make it a little more personal.

When Billy Graham was laid in honor at the US Capitol, Lora and I paid
our respects as his casket was being removed from the rotunda. It was a moving
experience because I put my faith in Christ after watching a Billy Graham film
called *The Hiding Place*. In a sense, I am Billy Graham's downline. Pop quiz:
Do you know his upline? It was an evangelist you've probably never heard of:
Mordecai Ham. I can't trace that lineage any further back than that, but I can't
wait until God reveals our spiritual Ancestry.com. We're going to have lots of
begats to thank!

One footnote.

Over the years, we've invested in hundreds of church plants and those investments range from $1,000 to $100,000. But the most common investment

amount is $5,000, like the investment we made in Cross Church. It's not the largest investment, but it's the most meaningful. And I'll explain why.

When National Community Church was less than a year old, we moved from a DC public school into the movie theaters at Union Station. The theater was depressingly dark, so we needed to add some stage lights, but those stage lights cost $5,000. That was money we did not have, but Bethel Church in Hampton Roads, Virginia, gave us $5,000 to buy them. I'm eternally grateful to Bethel Church and their pastor at the time, Ron Johnson. They were shareholders in everything God did during our Union Station days—and beyond. And the only way I know to pay them back is to pay it forward. Every time we invest $5,000 personally or corporately, we're flipping that original blessing!

Six Preachers

King Henry VIII made more than a few bad decisions. He married six times. He had a falling out with the Catholic Church. He ushered the divine rights of kings into the monarchy. And he had a tendency to kill anyone who disagreed with him. That said, he did make at least one really good decision. On April 8, 1541, he authorized Thomas Cranmer, the archbishop of Canterbury, to establish the college of Six Preachers.

The six preachers sat in designated stalls during services, a sort of medieval box seat. They often dined with the dean of Canterbury Cathedral, debriefing sermons. They were also required to preach twenty messages in their parishes as well as in the cathedral. Most remarkable is the fact that there has been an unbroken succession of six preachers from 1544 to the present, producing some of history's greatest preachers![19]

In football, it would be called a coaching tree. In science, it's called a mentoring chain. Either way, it brings us back to Paul's who's who list. We tend to heroize self-made men and women in our culture, but where you find success, there was succession. Remember Elijah and Elisha? We owe who we are to a very long list of people, most of whom we don't even know! And, of course, they owe their own thanks to a very long list of people.

I was recently speaking at a conference in Chicago where I met Juan

Martinez. I happened to mention my father-in-law, Bob Schmidgall. After the conference session, Juan said, "Your father-in-law led me to Christ." Juan eventually went to Bible college, but it wasn't easy making ends meet. Fortunately, he was able to get a scholarship that helped pay his way. Want to venture a wild guess as to whom that scholarship was named in honor of? Not only did my father-in-law lead Juan to Christ, but he also got him a scholarship more than a decade after he died. That's the double blessing in action.

Now let's get painfully practical.

Take Inventory

My first job was working as a gas-station attendant making minimum wage. One of my distinct memories is our monthly inventory. It was a high-stakes responsibility! If I missed an item in our inventory, it didn't get restocked. And the same goes for the blessings we fail to catalog. If you don't take inventory, you won't restock the blessing by flipping it. If, however, you take careful inventory, you'll be surprised by how blessed you are. I'll share a few fun examples from my inventory; then you can take your own inventory.

My undergraduate education began at the University of Chicago, and a full-ride scholarship helped pay my way. Again, I don't believe that scholarship was unrelated to the faith promise I made as a teenager working a minimum-wage job as a gas-station attendant. But when I transferred to Central Bible College, I had to pay my own way. What I didn't know is that my sweet, sweet grandmother Alene Johnson had saved a sum of money that she left to her three daughters as an inheritance. How she saved that money was a mystery to us all, but it paid off my college debt posthumously. When I inventory my blessings, that one is toward the top of the list. I can only imagine the sacrifices she made to make that possible. And there is only one way for me to thank her—by flipping that blessing for someone else!

Let's keep taking inventory.

One of the most memorable gifts I've ever been given is two tickets to Super Bowl XLV. After the Green Bay Packers beat the Chicago Bears in the 2011 NFC Championship game, I tweeted that I would preach for tickets. I was half joking, but a pastor in Dallas took me up on that offer. I would not have splurged for tickets for myself, but I was happy to preach for them! And to top it off, Super Bowl XLV landed on Josiah's ninth birthday! Can you say "Dad of the year"? Pastor Bryan Jarrett and Northplace Church didn't just give us two tickets; they gave us a memory we'll cherish forever.

Remember the talk I gave on opening day of the Ravens training camp? I took one of our staff members, Jim Tanious. I think Jim would have quit if I had not taken him, because he's a die-hard Ravens fan. Remember the last game of the season when the Ravens won the AFC North and Coach Harbaugh raised his lion spike? Before the game I called in a favor, and one of the Ravens coaches was kind enough to gift tickets to Jim, including a ticket for his daughter, Lily, who had never been to a game! As I watched that game on TV, I kept smiling as I pictured little Lily cheering for her team! Of course, it brought back some of my own Super Bowl memories!

A college scholarship and Super Bowl tickets are big-time blessings and easy to inventory. But some of the most meaningful blessings are the smallest acts of kindness!

After one of the first sermons I ever preached, a man came up to shake my hand, but this was no ordinary handshake. It was a Pentecostal handshake. At least that's what he called it! He hid a twenty-dollar bill in his hand and slipped it into mine when he shook my hand. He said, "Take your wife out to lunch." For the record, you don't have to be Pentecostal to give a Pentecostal handshake. But be careful—it might turn you into one!

Because that moment meant so much to me, I've tried to return that favor in fun ways. Sometimes it's a straight-up Pentecostal handshake, but I also love giving a hallelujah on Halloween. Most people give out candy, but I like dropping two-dollar bills in some of those buckets! And, yes, even that is flipping the blessing for me. The candy I got as a kid trick-or-treating is long forgotten, but I do remember the time I found a dollar bill at the bottom of my bag!

Big or small, inventory the blessing. How? Start with counting or recounting your blessings. What acts of kindness have altered your life? Who went out of their way to help you? What sacrifices have you been the beneficiary of? And who loved you when you least expected it or least deserved it? Once you identify who and what, start brainstorming how you can flip those blessings. Sometimes it's as simple as doing to others what has been done to you. But don't be afraid to get creative and put your unique fingerprint on it.

Peripheral Vision

I used to think vision simply meant dreaming big and thinking long, but I've come to appreciate a less celebrated type of vision that may be of equal importance. Peripheral vision is seeing what lies at the edges, which often means those who are most marginalized.

Anatomically, our vertical range of vision is approximately 150 degrees, while our horizontal field of view is 210 degrees.[20] Anything outside those parameters is invisible to us, and that's often where the blessing is hiding. Peripheral vision is noticing what others ignore. It's reading a room and reading between the lines. It's spotting potential where others see problems. It's finding opportunity where others see inconvenience.

In the Parable of the Good Samaritan, the Priest and the Levite turn a blind eye to their brother in need and walk right by. Why? They had vision, but it was tunnel vision. They were so focused on getting where they thought God wanted them to go that they missed an opportunity to be the blessing. Please don't read right past this: *sometimes it's our religious routines that cause us to miss the divine appointments God puts right in our path.* Why? Because those opportunities usually look like inconveniences! The Good Samaritan, on the other hand, noticed the need out of the corner of his eye.

Dave Schmidgall is one of our campus pastors at National Community Church, and he also leads our missions endeavors. He and his wife, Kate, have a huge heart for refugees. They have served in refugee camps, organized soccer leagues for refugee kids, and even taken refugees into their home.

At one of those soccer games, Dave spotted a Syrian man sitting by himself. With the help of Google Translate, Dave initiated a conversation that led to a friendship. Dave and Kate helped Bashir set up a business. They launched an initiative called Listen and Learn at our church, giving refugees the opportunity to cook their countries' cuisine while sharing their stories. They've helped kids get registered for school and adults get driver's licenses. Come on—if taking someone to the Department of Motor Vehicles isn't love, I don't know what is!

Not unlike the man who found himself on the side of the road, refugees need a helping hand. Most of them don't know the language and the culture of their new home. Many of them fled their countries under duress. So we've taken it upon ourselves to flip the blessing for them. As I've already noted, NCC helps resettle 65 percent of refugees in the DC area. But it started with Pastor Dave spotting Bashir out of the corner of his eye!

God is in the business of strategically positioning us in the right place at the right time—of that I'm sure. He is ordering our footsteps and preparing good works in advance.[21] And that means that the person next to you isn't there by accident. May God give us the peripheral vision to spot the divine appointments that are around us all the time.

A few years ago, I was getting some work done on our car. Yes, the car that earned my membership in the Junky Car Club. I asked our mechanic to fix a flat, change the oil, and check the fluids. When I went to pick it up, the bill seemed a little lower than it should have been, but far be it from me to argue about that. After charging my credit card, the gas-station attendant handed me my keys, except they weren't my keys. They were the keys of the woman who happened to be right behind me in line! I knew they could cancel my credit-card transaction, but I made a spontaneous decision. I turned to the woman behind me and said, "Merry Christmas! Your repair is paid for!" For the record, the bill was only forty-one dollars. So it caught me a little off guard when she started crying! She kept saying, "Thank you. Thank you." And I kept saying, "Merry Christmas! Merry Christmas!"

I'm not sure why she had such an emotional reaction to what was a relatively small gesture of generosity, but I have a few theories. Either she had fallen on hard financial times and couldn't afford the repair, or it had been way too long since she had been on the receiving end of a random act of kindness. Either way, few things are more fun than flipping those kinds of blessings! It can turn a rather mundane moment into an unforgettable memory! It can turn a ten-second encounter into a divine appointment that makes a difference for eternity.

The God Pocket

There is a subtext to the story of the Good Samaritan that is easily overlooked, and it has to do with money management.

> The next day he took out two denarii and gave them to the innkeeper. "Look after him," he said, "and when I return, I will reimburse you for any extra expense you may have."[22]

A denarius was a day's wage. In today's dollars, based on the median income in DC, this is $594 before taxes. What that tells me is this: the Good Samaritan created financial margin so that he could be a blessing in these kind of situations!

In his book *You Were Born for This,* Bruce Wilkinson shares about a divine appointment in Johannesburg, South Africa. Late one night after a speaking event, Bruce and his son, David, had a craving for ice cream. The restaurant they chose had just closed, but Bruce wasn't beyond begging. "Is there any way you could find some ice cream for two guys who would really appreciate it?" The server smiled and said, "I'll see what I can do."[23]

When she walked away, Bruce felt led to leave a rather large tip. In fact, he had a large wad of bills in his pocket, and he felt prompted to leave every last rand (the South African currency).

Bruce and David attempted to escape before the server could catch them, but she ran back out of the kitchen. With tears in her eyes, she said, "You know Jesus, don't you?" Bruce did not deny it. Then she said, "This is a miracle. I have a baby, and we couldn't pay rent, and the landlord was going to kick us out of our apartment tomorrow morning. I prayed to God on the way to work just this afternoon, 'Please, God, send us the money, or we'll be living on the street.'" She wiped away her tears and said, "Sir, this amount is exactly the rent I owe—*to the rand.* That's how I knew you know Jesus."[24]

Wouldn't it be wonderful if people knew that we knew Jesus by the tips we leave? And by tips I don't mean gospel tracts that look like fake bills! I was so inspired by Bruce's story that I decided to turn tipping into a little game. Sometimes I leave a large tip, as the Spirit leads. But I also love tipping people who don't normally get tipped. There are easier jobs than cleaning public bathrooms, right? It's often a thankless job, so I've started leaving tips. Sometimes I'll leave an anonymous tip on their cleaning rig. Sometimes I'll look them in the eye and thank them. Either way, it's another fun way to flip the blessing!

One last tip, pun intended.

Bruce Wilkinson keeps a stash of cash in what he calls the "God Pocket." He explains, "The God Pocket is a specific location in your wallet or purse where you keep money you have devoted to God so you can give it to someone in need as soon as He nudges you to do so."[25]

Pretty simple. Pretty practical. Pretty powerful.

Sounds like something the Good Samaritan would do!

Gospel Patrons

Do you know the name Selina Hastings? I'd be a little surprised if you did. Like the women who patronized Paul—and I mean that positively—Selina Hastings is an unsung hero. If she had been alive during the time of Christ, she would have thrown her hat in the ring with the women who underwrote Jesus's ministry.

In 1739, she joined the famed Fetter Lane Society.[26] Considered the first flowering of the Moravian church and the harbinger of Methodism,[27] its membership boasted the likes of John and Charles Wesley as well as George Whitefield. Selina Hastings, better known as the Countess of Huntingdon, was an English aristocrat and the heiress of old money. John Rinehart describes the five-foot, six-inch force of nature this way: "She rubbed shoulders with royalty, enjoyed a pinch of snuff, and really believed the Bible."[28]

When she was thirty-nine years old, Lady Huntingdon's husband passed away from a stroke. Five of her seven children would die before she did, two from smallpox. She could have turned inward, shriveled by the pain of loss. Instead, her generosity helped spark the Great Awakening both in England and in America. How? She proposed a partnership with none other than George Whitefield. Lady Huntingdon was to George Whitefield what Phoebe was to the apostle Paul.

Lady Huntingdon used her influence to open doors for George Whitefield and her wealth to finance his ministry. Whitefield is said to have preached as many as eighteen thousand sermons, which is remarkable considering he lived to the age of only fifty-five. It is estimated that before the American colonies declared independence, four-fifths of Americans had heard George Whitefield preach.[29] But his preaching would not have been possible without Lady Huntingdon's patronage!

There is one more reason I love Lady Huntingdon. She had vision beyond her times, even in her eighties. She didn't just finance 116 churches, plus a seminary to train pastors. She was out of the box. In 1790, she wanted to lease a large theater in East London that had been used for horse shows and convert it into a chapel. One of her senior advisers counseled against it because of the £500 price tag. While Lady Huntingdon was listening to his laundry list of objections, the mail arrived. One of the letters contained a promissory note for exactly £500! In today's currency, that's $97,846.50. Lady Huntingdon then advised her adviser: "Take this and pay for the chapel, and be no longer faithless but believing."[30]

Go thou and do likewise!

Take inventory.

Flip the blessing.

Repeat.

PLAYING THE LONG GAME

He was looking ahead to his great reward.

HEBREWS 11:26, NLT

In 1785, a French mathematician named Charles-Joseph Mathon de la Cour penned a parody mocking Benjamin Franklin's American optimism. This is how our forefathers took shots at one another before social media. Well, that and dueling to the death. Franklin is best remembered for his political and scientific achievements, but he also authored a periodical widely read in eighteenth-century America called *Poor Richard's Almanac*. How did Mathon de la Cour mock Franklin's American optimism? He fictionalized about "Fortunate Richard" leaving a small sum of money in his will that could be used only after it had collected interest for five hundred years.[1]

Instead of getting upset about getting roasted by the Frenchman, seventy-nine-year-old Franklin wrote a letter to Mathon de la Cour thanking him for an excellent idea. Benjamin Franklin bequeathed £1,000 to both his hometown of Boston and his adopted city of Philadelphia. The endowment was established with one stipulation. It was to be invested in a fund that earned interest and supported the public good for two hundred years. Then and only then would the funds be released.

Stop and think about that. Two hundred years? That took tremendous faith given the fact that the future of this newly formed nation called the United States of America was still very much in doubt when Franklin died on April 17, 1790.

For two hundred years, the interest on Franklin's endowment was given as seed money to tradesmen. Why? It was Franklin's way of paying it forward, flipping the blessing. A loan had helped Franklin start his own printing business, and the endowment was Benjamin Franklin's way of returning the favor!

Fast-forward two hundred years, and that original £2,000 investment was worth more than $5 million. Thinking long enables you to give big! In fact, it has the potential to become a generational blessing—a gift that keeps on giving.

Eternal Optimist

Generosity is born of optimism.

Optimism is an abundance of hope, an abundance of faith. It's epitomized by the little boy who gave his five loaves and two fish to Jesus. What was going through his mind? Here's my best guess: *If I give what I have to Jesus, maybe, just maybe, He can use it to feed far more people than just me!* When it comes right down to it, optimism is the willingness to skip a meal in order to feed a hungry world.

Generally speaking, pessimists are past-tense people. They let the negative things that have happened in their past overly inform their prognosis of the future. Instead of living openhanded and letting go of what God has entrusted to them, they live closefisted. Eventually, they are possessed by their possessions. The things they own, own them.

Optimists take a very different tack. They are focused on future-tense reward, believing that the best is yet to come. Optimists live openhanded because they are openhearted. The optimist's mantra is Jonathan's mindset: "Perhaps the LORD will act in our behalf."[2] It's a "go big or go home" approach to life that trusts God right down to the jot and tittle.

The optimism of Jonathan reminds me of Moses:

> It was by faith that Moses, when he grew up, refused to be called the son
> of Pharaoh's daughter. He chose to share the oppression of God's people
> instead of enjoying the fleeting pleasures of sin. He thought it was better
> to suffer for the sake of Christ than to own the treasures of Egypt, for he
> was looking ahead to his great reward.[3]

Moses was playing the long game! Why? He was an eternal optimist, something the Jewish people were very short on after four hundred years of slavery! A double-blessing mindset is focused on heavenly treasure, not earthly pleasure. Of course, it's not easy keeping eternity in focus. In the words of the French philosopher Blaise Pascal, "Our imagination so magnifies the present, because we are continually thinking about it, and so reduces eternity, because we do not think about it, that we turn eternity into nothing and nothing into eternity."[4]

Are you living for time or eternity? If you are living for eternity, it profoundly affects how you spend your time. Why? Because time is no longer a zero-sum game! You still need to keep a calendar, but it's much easier to be generous with your time when you know you can't run out of it.

Criticize by Creating

In 589 BC, the Babylonians laid siege to the city of Jerusalem. When they broke through the wall of Jerusalem three years later, they plundered the temple, razed the city, and took members of the creative class and upper class as prisoners of war. For many decades, these Jewish refugees lived as expats in Babylon. They weren't sure whether they would ever see Jerusalem again.

Their refugee status begged a question: How should we then live?[5] Should they enculturate, adopting and adapting to the customs of the Babylonians? Should they attempt to maintain their distinct traditions and unique identity as Jewish people? Should they undermine their captors? Or should they attempt to influence from the inside out, as Joseph, Daniel, and Esther did? These were practical questions they had to answer and difficult decisions they had to make. And there were conflicting opinions. But before I share those conflicting opinions, let's play multiple-choice.

When it comes to engaging a culture of "more" and "mine," I think we have four basic options. We can (a) mindlessly consume, (b) pompously condemn, (c) lazily copy, or (d) conscientiously create. You can probably guess which answer I'm advocating by the adverbs!

Too many Christians consume culture, condemn culture, or copy culture. In my opinion, those are cop-outs. Only one of the four options facilitates an outpouring of blessing. We're called to create culture and do it conscientiously! As cocreators we bestow blessing on the world around us.

I try to live by Michelangelo's maxim: "Criticize by creating."

Do we need to stand up for what's right? Of course we do! There is a sin of silence, and there are times when it takes tremendous courage to call a spade a spade! But taking potshots at culture is the easy way out. It's laziness at best and calling down curses at worst. As Christ followers, we should be more known for what we're *for* than what we're *against*. Translation? Quit cursing the darkness and start lighting candles. How? By producing better films, starting better businesses, writing better music, and drafting better legislation. How? With the help of the Holy Spirit. Why? Because cursing the darkness doesn't cut it. We're called to flip blessings.

Seventy Years from Now

During Israel's captivity, a prophet named Hananiah declared that God would break the yoke of Babylon in two years. He prophesied that the articles of the temple that Nebuchadnezzar had plundered would be returned, as would the remnant who had been taken captive. That sounds appealing, right? But it was fake news from a false prophet.

The prophet Jeremiah calls his bluff: "You have persuaded this nation to trust in lies."[6] Hananiah sat on a throne of lies, and Jeremiah knew it. Jeremiah prophesied a seventy-year captivity. That didn't help him with popularity polls— the people preferred Hananiah's shorter prediction—but Jeremiah was right.

Two years? Or seventy years?

What's the difference, besides sixty-eight years?

If you're going to live in Babylon for only two years, as Hananiah suggested, you don't even unpack your suitcase! You don't "own" the city; you "rent" it. Why? You're there for only one election cycle! But if you're going to be there for seventy years, as Jeremiah prophesied, it changes your mindset. You think long—seventy years longer! And thinking longer enables you to dream bigger. You start doing things that will make a difference to the third and fourth generations. And that enables you to be a bigger blessing!

Jeremiah penned an open letter to the Jewish exiles, and the advice he gave

is as relevant today as it was 2,500 years ago. You know a piece of this prophecy
because it's one of the most posterized promises in the entire Bible:

> "I know the plans I have for you," declares the LORD, "plans to
> prosper you and not to harm you, plans to give you hope and a
> future."[7]

We love that promise, right? But do we understand the context in which it
was given? Let me back up the truck a few verses. That promise is part of a
prophecy, and that prophecy is part of a theology of the city. Babylon was Israel's
archenemy. They had plundered Israel's temple and mocked Israel's God. You
might expect Jeremiah to suggest subterfuge or counsel a coup d'état, but he
does not. Consider the advice Jeremiah offers:

> Build houses and settle down; plant gardens and eat what they pro-
> duce. Marry and have sons and daughters; find wives for your sons
> and give your daughters in marriage, so that they too may have sons
> and daughters. Increase in number there; do not decrease.[8]

The exhortation to increase in number is reminiscent of the original blessing, right? But how exactly are the people to multiply? Jeremiah advocates the
long game. Don't just rent; put down roots. Don't just date; get married.

Translation: play the long game by doing things that will make a difference
seventy years from now! God's promise through Jeremiah—"I know the plans
I have for you"—is more than a pep talk or a poster. He is wallpapering their
hearts and minds. He is widening the aperture on their outlook. What God
wants to accomplish through your life is longer than your life span! Again, we
think right here, right now. But God is thinking nations and generations!

On a recent wedding anniversary, Lora and I were gifted tickets to the
Broadway show *Hamilton*. That'll be a fun blessing to flip! Every act was bril-
liantly produced and performed, but I love one line from one of the songs:
"What is a legacy? It's planting seeds in a garden you never get to see."[9] That's a
double-blessing mindset. It dreams big and thinks long, and the result is generational blessings.

Peace and Prosperity

After exhorting the Jewish exiles to play the long game, Jeremiah offered one last piece of priceless advice:

> Seek the peace and prosperity of the city to which I have carried you into exile. Pray to the LORD for it, because if it prospers, you too will prosper.[10]

Can I share a couple of convictions?

First, God's vision for your life is bigger than yours!

Second, God wants you to be a bigger blessing!

Remember the city block we're turning into a prototype campus and mixed-use marketplace? Think Chelsea Market in New York City, Armature Works in Tampa, Ponce City Market in Atlanta, or Anaheim Packing House in Los Angeles—just a few of my favorite places and spaces. It will include an event venue for concerts, conferences, and conventions. We'll leverage our kids' ministry space to operate as a child-development center Monday to Friday, meeting a real need in real time. Even our office space will include coworking space. Why not just build a traditional church building? We could do that, and there would be nothing wrong with that. But we're not just trying to build a church. We're trying to bless a city. In fact, we're bold enough to believe that the church ought to solve a city's problems for it. And when the city prospers because of it, so do we!

We have a core conviction: *the church belongs in the middle of the marketplace.* Jesus didn't just hang out in religious places with religious people. He hung out at wells, which were natural gathering places in ancient culture. We're building a postmodern well, a place where people can work and eat and play and pray. Like Ebenezers Coffeehouse, we'll have a double-blessing bottom line. Every penny of profit will fund kingdom causes. And we'll go about our business as if it's the Father's business, because it is!

Our marketplace will incubate entrepreneurs and facilitate business as mission. We'll create hundreds of jobs, and we'll do so conscientiously. Our vision is to create jobs for those who have the most difficult time finding them. That includes but isn't limited to returning citizens, resettled refugees, and the kids we're mentoring at our DC Dream Center. Our vision for this city block began with a prayer circle. More than two decades later, it's coming full circle as we holistically leverage it to bless our city in a way that is bigger than we could have ever imagined.

One final footnote.

In 2018, National Community Church was on the receiving end of a $14-million gift. That's not a misprint. Where did that blessing come from? From someone who is playing the long game, someone who is playing the giving game! That gift was given by someone with a mind for business and a heart for the kingdom.

Can I share a growing conviction? *The miracle is in the house!* And if it's not, God will send it through the door! Allow me one more conviction: maybe, just maybe, we should be discipling more entrepreneurs! If we're playing the long game, we won't just plant churches. We'll start businesses focused on double blessing—businesses that not only create jobs and create products but also help underwrite kingdom causes!

I hope this book helps you grow in the grace of giving. If we all played the long game, I'm absolutely convinced that every kingdom cause would be fully funded. May God raise up the next generation of Lydias and Phoebes! May God unleash the generosity and creativity of a thousand Barzillais!

Ask of Me

Show me the size of your dream, and I'll show you the size of your God. Of course, no matter how big your dream is, God is bigger still! We have a hard time believing God for *cities*. The irony? God is offering *nations*!

Only ask, and I will give you the nations.[11]

According to the United Nations, approximately 428,000 people move into cities every single day![12] Unfortunately, many churches are moving out of cities while the masses move in. A recent *Washington Post* article notes that 40 percent of religious buildings on Capitol Hill have been closed or converted for nonreligious use.[13] Why? To be blunt, we've failed to incarnate the gospel within the culture. We've failed to seek the peace and prosperity of the city outside the four walls of the church, shriveling up inside.

We're doing our level best to reverse that trend. As already outlined, we've turned a crack house into Ebenezers Coffeehouse. We've turned an abandoned apartment building into the DC Dream Center. And our next step is turning a city block into a prototype campus, child-development center, mixed-use marketplace, and coworking space.

I know some will question that vision and ask, *why?* Admittedly business as usual would be a lot easier! But business as usual goes out of business sooner or later, and that includes the Father's business. Again, faithfulness is *not* holding down the fort. Faithfulness is advancing the kingdom in new ways! And we happen to believe this: *there are ways of doing church that no one has thought of yet.*

Perhaps a better question than *why?* is *why not?*

In the words of George Bernard Shaw, "There are those that look at things the way they are, and ask *why?* I dream of things that never were, and ask *why not?*"[14]

National Community Church is a why-not church, and we have a why-not vision. We don't claim to be any better or any worse than any other church, but we're not afraid of daring to be different. Why? Because if you want to reach people no one is reaching, you have to do what no one is doing. If you want to reach people who are outside the box, you have to do things that are outside the box!

At last count, there were 116,607 people living below the poverty line in the nation's capital.[15] There are 6,904 people experiencing homelessness.[16] There are 853 children and youth in the care of Child and Family Services. And there are 1,540 kids who are educationally disengaged.[17] Why do I know these numbers? Because every number has a name, every name has a story, and every story matters to God. These are the statistics we're trying to change—one person at a time! Why? Because we have been blessed to bless!

Those statistics are the tip of the iceberg, but they reveal how much we're hurting beneath the surface. You can add other metrics to the mix, such as mental health. And you can fill in the blank based on where you live. But no matter how you slice it, we live in a fallen world surrounded by hurting people. That may feel a little overwhelming, but I'm not sure it's as bad as being prisoners of war in Babylon! The good news? God's kingdom is coming, and we are the conduits of His blessing.

Seeking the peace and prosperity of the city is posturing ourselves with open hands and open hearts. In the words of Emma Lazarus, inscribed on the Statue of Liberty, "Give me your tired, your poor, / Your huddled masses yearning to breathe free."[18] Sounds an awful lot like Matthew 25, doesn't it? Being a bigger blessing starts there—clothing the naked, feeding the hungry, and caring for the sick.

Jesus said, "Whatever you did for one of the least of these brothers and sisters of mine, you did for me."[19] That's the heart of the Great Commandment and the Great Commission. It's the way we play the long game, the giving game!

What are you believing God for? James, the brother of Jesus, reminded us, "You do not have because you do not ask God."[20] Jesus's words up the ante: "Ask and it will be given to you; seek and you will find; knock and the door will be opened to you."[21]

Blessing is yours for the asking, but the only way to *keep it* is to *give it away*. In the words of the martyred missionary Jim Elliot, "He is no fool who gives what he cannot keep to gain what he cannot lose."[22] The secret of the double blessing is simple: *you get it by giving it*.

This isn't a book you *read*. This is a book you *do*.

Whom will you bless today? How will you bless them?

What are you waiting for?

THE YEAR OF BLESSING

Bless the LORD, O my soul, and forget not all his benefits.

PSALM 103:2, KJV

Washington, DC, is a city of memorials and museums and monuments. When you climb the steps of the Lincoln Memorial and stand in the shadow of our sixteenth president, the larger-than-life statue evokes emotions residing in the deep recesses of the soul. The first time I visited the United States Holocaust Memorial Museum, I had to choke back tears. The same is true of the National Museum of African American History and Culture. The human suffering portrayed by both museums is palpable. And I won't forget walking into the US Capitol Rotunda to pay last respects to Billy Graham.

The nation's capital is dotted with sacred spaces, sacred places. But there is no more hallowed ground than Arlington National Cemetery, the final resting place for more than four hundred thousand veterans who gave their last full measure of devotion to their country.

On Veterans Day 1921, President Warren G. Harding presided over an interment ceremony honoring one of World War I's unidentified heroes. The remains of unknown soldiers from World War II, the Korean War, and the Vietnam War have since been laid to rest in the Tomb of the Unknown Soldier. The western panel reads, "Here rests in honored glory an American soldier known but to God."[1]

Since 1937, the Tomb of the Unknowns has been guarded around the clock by members of the elite Old Guard who walk the mat twenty-four hours a day, seven days a week. The guards march a precisely paced twenty-one steps, pause to pay respect for twenty-one measured seconds, then about-face and repeat that sacred sequence until relieved of duty.[2] Members of the Old Guard do not wear rank insignia so as not to outrank the unknown soldiers. Few rituals are more awe inspiring than the changing of the guard or the wreath-laying ceremonies on national holidays.

Why is the changing of guard performed with such attention to detail, even under the cover of dark when no one is watching? The answer is simple: the unknown soldier represents countless men and women who paid the ultimate price for their country. The blessings we enjoy every single day were paid for in full by the blood, sweat, and tears of unknown men and women and the families who lost them to the line of duty.

My point? Every blessing has a backstory, and that includes the freedoms we enjoy as Americans. Those freedoms were not free! They came at a tremendous cost. And if you fail to count that cost, you have not counted the blessing!

We've reached the end of this book, but we've barely scratched the surface of God's blessings. Simply put, *it's impossible to fully inventory the blessings of God.* Or their backstories! Only eternity will tell the full story of blessing, but every blessing was begotten by the original blessing. And when we pull the thread to the end, there is no end. There is eternal blessing.

At its core the Hebrew word *barak* means "to bless the one who blesses you."[3] That's where we began, and that's where we end. Most of God's blessings are a mystery, and it will take a good part of eternity to unravel Ariadne's thread. The good news?

When we've been there ten thousand years,
Bright shining as the sun,
We've no less days to sing God's praise
Than when we first begun.[4]

Just as we pray for needs, *spoken* and *unspoken,* we praise God for blessings, *known* and *unknown.* The Israelites actually offered a sacrifice for unintentional sin.[5] I'm afraid we're guilty of unintentional ingratitude, but God is gracious. For the blessings we can inventory, the words of Charles Wesley come to mind:

O for a thousand tongues to sing
My great Redeemer's praise!
The glories of my God and King,
The triumphs of His grace![6]

For the countless blessings we cannot begin to catalog, we sing the same.

Grace Period

In 1996, Lora and I inherited a core group of nineteen people and started pastoring National Community Church. There was nothing easy about those early years. It took three years to become self-supporting. It took five years to grow to 250 people. It wasn't quick. It wasn't easy. And I wouldn't have had it any other way! In hindsight, I call those first five years of church planting a *grace period*.

In law, a grace period is a period of time when a particular rule does not apply. In personal finance, it's waiving a late fee even though you've missed the deadline. In politics, it's an extra measure of goodwill at the beginning of a new term.

Spiritually speaking, a grace period is when God doesn't give you what you want when you want it. Why? Because you aren't ready for it. That's how blessings backfire! Good parents don't give their children everything they ask for.

What I learned during those first five years of church planting is that God needed to *grow me* before He could grow our church. You've heard it said that God won't allow you to be tested beyond what you can bear?[7] Well, God won't bless you beyond your level of spiritual maturity either. He loves you far too much to do that.

God's blessings are perfectly sequenced, and that requires great patience on our part. But in that process, we are conformed to the image of Christ. The good news? If you've made it all the way to the epilogue, you probably have the kind of patience God can bless! My point? We are living in a grace period, every one of us! Certainly there are blessings you've already received, for which you are eternally grateful. But isn't it awe inspiring to know that God is currently preparing *blessings for you* and *you for blessings*? And, I might add, He's preparing *blessings beyond your ability to ask or imagine!*

The Trough of Sorrow

In the world of entrepreneurship, *trough of sorrow* refers to the setbacks many start-ups experience in their early stages. It's virtually inevitable. And what's true in business is often true in life. Even Jesus experienced a trough of sorrow. Can you call forty days in the wilderness being tempted by the devil anything else?[8] But Jesus emerged from that season of testing with a greater anointing, a greater blessing.

Almost every marriage I know of goes through a trough of sorrow. So do dreams. So does faith. If you find yourself in that trough, I believe there is a blessing on the other side!

When Jesus came out of His forty-day trough, He made His way back to His hometown. On the Sabbath, He unrolled the scroll of Isaiah and began reading:

> The Spirit of the Lord is on me,
>   because he has anointed me
>   to proclaim good news to the poor.
> He has sent me to proclaim freedom for the prisoners
>   and recovery of sight for the blind,
>   to set the oppressed free,
>   to proclaim the year of the Lord's favor.[9]

What happened next? Jesus rolled up the scroll and handed it back to the altar boy. Then He said, "Today this scripture is fulfilled in your hearing."[10] What He said was shocking, no doubt. But not as shocking as what He *did not* say! His audience knew Isaiah's prophecy by heart, so they knew He stopped reading midsentence.

After proclaiming "the year of the LORD's favor," Isaiah declared "the day of vengeance of our God."[11] But Jesus did not do the same. The question is, why not? Simply put, Jesus didn't come to condemn the world.[12] He came to save the world from its sin, and that includes saving you. Do you have the *blessed assurance* of salvation? It's as simple as opening a gift, but that gift must be received.

To "as many as received Him, to them He gave the right to become children of God."[13]

"In the time of my favor I heard you,
    and in the day of salvation I helped you."

I tell you, now is the time of God's favor, now is the day of salvation.[14]

Before you began reading this book, I prayed that God would begin a new season of blessing in your life. Can I push the envelope a little further? May this book benchmark the year of the Lord's favor, the year of blessing!

Nostalgia for God

A hundred years ago, a pair of English ornithologists took some birds from their mother's nest on the island of Skokholm off the coast of Wales. They tagged those birds and transported them to various places far from home. Then they released them to see whether those birds could find their way home.

One of those birds was flown by airplane to Venice. Despite the tremendous distance of about a thousand miles and despite the fact that this species of bird was not native to the region around Venice, the bird found its way back home by a path it had never flown—in just over 341 hours! That experiment was repeated with even greater distances. Two birds were transported by train in a closed box to London, then flown by airplane to Boston. Only one of the two birds survived that trip. The lone survivor, bird No. AX6587, flew all the way across the Atlantic Ocean and found its way back to its mother's nest in twelve days and twelve hours![15]

Pretty impressive, right? Even ornithologists are amazed by this inbuilt capacity called the homing instinct. It's the inherent ability within certain animals to find their way home across great distances despite unfamiliar terrain.

There is a similar instinct hardwired into the human soul—the longing to be blessed by God. Why? It's our earliest memory! In the words of Saint Augustine, "You have made us for yourself, and our heart is restless until it rests in you."[16] The seventeenth-century French philosopher Blaise Pascal called it the God-shaped hole. Pope Francis called it "nostalgia for God."[17]

We cannot reach the full measure of our potential or find the full measure of meaning in life without God. Why? That's whose image we bear. That's whose nest we come from. That's who blessed us in the beginning.

Remember the prodigal son? I think it was nostalgia for God, a holy home-sickness, that jogged his memory and turned his heart toward home. The prodigal who had disowned his father now sought his blessing. And so do we. If this book helps you find your way back to God, it has served its purpose. May you find faith with your fingerprint on it.

The prodigal was so far from home, but not so far that God's grace could not lead him home. And when it did, he found his father watching and waiting for his return. You will too! The father ran to his son, with his arms wide open. Then he threw a party, more than a three-minute party! He celebrated his son, and God will do the same for you. His ancient instinct has not changed. There is nothing God wants to do more than to give you His full blessing.

God wants to bless you beyond your ability to ask or imagine. There, I said it again. But by now you know the secret to the double blessing: *you get it by giving it.*

Count your blessings.

Flip your blessings.

Repeat as often as possible!

DISCUSSION QUESTIONS

Chapter 1—Double Portion

1. Before the prophet Elijah died, his apprentice, Elisha, asked Elijah to bless him with "a double portion of your spirit." How would you describe this double portion?
2. Mark writes that our legacy is "measured by the fruit we grow on other people's trees." What does he mean by this statement? Whose trees are you growing fruit on?
3. How would you describe a brave prayer?
4. Why does a comeback in life require a prior setback? Do you have an example from your own experiences?
5. Are you convinced that you have "every spiritual blessing in Christ"? Why or why not?

Chapter 2—Umbrella Blessing

1. Mark compares the blessing of God to an umbrella. What does he mean by this analogy?
2. Do God's blessings come with any conditions? Explain your answer.
3. In regard to the way God responds to our sin, what is the distinction between penalty and consequence?
4. Why is obedience "the first habit of highly blessed people"?
5. Have you ever experienced a blessing that seemingly came out of nowhere? Share the details.

Chapter 3—The X Factor

1. When you think about doing something bold for God, are you confident He has your back? Why or why not?
2. How would you define "flip the blessing"?
3. Have you ever experienced a boomerang blessing—something posi-

tive happening months, years, or maybe even decades later? Share the story.

4. What does it mean that "the X factor is the favor of God"? Have you experienced this?

5. The apostle James wrote: "You have not because you ask not" (Mark's paraphrase of James 4:2). Is there something you feel called to ask God for, boldly desiring the X factor?

Chapter 4—The Avogadro Constant

1. What does Mark mean when he writes that God blesses "those who have the humility and courage to be themselves, without pretense"?

2. Why does Scripture place such importance on the power of words?

3. Have you had a moment in your life when someone's words made all the difference? What was the outcome of those words?

4. What do you think are some of the common lies the Enemy tells people?

5. The priestly blessing says,

The LORD bless you
    and keep you;
The LORD make his face shine on you
    and be gracious to you;
The LORD turn his face toward you
    and give you peace. (Numbers 6:24–26)

Share which of these phrases in this six-fold blessing is most meaningful to you.

Chapter 5—God in the Hands of Angry People

1. A. W. Tozer famously said, "What comes into our minds when we think about God is the most important thing about us." Why is this true?

2. How would you describe God's anger? How does this anger affect your relationship with Him?

3. Mark writes, "Without a revelation of God's love, you'll relate to Him out of fear rather than affection." When you think about God, do you feel fear, affection, or both? Elaborate on your answer.

4. The Bible says in Zechariah 2:8 that you are the apple of God's eye. Is this truth easy or difficult to accept? Why?

5. Scripture proclaims that nothing can separate us from the love of God (Romans 8:38–39). How might you grow in your confidence of this truth?

Chapter 6—Fight for It

1. Why is it important in life to know which battles to fight?

2. What is Mark getting at when he writes, "The blessing of God doesn't just fall into our laps"?

3. How do disappointments and failures—"scars"—in life benefit us?

4. In your experience as both a leader and a follower, what is the value of someone who leads "with a limp"?

5. Give examples of God's blessings you have experienced thus far in your spiritual journey.

Chapter 7—Blessings in Disguise

1. How has God used some of your "scars" to help others heal?

2. In your life, have you had situations where things seemed to be at their worst right before they got better? Share about one of these.

3. "Someday, we'll thank God for the prayers He didn't answer as much as the ones He did," Mark says. What prayers are you glad God didn't answer?

4. Recall some situations when someone's criticism of you or something you did actually turned out to bless or strengthen you.

5. Mark writes that in many cases, "the obstacle is the way." Have you experienced this? Explain your answer.

Chapter 8—Living in Wide-Eyed Wonder

1. How would you describe "living in wide-eyed wonder"?

2. Why are cynicism and skepticism hindrances in following Christ?

3. What does Mark mean when he writes, "Whatever you don't turn into praise turns into pride"?

4. The apostle Paul wrote, "Rejoice always, pray continually, give thanks in all circumstances" (1 Thessalonians 5:16–18). On a scale of 1 (low) to 10 (high), how would you rate yourself in following this advice? What might help you improve your rating?

5. What is your "bravest prayer"—the prayer you have prayed the most or the longest that God has not yet answered? Will you continue praying this prayer? Why or why not?

Chapter 9—The Law of Measures

1. Mark writes, "Don't despise the day of small beginnings!" Do you recall an event or endeavor in your life that started small but ended up big? Share the details.

2. Jesus said, "Where your treasure is, there your heart will be also" (Matthew 6:21). In today's world, how would you define treasure? How is treasure connected to the heart?

3. What is the difference between a scarcity mentality and an abundance mentality?

4. Mark writes that because God is the source of everything we are and have, "we don't own anything." How should this truth affect our relationship with money and material possessions?

5. What are the qualities of a good steward? How do they influence a Christ follower's life?

Chapter 10—Seed the Clouds

1. Why do you think faith is so important to God? Share some of your thoughts.

2. Mark writes, "If you wait until you're ready, you'll be waiting the rest of your life." Can you identify some dream areas of your life where you seem stalled?

3. How might more attention to prayer help you expand your willingness to take steps of faith?

4. "Don't get paralyzed by the size of your dream," Mark writes. "Sow a

seed, and see what God does!" Can you recall a seed you sowed in the past that God grew and multiplied?

5. List a few seeds related to your dreams that you can sow. Where do you need to "drive your stake into the ground"?

Chapter 11—Opportunity Cost

1. Rather than just continuing to acquire more, how might we go about thoughtfully determining "how much is enough"?

2. Have you ever been blessed by someone's radical generosity? What happened, and what did it mean to you?

3. Mark writes, "The most profound form of joy is found on the giving side of life." Why do you think this is true?

4. Besides the giving of money, make a list—as long as possible—of other ways to be generous.

5. What might be something—big or small—you could do today that would flip the blessing for another person?

Chapter 12—The Giving Game

1. Why does sin cause so many problems in life?

2. Have you ever received the gift of undivided attention from another person? Describe what that meant to you.

3. Mark writes, "If you were truly selfish, you would be more generous." What does he mean by that?

4. Mark presents four levels of generosity:

   - Give spontaneously
   - Give consistently
   - Give proportionately
   - Give radically

   Do a self-evaluation (no need to share this with anyone). On a 1 (low) to 10 (high) scale, how would you rate yourself on each of these levels?

5. Although we often associate giving with money, what are other creative ways to give away treasure, time, and talents?

Chapter 13—Pay It Forward

1. Mark points out that the only place in Scripture where God asks us to test Him is in His response to our tithing. Why do you think God chose this topic to issue an opportunity to challenge Him?

2. How would you define the term *firstfruits*? What would you list as your firstfruits?

3. Mark writes that "the tithe is *not* a threat; it's a promise!" Does *threat* or *promise* best describe the way you think about tithing? Elaborate on your answer.

4. Jesus taught His disciples to "lead with blessing" rather than to determine if someone was worthy of blessing before giving it. In what ways might you lead with blessing in your daily experiences?

5. To whom can you "pay forward" a blessing today?

Chapter 14—Kingdom Calculus

1. Martin Luther said, "I have held many things in my hands, and I have lost them all. But whatever I have placed in God's hands, that I still possess." What did he mean by this?

2. Why is greed never satisfied?

3. Mark describes *kingdom calculus* like this: "If you put what you have in your hands into the hands of God, it doesn't just add up. It multiplies!" Have you seen this happen in your life? Share the story.

4. What might be some things God wants you to let go of?

5. Mark tells how his approach to money was faulty because he was focused on getting rather than giving. He writes, "When I started setting giving goals, the game changed. It flipped a switch in my spirit." What intrigues you about this change in focus as it relates to personal financial planning?

Chapter 15—The Eighth Wonder of the World

1. What is your definition of a hero?

2. In this chapter, Mark asks, "What if the joy of blessing others was the only honor we sought? What if all we wanted was to add value to others?" If we sought to live like this, how might our lives change?

3. How can we develop better spiritual peripheral vision—the ability to spot opportunities to bless others around us?

4. Mark advises, "If you don't take inventory [of your blessings], you won't restock the blessing by flipping it." Take a few minutes to list some of your blessings.

5. Now that you have taken inventory, what are some ways you could flip the blessings you have listed? Remember, some of the most meaningful blessings are the smallest acts of kindness.

Chapter 16—Playing the Long Game

1. In a general sense, would you describe yourself as a pessimist or an optimist? Thoughtfully explain your answer, and don't be too hard or too easy on yourself!

2. Mark writes, "A double-blessing mindset is focused on heavenly treasure, not earthly pleasure." What is your definition of heavenly treasure?

3. As believers in Jesus, we are promised life eternal; in other words, life is not limited by time. How might a more intentional awareness of eternity change how you live now?

4. Mark writes that as Christ followers, "we're called to create culture and do it conscientiously!" What does he mean by this? How might this idea affect your attitudes and your life?

5. In conclusion, a central theme of this book is that "we have been blessed to bless." Make a list of the blessings you want to give others—now, in the near future, and even to the next generation.

ACKNOWLEDGMENTS

So many people have invested their time, talent, and treasure into this particular book.

Thanks to the entire team at WaterBrook and Multnomah! It takes teamwork to make the dream work! A special thanks to Tina, Andrew, Campbell, Chris, and Brett for your vision for this book! Thanks to Andrew, Helen, Abby, Kayla, and Dan for your editing eyes! Your attention to detail made a big difference! Thanks to Laura, Lori, Jennifer, Ericka, Ginia, Mark, and so many others whose fingerprints are all over this book.

A special thanks to my agent, Esther Fedorkevich, as well as Whitney and the entire team at the FEDD agency!

I'm beyond grateful for the privilege of pastoring National Community Church in Washington, DC. A special thanks to our executive leadership team—Joel, Jim, and Heather; our stewardship team—Sarah, Heather, and Brian; as well as our staff, leaders, volunteers, and congregation.

Thanks to those who have modeled the double blessing lifestyle—you know who you are!

Finally, the greatest joy of my life is being a husband to my wife, Lora, and a father to my children, Parker, Summer, and Josiah. Thanks for letting me share two of our family values—gratitude and generosity—with those who read this book.

NOTES

Preface: Ariadne's Thread

1. *Encyclopaedia Britannica Online*, s.v. "Ariadne," www.britannica.com
   /topic/Ariadne-Greek-mythology.

2. Mark Batterson, *Soulprint: Discovering Your Divine Destiny* (Colorado
   Springs: Multnomah, 2011), 57.

3. Genesis 1:28, NLT.

4. John 16:33.

5. John 16:33.

6. "Strong's H1288—Barak," Blue Letter Bible, www.blueletterbible.org
   /lang/lexicon/lexicon.cfm?t=kjv&strongs=h1288, author's paraphrase.

7. "Strong's G3107—Makarios," Blue Letter Bible, www.blueletterbible.org
   /lang/lexicon/lexicon.cfm?t=kjv&strongs=g3107; "Strong's G2128—
   Eulogētos," Blue Letter Bible, www.blueletterbible.org/lang/lexicon
   /lexicon.cfm?t=kjv&strongs=g2128.

8. "Winston Churchill Quotes," BrainyQuote, www.brainyquote.com
   /quotes/winston_churchill_131192.

9. Genesis 12:2–3.

10. Genesis 1:28, NLT.

11. Genesis 14:18–20.

12. Genesis 32:28; 49:1–27.

13. Exodus 3:1–4:17.

14. Exodus 13:21.

15. Numbers 6:22–26.

16. Deuteronomy 28:1–14.

17. Joshua 3:7–17; 6:1–21; 14:6–13.

18. 1 Corinthians 10:16, ESV.

19. Acts 13:34, NLT.

20. Luke 24:50.

21. Philippians 4:7.

22. Ephesians 1:3.

23. Revelation 22:14.

Chapter 1: Double Portion

1. Isaiah 61:3.

2. 2 Kings 2:9.

3. 2 Kings 2:9.

4. David Pyles, "A Double Portion of Thy Spirit," Berean Christian Bible Study Resources, www.bcbsr.com/survey/eli.html.

5. Wikipedia, s.v. "Amos Alonzo Stagg," last modified March 9, 2019, 15:46, http://en.wikipedia.org/wiki/Amos_Alonzo_Stagg.

6. Collin Hansen, "Football's Pious Pioneer: Amos Alonzo Stagg Instilled in Football Christian Values That Remain Apparent Today," *Christianity Today*, www.christianitytoday.com/ch/news/2005/jan14.html?start=2.

7. Amos Alonzo Stagg, quoted in John Wooden and Steve Jamison, *The Wisdom of Wooden: My Century On and Off the Court* (New York: McGraw Hill, 2010), 19.

8. Wikipedia, s.v. "Amos Alonzo Stagg."

9. 2 Kings 2:10.

10. 1 Corinthians 3:6.

11. Isaiah 61:7.

12. 1 Timothy 5:17.

13. Zechariah 9:12, ESV.

14. Zechariah 2:8.

15. Deuteronomy 10:15.

16. Romans 8:37.

17. Psalm 84:10.

18. 2 Peter 3:8.

19. Hebrews 13:8.

20. Ephesians 1:3.

21. 2 Corinthians 1:20.

22. Job 1:21.

23. Job 42:10, NLT.

24. Psalm 56:8, NLT.

25. Job 42:12, NLT.

26. Exodus 22:4.

27. John 10:10.

28. Deuteronomy 28:2, ESV.

29. Romans 8:28.

Chapter 2: Umbrella Blessing

1. "Jonas Hanway," Westminster Abbey, www.westminster-abbey.org/abbey
-commemorations/commemorations/jonas-hanway.

2. Wikipedia, s.v. "Foundling Hospital," last modified May 7, 2019, 3:43,
https://en.wikipedia.org/wiki/Foundling_Hospital.

3. Ed Young, "Under the Umbrella of Authority," video, 2:01, September 27,
2014, www.youtube.com/watch?v=SYGReK0919E.

4. Deuteronomy 28:1.

5. Exodus 12:7.

6. Charles Wesley, "O for a Thousand Tongues to Sing," 1739, public
domain.

7. Deuteronomy 28:2, ESV.

8. Eugene Peterson has written a wonderful book by this title, *A Long
Obedience in the Same Direction: Discipleship in an Instant Society*
(Downers Grove, IL: InterVarsity, 2000).

9. Jeremiah 1:12, ESV.

10. 2 Chronicles 16:9, NLT.

11. Psalm 23:6, ESV.

12. "Psalm 23 in Hebrew," Hebrew for Christians, www.hebrew4christians
.com/Scripture/Ketuvim/Psalms/Psalm_23/psalm_23.html.

13. Wikipedia, s.v. "Mandelbrot Set," last modified April 25, 2019, 14:35,
https://en.wikipedia.org/wiki/Mandelbrot_set.

14. Lamentations 3:22–23, ESV.

15. Deuteronomy 28:3–13.

16. While rabbinic tradition is not on par with Scripture itself, it's a helpful
commentary. This idea is drawn from Lawrence Kushner, *Eyes Remade
for Wonder: A Lawrence Kushner Reader* (Woodstock, VT: Jewish Lights,
1998), 50.

17. Matthew 5:45, esv.

18. Wikipedia, s.v. "Prevenient Grace," last modified May 3, 2019, 1:31, https://en.wikipedia.org/wiki/Prevenient_grace.

19. Deuteronomy 28:8.

20. This idea was popularized by Malcolm Gladwell, but it was first articulated by Anders Ericsson. If you haven't read it, I recommend reading Anders Ericson and Robert Pool, *Peak: Secrets from the New Science of Expertise* (New York: Mariners Books, 2016).

21. Dorothy L. Sayers, "Why Work?," in *Letters to a Diminished Church: Passionate Arguments for the Relevance of Christian Doctrine* (Nashville: W Publishing, 2004), 132.

22. 2 Corinthians 12:9.

23. Genesis 1:28, NLT.

24. "Strong's H7235—Rabah," Blue Letter Bible, www.blueletterbible.org /lang/lexicon/lexicon.cfm?t=kjv&strongs=h7235.

25. John 14:12.

26. Ephesians 3:20, esv.

27. Matthew 13:8.

28. BJ Gallagher, "The Ten Awful Truths—and the Ten Wonderful Truths—About Book Publishing," *Huffpost,* December 6, 2017, www.huffpost .com/entry/book-publishing_b_1394159.

29. Deuteronomy 28:11.

Chapter 3: The X Factor

1. Elliot Forbes, ed., *Thayer's Life of Beethoven*, rev. ed., vol. 2 (Princeton, NJ: Princeton University Press, 1967), 920.

2. Jonathan Kandell, "The Glorious History of Handel's Messiah," *Smithsonian* magazine, December 2009, www.smithsonianmag.com/arts-culture /the-glorious-history-of-handels-messiah-148168540.

3. Eric W. Nye, "Pounds Sterling to Dollars: Historical Conversion of Currency," www.uwyo.edu/numimage/currency.htm.

4. "Messiah and George Frideric Handel," Christianity.com, April 28, 2010, www.christianity.com/church/church-history/timeline/1701-1800/messiah -and-george-frideric-handel-11630237.html.

5. Psalm 84:11, ESV.

6. Matthew 7:9–11.

7. Warren Cole Smith, "*The Drop Box* Director on Coming to Christ," *World*, March 3, 2015, https://world.wng.org/2015/03/the_drop_box _director_on_coming_to_christ.

8. 2 Corinthians 10:5.

9. Deuteronomy 33:11.

10. "Martin Luther King Jr., "What Is Your Life's Blueprint?" (speech, Barratt Junior High School, Philadelphia, PA, October 26, 1967), https://projects .seattletimes.com/mlk/words-blueprint.html.

11. Cambridge Dictionary, s.v. "X Factor," https://dictionary.cambridge.org /us/dictionary/english/x-factor.

12. Oxford Living Dictionaries, s.v. "X Factor," https://en.oxforddictionaries .com/definition/us/X_factor.

13. Deuteronomy 33:16.

14. Galatians 3:29.

15. Exodus 9:1.

16. James 4:2.

Chapter 4: The Avogadro Constant

1. Wikipedia, s.v. "Avogadro Constant," last modified May 9, 2019, 2:52, https://en.wikipedia.org/wiki/Avogadro_constant.

2. Numbers 6:24–26.

3. "Who, What, Why: Why Does the Military Insist on Saluting?," BBC, January 5, 2015, www.bbc.com/news/blogs-magazine-monitor-3067 9406.

4. Exodus 3:14.

5. Matthew 18:6.

6. There are four fundamental forces in physics, but many physicists believe in the existence of a more mysterious fifth force that they can't quite define as a data point. I use the term figuratively, but I do believe that the Spirit of God is what animates the human spirit.

7. Acts 17:28.

8. Proverbs 18:21, ESV.

9. Mark 14:9.

10. 1 Peter 2:9.

11. Thanks to John Ortberg for this concept. I've adapted it, but the idea originated with him.

12. Proverbs 25:11, NET.

13. Revelation 12:10–11.

14. 1 Peter 1:18–19.

15. Ephesians 1:7.

16. Hebrews 9:22.

17. Hebrews 10:19.

18. 1 John 1:7.

19. 1 Peter 2:24.

20. Hebrews 9:14.

21. John Pickrell, "95% of Thoroughbreds Linked to One Superstud," New Scientist, September 6, 2005, www.newscientist.com/article/dn7941-95 -of-thoroughbreds-linked-to-one-superstud.

22. Melissa Helser and Jonathan David Helser, "No Longer Slaves (Live)," by Brian Johnson, Jonathan David Helser, and Joel Case, *We Will Not Be Shaken (Live)*, copyright © 2015, Bethel Music.

23. William Cowper, "There Is a Fountain," 1772, public domain.

24. Luke 2:14, NKJV.

25. Deuteronomy 8:18.

26. 2 Corinthians 9:11.

27. Wikipedia, s.v. "Shalom," last modified May 28, 2019, 9:49, https://en .wikipedia.org/wiki/Shalom.

28. Genesis 35:11, NLT.

29. Wikipedia, s.v. "Vulcan Salute," last modified May 21, 2019, 20:03, https://en.wikipedia.org/wiki/Vulcan_salute.

30. Numbers 6:24–26.

Chapter 5: God in the Hands of Angry People

1. "Famous Kin of Jonathan Edwards," FamousKin.com, https://famouskin .com/famous-kin-menu.php?name=13924+jonathan+edwards.

2. Romans 3:23.
3. Proverbs 6:16–19, NKJV.
4. Malachi 2:16.
5. Mark 10:9.
6. Jonathan Edwards, "Sinners in the Hands of an Angry God," in *Sinners in the Hands of an Angry God and Other Puritan Sermons*, ed. David Dutkanicz (Mineola, NY: Dover, 2005), 178.
7. Proverbs 9:10.
8. Romans 2:4.
9. A. W. Tozer, *The Knowledge of the Holy* (New York: HarperOne, 1961), 1.
10. Zechariah 2:8.
11. Deuteronomy 10:15.
12. Isaiah 62:12.
13. Job 1:8.
14. Romans 8:34.
15. Psalm 23:6.
16. Exodus 15:13.
17. Jeremiah 31:3.
18. Song of Songs 8:6.
19. Zephaniah 3:17.
20. 1 John 4:16.
21. Barbara Ehrenreich, *Living with a Wild God: A Nonbeliever's Search for the Truth About Everything* (New York: Hachette, 2014), 2.
22. Eric Metaxas, "National Prayer Breakfast," C-SPAN, February 2, 2012, video, www.c-span.org/video/?304149-1/national-prayer -breakfast.
23. Revelation 2:17.
24. Numbers 6:27.
25. "The Names of God in the Old Testament," Blue Letter Bible, www .blueletterbible.org/study/misc/name_god.cfm.
26. Diana Nyad, *Find a Way: The Inspiring Story of One Woman's Pursuit of a Lifelong Dream* (New York: Vintage Books, 2015), 15.

27. "Long-Distance Swimmer Diana Nyad," *National Geographic*, November 13, 2013, www.nationalgeographic.com/adventure/features/adventurers -of-the-year/2014/diana-nyad.

28. Diana Nyad, quoted in Greg Myre, "On Fifth Try, Diana Nyad Completes Cuba-Florida Swim," NPR, September 2, 2013, www.npr .org/sections/thetwo-way/2013/09/02/218207861/diana-nyad-in -homestretch-of-cuba-florida-swim.

29. Diana Nyad, *Find a Way*, 27–28 (modified to not include Greek accent).

30. Gabriel Barkay, "The Riches of Ketef Hinnom: Jerusalem Tomb Yields Biblical Text Four Centuries Older Than Dead Sea Scrolls," BAS Library, www.baslibrary.org/biblical-archaeology-review/35 /4/4.

31. Deuteronomy 6:6–9.

32. Deuteronomy 6:4.

33. Wikipedia, s.v. "Tefillin," last modified May 7, 2019, 20:54, https://en .wikipedia.org/wiki/Tefillin.

34. "Shekinah," Bible Hub, https://biblehub.com/topical/s/shekinah .htm; "3519b. Kabod," Bible Hub, https://biblehub.com/hebrew /3519b.htm.

35. Matthew 11:28, NASB.

Chapter 6: Fight for It

1. Angela Duckworth, *Grit: The Power of Passion and Perseverance* (New York: Scribner, 2016), 250.

2. Hudson Strode, "Sisu: A Word That Explains Finland," *New York Times*, January 14, 1940, www.nytimes.com/1940/01/14/archives/sisu-a-word -that-explains-finland.html.

3. Strode, "Sisu."

4. Luke 18:1–5.

5. Ephesians 1:3.

6. "Louis Pasteur," Wikiquote, last modified December 26, 2018, 17:14, https://en.wikiquote.org/wiki/Louis_Pasteur.

7. Genesis 32:24–31.

8. Genesis 32:30.

9. Genesis 25:26.

10. Kate Patterson, *The Promise of Blessing* (Edinburgh: Muddy Pearl, 2015), 14.

11. Galatians 6:17, NLT.

12. Bryan Stevenson, *Just Mercy: A Story of Justice and Redemption* (New York: Spiegel & Grau, 2014), 45–46.

13. "The Reagan Wit," CBS News, July 20, 2014, www.cbsnews.com /news/the-reagan-wit.

14. Ronald Reagan, quoted in M. J. Stephey, "Top 10 Memorable Debate Moments," *Time,* http://content.time.com/time/specials/packages /article/0,28804,1844704_1844706_1844612,00.html.

15. 2 Timothy 4:3.

16. Matthew 13:44.

17. Matthew 13:45–46.

18. 1 Peter 5:4.

19. Wikipedia, s.v. "God Moves in a Mysterious Way," last modified April 19, 2019, 14:04, https://en.wikipedia.org/wiki/God_Moves_in_a_Mysterious _Way.

20. James 4:6.

21. Oswald Chambers, "Getting There," My Utmost for His Highest, https:// utmost.org/classic/getting-there-3-classic.

Chapter 7: Blessings in Disguise

1. "Letter to John Stuart (January 23, 1841)," Lincoln's Writings: The Multi-Media Edition, http://housedivided.dickinson.edu/sites/lincoln /letter-to-john-stuart-january-23-1841.

2. Henry Whitney, quoted in Joshua Wolf Shenk, "Lincoln's Great Depression," *Atlantic,* October 2005, www.theatlantic.com/magazine /archive/2005/10/lincolns-great-depression/304247.

3. Deuteronomy 31:6.

4. Isaiah 61:3.

5. "How Spurgeon Scheduled His Week," Spurgeon Center, June 27, 2017, www.spurgeon.org/resource-library/blog-entries/how-spurgeon-scheduled-his-week.

6. Robert H. Ellison, "Charles H. Spurgeon: A Brief Biography," The Victorian Web, www.victorianweb.org/religion/sermons/chsbio.html.

7. C. H. Spurgeon, "The Minister's Fainting Fits," in *Lectures to My Students: A Selection from Addresses Delivered to the Students of the Pastors' College, Metropolitan Tabernacle* (London: Passmore and Alabaster, 1883), 173–74.

8. DSM-V: *The Diagnostic and Statistical Manual of Mental Disorders*.

9. Thomas Fuller, *A Pisgah Sight of Palestine and the Confines Thereof; with the History of the Old and New Testament Acted Thereon* (1650; London: William Tegg, 1869), 208.

10. Hebrews 4:15.

11. Galatians 3:13–14.

12. "Second Temple: Israel's Messenger," August 28, 2005, Promises to Israel, https://promisestoisrael.org/second-temple.

13. Zechariah 4:7.

14. "Famous Words of Lincoln and Lydgate," Scott Dunlop & Bivium, https://scottdunlop.wordpress.com/2007/09/07/famous-word-of-lincoln-and-lydgate-you-cant-please-all-of-the-people-all-of-the-time.

15. Marcus Aurelius, *Meditations*, trans. Gregory Hays (New York: Modern Library, 2002), 60.

16. Ryan Holiday has written a wonderful book by this title, *The Obstacle Is the Way: The Timeless Art of Turning Trials into Triumph* (New York: Penguin, 2014).

17. Thanks to Pastor Zeb Mengistu for this thought. He shared this while I gave him a tour of our new campus on Capitol Hill in March 2019.

18. Genesis 50:20.

19. Zechariah 8:13, NLT.

20. Hebrews 12:2.

21. Psalm 51:17.

22. Genesis 47:7, NLT.

23. Genesis 47:10, NLT.

Chapter 8: Living in Wide-Eyed Wonder

1. "Mission Status," Jet Propulsion Laboratory, https://voyager.jpl.nasa.gov
   /mission/status.

2. Hannah Ashworth, "How Long Is Your DNA?," Science Focus, www
   .sciencefocus.com/the-human-body/how-long-is-your-dna.

3. Psalm 139:14.

4. Michael Cannon, "On Average, How Many Chemical Reactions Happen
   in the Body in One Second?," Quora, April 14, 2016, www.quora.com
   /On-average-how-many-chemical-reactions-happen-in-the-body-in
   -one-second.

5. 3 John 2, NKJV.

6. G. K. Chesterton, *The Autobiography of G. K. Chesterton* (San Francisco:
   Ignatius, 2006), 325.

7. Elizabeth Barrett Browning, *Aurora Leigh*, in *Aurora Leigh, and Other
   Poems* (New York: James Miller, 1866), 265.

8. Matthew 6:26, ASV.

9. Matthew 6:28, ESV.

10. "New Study Doubles the Estimate of Bird Species in the World," Ameri-
    can Museum of Natural History, www.amnh.org/about/press-center
    /new-study-doubles-the-estimate-of-bird-species-in-the-world.

11. "Types of Lilies: A Visual Guide," FTD by Design, June 19, 2017, www
    .ftd.com/blog/share/types-of-lilies.

12. Thomas Carlyle, "The Hero as Divinity," in *On Heroes, Hero-Worship,
    and the Heroic in History: Six Lectures* (New York: Wiley and Putnam,
    1846), 8.

13. Lewis Thomas, *The Lives of a Cell: Notes of a Biology Watcher* (New
    York: Penguin Books, 1974), 21.

14. Revelation 5:13, NLT.

15. "Western Meadowlarks: Sounds," The Cornell Lab of Ornithology, www
    .allaboutbirds.org/guide/Western_Meadowlark/sounds.

16. "Pythagoras Quotes," AZ Quotes, www.azquotes.com/quote/1367132.

17. Luke 19:40.

18. Isaiah 55:12.

19. Peter Wohlleben, *The Hidden Life of Trees: What They Feel, How They Communicate,* trans. Jane Billinghurst (Vancouver: Greystone Books, 2015), 131–32.

20. Wohlleben, *Hidden Life of Trees,* 7.

21. Wohlleben, *Hidden Life of Trees,* 163.

22. Wohlleben, *Hidden Life of Trees,* 29.

23. Wohlleben, *Hidden Life of Trees,* 224.

24. Psalm 24:1.

25. Psalm 50:10.

26. Hayim Nahman Bialik and Yehoshua Hana Ravnitzky, eds., *The Book of Legends: Legends from the Talmud and Midrash,* trans. William G. Braude (New York: Schocken Books, 1992), 772:125.

27. *Book of Legends,* 535:262.

28. *Book of Legends,* 533:253.

29. *Book of Legends,* 533:250.

30. *Book of Legends,* 535:259.

31. Midrash Tanchuma, Korach 12.

32. *Book of Legends,* 533:250.

33. Jamie Ducharme, "7 Surprising Health Benefits of Gratitude," *Time,* November 20, 2017, http://time.com/5026174/health-benefits-of -gratitude.

34. Psalm 96:1.

35. A little tip of the cap to a song I sang as a kid, "Count Your Blessings" by Johnson Oatman Jr., 1897, public domain.

36. 1 Thessalonians 5:16–18.

37. Lamentations 3:22–23.

38. Luke 17:15–16, NLT.

39. Mark 8:22–25.

40. Wikipedia, s.v. "Roman Plague of 590," last modified February 17, 2019, 14:01, https://en.wikipedia.org/wiki/Roman_Plague_of _590.

41. Wikipedia, s.v. "God Bless You," last modified May 10, 2019, 11:53, https://en.wikipedia.org/wiki/God_bless_you.

42. Wikipedia, s.v. "Germ Theory of Disease," last modified May 10, 2019, 16:39, https://en.wikipedia.org/wiki/Germ_theory_of_disease.

43. Leonard Sweet, *SoulSalsa: 17 Surprising Steps for Godly Living in the 21st Century* (Grand Rapids, MI: Zondervan, 2000), 18.

Chapter 9: The Law of Measures

1. Joshua 1:3.

2. Luke 6:38.

3. Matthew 6:21.

4. 2 Corinthians 8:7.

5. Luke 16:10, NLT.

6. Matthew 25:26.

7. James 1:17.

8. Deuteronomy 8:18.

9. Mark 6:35–44.

10. Luke 21:1–2, NLT.

11. "Widow's Mites," Forvm Ancient Coins, www.forumancientcoins.com/catalog/roman-and-greek-coins.asp?vpar=812. Also see "Lesson of the Widow's Mite," Wikipedia, https://en.m.wikipedia.org/wiki/Lesson_of_the_widow%27s_mite.

12. Luke 21:3–4, NLT.

13. "James Cash Penney," The Truth . . . What Is It?, February 12, 2013, https://poptop.hypermart.net/testjcp.html.

14. Civilla D. Martin, "God Will Take Care of You," quoted in "J. C. Penney," Christianity.com, April 28, 2010, www.christianity.com/church/church-history/timeline/1901-2000/jc-penney-11630672.html.

15. Matthew 11:28.

16. "J. C. Penney," Christianity.com.

17. Isadore Barmash, "J. C. Penney of Store Chain Dies; Built Business on 'Golden Rule,'" *New York Times*, February 13, 1971, www.nytimes.com/1971/02/13/archives/j-c-penney-of-store-chain-dies-built-business-on-golden-rule-j-c.html.

Chapter 10: Seed the Clouds

1. Wikipedia, s.v. "Project Stormfury," last modified September 20, 2018, 23:29, https://en.wikipedia.org/wiki/Project_Stormfury.
2. Ginger Strand, *The Brothers Vonnegut: Science and Fiction in the House of Magic* (New York: Farrar, Straus and Giroux, 2015), 52.
3. Strand, *Brothers Vonnegut*, 58.
4. Ecclesiastes 11:4.
5. Mark 16:20, KJV.
6. Ephesians 2:10.
7. Joshua 3:8.
8. 1 Kings 18:41.
9. 1 Kings 18:42, NLT.
10. I first heard this phrase, I believe, from our pastor of prayer, Heidi Scanlon.
11. Jeremiah 1:12, ESV.
12. Philippians 1:6.
13. 1 Kings 18:44, NLT.
14. Jessica, email message to author.
15. Jessica, email message to author.
16. Strand, *Brothers Vonnegut*, 58.
17. Ecclesiastes 11:6.
18. Hebrews 12:2.
19. Numbers 13–14.
20. Joshua 14:12.
21. Matthew 17:20.

Chapter 11: Opportunity Cost

1. Adam Grant, *Originals: How Non-Conformists Move the World* (New York: Penguin Books, 2016), 2.
2. Luke 14:28, NLT.
3. Matthew 13:45–46.
4. You can read more of Stanley's story in his book *God Owns My Business* (Chicago: Wingspread, 2013).

5. Acts 2:45.

6. Wikipedia, s.v. "Keeping Up with the Joneses," last modified April 7, 2019, 23:52, https://en.wikipedia.org/wiki/Keeping_up_with_the_Joneses.

7. Acts 20:35.

8. "3107. Makarios," Bible Hub, https://biblehub.com/greek/3107.htm.

9. 1 Chronicles 4:10.

10. Isaiah 54:2.

11. "How the Grinch Stole Christmas," Quotegeek.com, http://quotegeek .com/television-quotes/how-the-grinch-stole-christmas/9900.

12. Proverbs 18:16, KJV.

13. 2 Corinthians 9:11.

14. "3107. Makarios," Bible Hub, https://biblehub.com/greek/3107.htm.

15. Matthew 19:20.

16. Matthew 19:21.

17. Matthew 19:29.

Chapter 12: The Giving Game

1. Wikipedia, s.v. "Newton's Laws of Motion," last modified April 25, 2019, 17:40, https://en.wikipedia.org/wiki/Newton%27s_laws_of_motion.

2. Matthew 7:2.

3. Acts 20:35.

4. Elizabeth Dunn, Lara Aknin, and Michael Norton, quoted in Laura Vanderkam, *All the Money in the World: What the Happiest People Know About Wealth* (New York: Portfolio/Penguin, 2013), 161–62.

5. Matthew 25:34–40.

6. 2 Corinthians 8:7.

7. "4052. Perisseuó," Bible Hub, https://biblehub.com/greek/4052.htm.

8. Mark 6:35–44.

9. 2 Corinthians 8:5, MSG.

10. These words are often attributed to Aristotle, but they are Will Durant's summary of Aristotle's sentiment in *The Story of Philosophy: The Lives and Opinions of the Greater Philosophers* (New York: Pocket Books, 1961), 98.

11. 1 Corinthians 16:2.

12. 2 Corinthians 8:11, NLT.

13. 2 Corinthians 8:2.

14. 2 Corinthians 8:3.

15. "The Science Behind Smiling," Pick the Brain, November 12, 2016, www
    .pickthebrain.com/blog/the-science-behind-smiling.

16. "Science Behind Smiling."

17. Jennie Jerome, quoted in Mary Mkandawire, "Leadership Is Influence,"
    Dr. Mary: Living on Purpose, August 14, 2015, https://drmaryliving
    onpurpose.com/2015/08/14/leadership-is-influence.

18. Mark 5:30.

19. Mark 5:31.

20. Hebrews 13:2, ESV.

21. Victoria, quoted in Mkandawire, "Leadership Is Influence."

22. C. S. Lewis, "Answers to Questions on Christianity," in *God in the Dock:
    Essays on Theology and Ethics*, ed. Walter Hooper (Grand Rapids, MI:
    Eerdmans, 1970), 52.

23. Lewis, "Answers to Questions," 52.

24. Wikipedia, s.v. "Wonder Twins," last modified February 19, 2019, 00:23,
    https://en.wikipedia.org/wiki/Wonder_Twins.

25. A little tip of the cap to the classic Christmas movie *Elf,* directed by Jon
    Favreau, New Line Cinema, 2003.

26. Bob Goff, *Everybody, Always: Becoming Love in a World Full of Setbacks
    and Difficult People* (Nashville: Nelson Books, 2018), 107.

Chapter 13: Pay It Forward

1. "Religion: Dynamic Kernels," *Time,* July 30, 1945, http://content.time
   .com/time/magazine/article/0,9171,801686,00.html.

2. Malachi 3:10.

3. Brenda Ervin, "The Biblical Wheat Experiment," *Lutheran Digest,*
   October 25, 2010, http://lutherandigest.com/2010/10/25/the-biblical
   -wheat-experiment.

4. John 12:24, NLT.

5. Ervin, "Biblical Wheat Experiment"; US Inflation Calculator, using the years 1952 and 2019, respectively, and a purchase amount of $150,000, www.usinflationcalculator.com.

6. "Strong's G3198—Melchisedek," Blue Letter Bible, www.blueletterbible .org/lang/lexicon/lexicon.cfm?Strongs=G3198&t=ESV.

7. See, for example, Dictionary.com, s.v. "tithe," www.dictionary.com /browse/tithe.

8. Hayim Nahman Bialik and Yehoshua Hana Ravnitzky, eds., *The Book of Legends: Legends from the Talmud and Midrash,* trans. William G. Braude (New York: Schocken Books, 1992), 533:250.

9. *Pay It Forward,* directed by Mimi Leder, Warner Bros., 2000.

10. Joshua 2:12.

11. Wikipedia, s.v. "Rahab," last modified May 9, 2019, 11:39, https://en .wikipedia.org/wiki/Rahab.

12. Matthew 1:5.

13. Matthew 10:10, NLT.

14. Matthew 10:16, NLT.

15. Matthew 10:12–13, NLT.

16. Matthew 7:6.

17. Matthew 5:21–48.

18. Matthew 5:38, ESV.

19. Matthew 5:39.

20. *Merriam-Webster,* s.v. "ex nihilo," www.merriam-webster.com/dictionary /ex%20nihilo.

21. 2 Corinthians 9:7.

Chapter 14: Kingdom Calculus

1. Wikipedia, s.v. "Jules Léotard," last modified April 16, 2019, 18:07, https://en.wikipedia.org/wiki/Jules_L%C3%A9otard.

2. Amy Chillag and Bianca Britton, "For Cirque de Soleil's Trapeze Artists, It's Hard Work to Fly Right," CNN, March 27, 2017, www .cnn.com/2016/10/12/travel/cirque-du-soleil-trapeze-vargas/index .html.

NOTES

3. John Wesley, quoted in "John D. Rockefeller—the Man Who Gave Away Shiny New Dimes," Wealthymatters.com, June 2, 2012, https://wealthymatters.com/2012/06/02/john-d-rockefeller-the-man-who-gave-away-shiny-new-dimes.

4. "Martin Luther Quotes," BrainyQuote, www.brainyquote.com/quotes/martin_luther_390009.

5. John 6:5.

6. John 6:7.

7. John 6:6, NLT.

8. John 6:9, NLT.

9. Genesis 1:28, NLT.

10. Adapted from Abraham Cohen, *Everyman's Talmud: The Major Teachings of the Rabbinic Sages* (New York: Schocken Books, 1975), 187–88.

11. Cohen, *Everyman's Talmud*, 188.

12. Cohen, *Everyman's Talmud*, 188.

13. Adam Grant, *Give and Take: Why Helping Others Drives Our Success* (New York: Viking, 2013), 4.

14. John Ortberg has written a book on this subject titled *When the Game Is Over, It All Goes Back in the Box* (Grand Rapids, MI: Zondervan, 2007).

15. Adam Grant cited a study of CEOs in his book *Give and Take*, 35–36.

16. Matthew 12:34.

17. Nissan Mindel, "Sir Moses Montefiore," Chabad.org, www.chabad.org/library/article_cdo/aid/112353/jewish/Sir-Moses-Montefiore.htm.

18. Menachem Levine, "Sir Moses Montefiore: A Brief History," Aish.com, November 10, 2018, www.aish.com/jw/s/Sir-Moses-Montefiore-A-Brief-History.html.

19. Levine, "Sir Moses Montefiore."

20. Gary Thomas, "Wise Christians Clip Obituaries," *Christianity Today*, October 3, 1994, www.christianitytoday.com/ct/1994/october3/4tb024.html.

21. 1 Timothy 6:10.

22. Mark Batterson, *The Circle Maker: Praying Circles Around Your Biggest Dreams and Greatest Fears* (Grand Rapids, MI: Zondervan, 2016), 192.

23. Mark 8:36, NKJV.

24. Matthew 10:39, ESV.

25. James O'Shea, "Chuck Feeney, Unsung Hero, Honored by IrishCentral, Guinness," IrishCentral, August 6, 2015, www.irishcentral.com/culture /chuck-feeney-unsung-hero-honored-by-irishcentral-guinness.

26. Steven Bertoni, "Chuck Feeney: The Billionaire Who Is Trying to Go Broke," *Forbes,* September 18, 2012, www.forbes.com/sites/steven bertoni/2012/09/18/chuck-feeney-the-billionaire-who-is-trying-to -go-broke.

27. Wikipedia, s.v. "Chuck Feeney," last modified April 30, 2019, 19:32, https://en.wikipedia.org/wiki/Chuck_Feeney.

Chapter 15: The Eighth Wonder of the World

1. Alfred F. Young, *The Shoemaker and the Tea Party: Memory and the American Revolution* (Boston: Beacon, 1999), 44.

2. Wikipedia, s.v. "Lydia Darragh," last modified May 8, 2019, 20:47, https://en.wikipedia.org/wiki/Lydia_Darragh.

3. Alissa Walker, "10 of History's Deadliest Construction Projects," Gizmodo, August 28, 2014, https://gizmodo.com/10-of-historys -deadliest-construction-projects-1588099877.

4. Wikipedia, s.v. "William C. Gorgas," last modified May 3, 2019, 19:10, https://en.wikipedia.org/wiki/William_C._Gorgas.

5. Chris Myers Asch and George Derek Musgrove, *Chocolate City: A History of Race and Democracy in the Nation's Capital* (Chapel Hill: University of North Carolina Press, 2017), 49–53.

6. "A Slave Who Sued for Her Freedom," *Atlantic,* May 1, 2018, www .theatlantic.com/video/index/559364/ann-williams.

7. "Her Story: From Anna to Ann Williams," Anna, http://annwilliams film.com/herstory.

8. Exodus 17:12–14.

9. 2 Samuel 19:32.

10. 2 Samuel 17:28–29.

11. 2 Samuel 19:36, NLT.

12. 2 Samuel 19:39, ESV.

13. Romans 16:2, ESV.

14. John Rinehart, *Gospel Patrons: People Whose Generosity Changed the World* (Reclaimed Publishing, 2013), 31.

15. Luke 8:1–3, NLT.

16. "Angel Investor," Investopedia, March 31, 2019, www.investopedia.com /terms/a/angelinvestor.asp.

17. Catholic News Service, "Feast of St. Mary Magdalene," Catholic Sun, July 22, 2018, www.catholicsun.org/2018/07/22/feast-of-st-mary -magdalene.

18. "Einstein's 8th Wonder of the World," ClearWealth Asset Management, www.clearwealthasset.com/einsteins-8th-wonder-of-the-world.

19. Wikipedia, s.v. "Six Preachers," last modified March 11, 2017, 22:38, https://en.wikipedia.org/wiki/Six_Preachers.

20. Wikipedia, s.v. "Field of View," last modified March 13, 2019, 23:52, https://en.wikipedia.org/wiki/Field_of_view.

21. Ephesians 2:10.

22. Luke 10:35.

23. Bruce Wilkinson, *You Were Born for This: 7 Keys to a Life of Predictable Miracles* (Colorado Springs: Multnomah, 2009), 153–54.

24. Wilkinson, *Born for This*, 154–55.

25. Wilkinson, *Born for This*, 159.

26. "Lady Huntingdon and Her Friends," Revival Library, www.revival -library.org/index.php/catalogues-menu/1725/lady-huntingdon-and -her-friends.

27. Wikipedia, s.v. "Fetter Lane Society," last modified January 18, 2019, 10:02, https://en.wikipedia.org/wiki/Fetter_Lane_Society.

28. Rinehart, *Gospel Patrons*, 58.

29. E. A. Johnston, *George Whitefield: A Definitive Biography* (Tentmaker, 2009), 2:504–5. See also: http://lists.project-wombat.org/pipermail /project-wombat-fm-project-wombat.org/2018-March/000747.html.

30. Rinehart, *Gospel Patrons*, 82–83.

Chapter 16: Playing the Long Game

1. Peter Jeppson, "Benjamin Franklin's Experiment with Compound Interest Will Astound You," Money Mastery, January 23, 2016, https://money mastery.com/benjamin-franklins-experiment-with-compound-interest -will-astound-you.
2. 1 Samuel 14:6.
3. Hebrews 11:24–26, NLT.
4. "Blaise Pascal Quotes," Goodreads, www.goodreads.com/quotes/395165 -our-imagination-so-magnifies-the-present-because-we-are-continually.
5. A little tip of the cap to Francis Schaeffer's classic *How Should We Then Live? The Rise and Decline of Western Thought and Culture* (Wheaton, IL: Crossway Books, 1983).
6. Jeremiah 28:15.
7. Jeremiah 29:11.
8. Jeremiah 29:5–6.
9. Leslie Odom Jr., Lin-Manuel Miranda, and Original Broadway Cast of *Hamilton*, "The World Was Wide Enough," by Lin-Manuel Miranda, *Hamilton (Original Broadway Cast Recording)*, copyright © 2015, Hamilton Uptown LLC.
10. Jeremiah 29:7.
11. Psalm 2:8, NLT.
12. International Organization for Migration, *World Migration Report 2015: Migrants and Cities—New Partnerships to Manage Mobility*, 2015:1, www.iom.int/sites/default/files/country/docs/syria/IOM-World-Migration -Report-2015-Overview.pdf.
13. Michelle Boorstein, "Does a Religious Community Need Its Own Building to Flourish?," *Washington Post*, November 23, 2018, www .washingtonpost.com/local/social-issues/does-a-religious-community -need-its-own-building-to-flourish/2018/11/23/d350ca6c-ed1d-11e8 -baac-2a674e91502b_story.html?utm_term=.b3ffff5bc0c1.
14. George Bernard Shaw, *Back to Methuselah: A Metabiological Pentateuch* (New York: Brentano's, 1921), 6.
15. "QuickFacts: District of Columbia," United States Census Bureau, www .census.gov/quickfacts/fact/table/dc/PST045217.

16. Martin Austermuhle, "D.C. Homeless Population Decreases for Second Year, but Advocates Worry Many Are Still at Risk," WAMU, May 8, 2018, https://wamu.org/story/18/05/08/d-c-homeless-population-decreases-second-year-advocates-worry-many-still-risk.

17. "Breakdown of Foster Care System," Best Kids, www.bestkids.org/uploads/2/7/0/6/27067547/bestkidsbrochureupdated_2019.pdf.

18. Emma Lazarus, "The New Colossus," Poetry Foundation, www.poetryfoundation.org/poems/46550/the-new-colossus.

19. Matthew 25:40.

20. James 4:2.

21. Matthew 7:7.

22. Jim Elliot, quoted in Elisabeth Elliot, *Through Gates of Splendor* (Wheaton, IL: Tyndale, 1981), 172.

Epilogue: The Year of Blessing

1. "The Tomb of the Unknown Soldier," Arlington National Cemetery, www.arlingtoncemetery.mil/Explore/Tomb-of-the-Unknown-Soldier.

2. Elizabeth M. Collins, "The Tomb of the Unknowns," US Army, April 26, 2010, www.army.mil/article/38013/the_tomb_of_the_unknowns.

3. "Strong's H1288—Barak," Blue Letter Bible, www.blueletterbible.org/lang/lexicon/lexicon.cfm?t=kjv&strongs=h1288.

4. John Newton, "Amazing Grace," *The Broadman Hymnal* (Nashville: Broadman, 1940), public domain.

5. Numbers 15:22–29.

6. Charles Wesley, "O for a Thousand Tongues to Sing," 1739, public domain.

7. 1 Corinthians 10:13.

8. Luke 4:1–12.

9. Luke 4:18–19.

10. Luke 4:21.

11. Isaiah 61:2.

12. John 3:17.

13. John 1:12, NASB.

14. 2 Corinthians 6:2.

15. Bernd Heinrich, *The Homing Instinct: Meaning & Mystery in Animal Migration* (New York: Houghton Mifflin Harcourt, 2014), 67–68.

16. Augustine, *Confessions*, trans. Henry Chadwick (New York: Oxford University Press, 1991), 3.

17. Francis, *The Name of God Is Mercy,* trans. Oonagh Stransky (New York: Random House, 2016), 68.

NEW! CHASE THE LION WEEKLY PLANNER!

This undated week-at-a-glance 12-month planner features excerpts from *Chase the Lion* sprinkled throughout to encourage the user to face their fears, defy the odds, and hold tight to God.

Each week has space in the margin for trackable items such as the week's goals, goals met, prayer requests, to-do lists, etc.

The perfect companion product to *New York Times* bestselling author Mark Batterson's compelling manifesto, Chase the Lion!

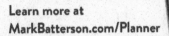

**Learn more at
MarkBatterson.com/Planner**

LEARN TO HEAR GOD'S VOICE MORE CLEARLY!

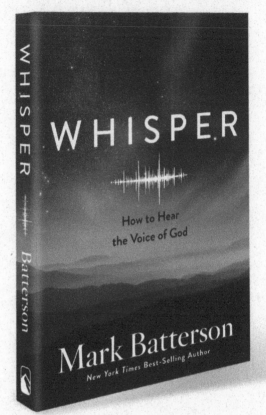

The voice that spoke the cosmos into existence is the same voice that parted the Red sea, and made the sun stand still in the midday sky. One day, this voice will make all things new, but it's also speaking to you now!

That voice is God's voice, and what we've learned from Scripture is that He often speaks in a whisper. Not to make it difficult to hear Him, but to draw us close.

Many people have a tough time believing God still speaks. Sure, in ancient times and in mysterious ways, God spoke to His people, but is He still speaking now?

Start reading chapter one at MarkBatterson.com/Whisper

@markbatterson

ABOUT THE TYPE

This book was set in Garamond, a typeface originally designed by the Parisian type cutter Claude Garamond (c. 1500–61). This version of Garamond was modeled on a 1592 specimen sheet from the Egenolff-Berner foundry, which was produced from types assumed to have been brought to Frankfurt by the punch cutter Jacques Sabon (c. 1520–80).

Claude Garamond's distinguished romans and italics first appeared in Opera Ciceronis in 1543–44. The Garamond types are clear, open, and elegant.